I0130251

Radical
Criminology

issue five ★ fall 2015

ISSN: 1929-7904
ISBN: 978-0692512364

a publication of the
Critical Criminology Working Group
at Kwantlen Polytechnic University
(12666 72 Avenue, Surrey, BC V3W 2M8)
www.radicalcriminology.org

punctum books * brooklyn, ny
www.punctumbooks.com

* Radical Criminology * Issue 5 *
August 2015 * ISSN 1929-7904

General Editor: Jeff Shantz

Feature Guest Editors: Carrie B. Sanders
Public Criminology & Lauren Eisler

Production Editor: PJ Lilley

Advisory Board: Olga Aksyutina, Institute for African Studies of Russian Academy of Sciences, Moscow; **Davina Bhandar** (Trent U.); **Jeff Ferrell** (Texas Christian U.); **Hollis Johnson** (Kwantlen Polytechnic U.); **Michael J. Lynch** (U. of South Florida); **Mike CK Ma** (Kwantlen Polytechnic U.); **Lisa Monchalin** (Kwantlen Polytechnic U.); **Heidi Rimke** (U.Winnipeg); **Jeffrey Ian Ross** (U.Baltimore); **Herman Schwendinger**, independent scholar

cover art: ***16:9clue*** *(flickr, CC-BY) see pg. 12*

Unless otherwise stated, contributions express the opinions of their writers and are not (necessarily) those of the Editors or Advisory Board. Please visit our website for more information.

* Contact Us *

email: editors@radicalcriminology.org

website: http://journal.radicalcriminology.org

Mailing address: Kwantlen Polytechnic University,
ATTN: Jeff Shantz, Dept. of Criminology
12666 72 Avenue | Surrey, BC, Canada V3W 2M8

∗

Our website uses the Open Journal System, developed by the Public Knowledge Project at Simon Fraser University:

journal.radicalcriminology.org

∗

As an online, open access publication, all our content is freely available to all researchers worldwide ensuring maximum dissemination.

∗

paperback copies with full color cover are available at cost through

punctum books ∗ brooklyn, ny

www . punctumbooks . com

"SPONTANEOUS ACTS OF SCHOLARLY COMBUSTION"

IN THIS ISSUE...

Editors note: Our FEATURES are double-blind peer-
reviewed, while our COMMENTARIES are not. →→

EDITORIAL

TIME FOR CRIMINOLOGY: THE ESTABLISHED IS NOT ENOUGH

The present period has a certain premonitory feel about it. A sense of historic promise. There is a real air of change. The mood is one of resistance, of uprising.

In terms of social sciences, it could be said that the current period of austerity and state violence, and resistance to them, is a period of criminology. Some of the most compelling, incisive social commentary has come in the form of criminological works (see *The New Jim Crow* by Michelle Alexander or *Locked Down, Locked Out* by Maya Schenwar as only a couple of examples[1]). And around the world we are seeing critical, indeed radical, criminological approaches press forward with a renewed urgency.

During more placid periods of socialization and social democratic recuperation (under the postwar welfare state, for example) sociology came to the fore as the social science of the day. Now, after almost four decades of neoliberal capitalist austerity (imposed on the working class, the poor) the softer managerialism of the welfare state has been stripped away, the liberal democratic state is more

---

[1] Full titles in the bibliography, page 11

7

clearly streamlined to its purely repressive, its *brutal* aspect—its criminological aspect.

And these repressive aspects are being exerted at all levels, high and low, dramatic and subtle. They are expanded through regimes and practices of surveillance, border restraints, detention, deportation, murders by police and militarized policing. Indeed militarization in general continues apace—wars, invasions, occupations, even in operations signaled as earthquake or hurricane "disaster relief", and especially in the repression of refugees displaced by all of these dislocations. It is also exercised through neo-colonialism (really continued colonialism) and targeting of indigenous communities by states (and their extractives industry sponsors).

And all of this is given cover by new laws against "bad thoughts" which have been passed in the US, the UK, and, more recently, Canada (as in Bill C-51, see Shantz 2014). These bad thoughts laws are emerging in the so-called liberal democracies that supposedly pride themselves on freedom of thought and expression.

Given the colonial and racist histories of the Canadian and US states, austerity and repressive mechanisms have been particularly violent in relation to racialized and indigenous people and communities. Not surprisingly, given the settler colonial and slave structures of the North American states, resistance has once again been sharpest among indigenous and African American communities. And these communities in struggle are developing the strategies and tactics for opposing repressive police state austerity as well as honing theoretical perspectives on the nature and character of (neo)liberal democracy.

The movements in the streets and on the land are in many ways reaching more thoroughgoing conclusions than are many criminologists. In the wake of the Eric Garner murder by police and police tantrum of refusal to pursue low level activities in New York City, residents of poor and racialized neighborhoods noted that their lives were less stressful and violent and that communities felt safer *in the absence of police* (Ford 2014; Hager 2015). And crime worries did not increase. Thus an organic abolitionism arose, gained from experience (or was reinforced for those who had been subjected to police violence and knew they would be better off without police in their faces).

It should be clear that radical criminology must further develop its anti-colonial and anti-racist analysis. As well it must recognize developing aspects of ownership and control (as in extractives industry battles) and class in relationship to manufactured economic crisis and austerity policies (as in the policing of poor neighborhoods and the carceral management of poverty). The question of public criminology has recently re-emerged and it is typically conceived as taking criminology, criminological insights, to the people, the public. Even more, at present, it might be more appropriate to bring the insights of the people (the exploited, oppressed, repressed) to criminology.

At the same time we must go forward without some of our most important teachers—those who developed and sustained critical criminology in an earlier period of uprisings in the 1960s and 1970s. In the last few years alone we have lost some of our great mentors—Nils Christie, Stan Cohen, Julia Schwendinger, and Jock Young to name only a few. Closer to home, my own department, last year, suffered the loss of one of our trusted voices, Tom Allen, whose views were informed by life as a prisoner as well as a criminologist. Their guidance is missed but they leave us crucial lessons. We gain significant insights by returning especially to their earlier works. The struggles of the present period find important precursors in the struggles of the Berkeley School as documented, for example, by the Schwendingers (2014). These are histories of an engaged, rooted criminology directly involved in resistance struggles in alliance and solidarity with specific exploited, oppressed, and repressed communities.

Once again criminology must throw itself unequivocally against the systems of injustice that we too often take as mere objects of study. These are not systems of justice; they are not eternal, they are not natural, they are not neutral, they are not legitimate human endeavors. We must be unflinching and uncompromising in our analysis and in our actions. At the same time we must work to develop alternatives. And in the present period, happily, many are thinking about this too.

It is still too early to tell if this is becoming one of those moments in which, as Henri Lefebvre suggests, people will not, indeed cannot, continue living as they did before, when the established is not enough, and they shatter the bounds of everyday life (1991, 297). Nevertheless, it is clear that critically important change is happening.

And criminologists, as those who live by studying and analyzing institutions, structures, and relations of justice and punishment (and the state that makes monopoly claims on both) have, as much as ever, a duty to contribute to it. In the communities of the surveilled, the repressed, the governed, and the ones killed by the state, new questions are being asked and new, better, answers are being given. It is there that a renewed criminology must locate itself. With, and for, the communities, against the (neo)liberal capitalist state and its criminal "justice."

Jeff Shantz, June 2015,
Surrey, B.C. (unceded coast salish territories)

REFERENCES

Alexander, Michelle. 2010. *The New Jim Crow: Mass Incarceration in the Age of Colorblindness*. New York: The New Press

Ford, Matt. 2014. "The Benefits of Fewer NYPD Arrests." *The Atlantic* Dec. 31. http://www.theatlantic.com/national/archive/2014/12/the-benefits-of-fewer-nypd-arrests/384126/

Hager, Eli. 2015. "Life Without Police." *The Marshall Project* https://www.themarshallproject.org/2015/01/08/life-without-police

Lefebvre, Henri. 1991. *Critique of Everyday Life*. London: Verso

Schenwar, Maya. 2014. *Locked Down, Locked Out: Why Prison Doesn't Work and How We Can Do Better*. San Francisco: Berrett-Koehler

Schwendinger, Herman and Julia Schwendinger. 2014. *Who Killed the Berkeley School?: Struggles Over Radical Criminology*. Brooklyn: punctum

Shantz, Jeff. 2014. "Punishing Bad Thoughts: Next Generation Canadian State Repression." *Toronto Media Co-op* http://toronto.mediacoop.ca/story/punishing-bad-thoughts-next-generation-canadian-st/32901

RECOMMENDED

The Ferguson Syllabus:
http://sociologistsforjustice.org/ferguson-syllabus/

The Charleston Syllabus:
http://aaihs.org/resources/charlestonsyllabus/

ON OUR COVER...

" ¡ES POSIBLE!"

by **16:9clue**

(May 29, 2011 | CC-BY2.0 | found on flickr:
https://www.flickr.com/photos/53255320@N07/6681093463)

image is from *Cuitat Vella, Valencia* in Spain

and came out of the anti-austerity 15-M movement of
the Indignants (*Indignados*)

Of it, the artist quotes Wikipedia in asserting:

**"The series of protests demands a
radical change in Spanish politics,
as protesters do not consider
themselves to be represented by any
traditional party nor favoured by the
measures approved by politicians.**

**(en.wikipedia.org/wiki/2011_
Spanish_protests)"**

[features: PUBLIC CRIMINOLOGY]

ENGAGING AND DEBATING THE ROLE OF PUBLIC CRIMINOLOGY: AN INTRODUCTION

CARRIE B. SANDERS[1] AND LAUREN EISLER[2],
GUEST EDITORS

---

[1] Carrie B. Sanders is an Associate Professor of Criminology at Wilfrid Laurier University. Her theoretical areas of interest are interpretive sociological theories, social shaping of technology and critical criminology. Her research interests include policing, crime analysis, information technologies, surveillance, and public criminology. Her research has been published in high impact journals such as: *Gender & Society; British Journal of Criminology; Qualitative Sociology Review; Sociology; Policing & Society: An International Journal, Canadian Review of Sociology, Science & Public Policy, Social Science and Medicine*. Her research has received funding by the Social Sciences and Humanities Research Council of Canada.

[2] Lauren D. Eisler is currently the Acting Dean of the Faculty of Human and Social Sciences at the Brantford campus of Wilfrid Laurier University and an Associate Professor in Criminology. Her theoretical interests are critical and post-modernist. Her research interests include institutional responses to the marginalized and youth in conflict with the law and public criminology. She has published in *Critical Criminology*, with Oxford University Press, and with Fernwood Publishers.

In his 2004 presidential address to the American Sociological Association, Michael Burawoy implored sociologists to engage "publics beyond the academy in dialogue about matters of political and moral concern" (2004: 5) and to "promote dialogue about issues that affect the fate of society, placing the values to which we adhere under a microscope" (Burawoy et al., 2004: 104). This edited volume is dedicated to discussing, debating and illustrating how academic research can contribute to public discourse, understanding and action in regards to crime and its control. Specifically, the issue provides empirical accounts of the ways in which academic research can: i) evaluate and reframe cultural images of crime and criminals, ii) evaluate and assess rule making and breaking, and, iii) evaluate and critique the justice system.

Burowoy's public sociology has been described as "advocacy on behalf of 'the public', against trends of exclusion and injustice, and for human rights and social justice." (Carlen *et al.*, 2000: 206). Public sociology builds upon C.Wright Mills' (1959: 226) conception of the sociological imagination, which required sociologists to situate human biography in history and in social structure to understand how personal troubles are connected to public issues. Mills encouraged researchers to actively link the micro to the macro and to recognize that if sociology is "to be of any significance, [it] must link the inner lives of people to the structures of power and ideology and the historical period in which they live" (Young, 2012: 3). Mills' sociological imagination, therefore, draws an important distinction between 'personal troubles of a milieu' and the 'public issues of social structure' (1959). Without a sociological imagination, personal troubles remain that—"personal, individual and isolated pains often tinged with self-blame and doubt, with imaginative help, the personal troubles of the many become collective issues: the personal becomes the political" (Young, 2012: 4).

Criminologists employing a "criminological" imagination have been able to draw attention to harm and inequity (Young, 2012). For example, Jeff Ferrell (in this issue) links the personal challenges individuals face in regard to finding permanent work and housing as resulting from broader societal and economic structures. The changing structure of society, he argues, has led to the further marginalization and criminalization of the underclass. Specifically the political and economic changes in North America are casting people *adrift*. Thus, the changing structure of North American society has forced people into non-stop dispersion; rendering *drift* a contemporary crisis.

For academics to move beyond merely identifying harm to *using* their research to address or change the identified harms requires a "political imagination" (Burowoy, 2012). For Burawoy (2012), a "political imagination depends on an organic connection between sociologists and their publics... [and] ... is an essential intervention, necessary to save the university under siege from state and market" (2012: x-xi). In this regard, a political imagination requires researchers to move beyond strictly conducting university funded research to, instead, build and extend relations with the communities they are studying in order to address and fight social inequality and harm. As Barak (2007) explains, "working with those in the 'struggles for justice' allows ...criminologists to help shape the 'progressive' discourse, language and representation of crime and justice, and ultimately the policies that are adopted and acquiesced to by societies in their 'fights' against crime and injustice" (205). Both Andrew Hathaway and Patricia Erickson's commentaries (in this issue) on the regulation of cannabis in Canada highlight the importance of academic research for informing policy development, but also the challenge academics face in the political are-na. For example, Andrew Hathaway's provides a reflexive critique of his own challenges in influencing Canadian drug policies. In this account, he explores how public poli-cy discussions concerning drug use have progressed little, and considers the federal government's commitment to upholding prohibition despite contradictory research evi-dence suggesting that the time has come to end the war on drugs. In this commentary, Hathaway discusses the chal-lenges of academic research informing public policy and, in the process, identifies broader issues facing public criminology.

There are few topics of greater public concern than crime, criminality and crime control. Media accounts of crime can spark "moral panic" (Becker, 1967), and "as a consequence, people often have stronger opinions on crime and justice than on much of the subject matter of so-ciology, economics and political science" (Uggen and In-derbitzin, 2010: 730). For example, Brennan, Ches-ney-Lind, Vandenberg and Wulf-Ludden's article in this issue on media portrayals of female drug offenders draws important attention to the role media may play in the dra-matic and persistent racial/ethnic disparities that pervade the American criminal justice system. Further, Christopher Schneider's article, on the use of social media (in his case facebook) during the 2011 Vancouver riots illuminates the importance of media in publics understanding of crime and its control. In this account, Schneider illustrates how social media was used to (1) document the events as they unfolded and (2) shape the outcome of how the riot was defined and interpreted in news media reports.

As a result of the emotionally charged discourse con-cerning crime and its control (Garland 2001: 10) "legisla-tors and politicians…have replaced academics and re-searchers in influencing media reports and criminal justice policy" (Uggen and Inderbitzin, 2010: 730). This 'perceived failure' in criminology to influence social policy has led to a growing interest in public criminology where academics can attempt to shape "the ways in which crime has been apprehended and governed" (Loader and Sparks, 2011: 7) and to promote the development of "sound policy and averting moral panics precipitated by extreme rare cases" (Uggen and Inderbitzen, 2010: 738). For example, Bernard Schissel's article (in this issue) on human rights, children, and youth highlights the need for criminologists to broaden their mandate and speak to issues of social justice prior to addressing issues of crime and justice.

Public criminology, we believe, provides a vital opportunity for researchers to counter the current political climate of anti-intellectualism, which has emerged in recent years. Anti-intellectualism is characterized by mistrust and derision aimed at intellectuals, scholars, and scientists and the argument that the majority of research is of no practical importance. This contempt for intellectuals and for scientific research and a reliance on ideologically driven policy is perhaps best reflected in the recent words of the Canadian Prime Minister when responding to reports of a foiled terrorist attack on Via Rail in the spring of 2013. On Monday, April 22nd, 2013 police arrested two men alleged to have Al-Qaeda connections and support who planned to plant bombs on a Canada's Via Rail train traveling between Toronto and New York. This arrest came shortly after two bombs exploded near the finish line at the Boston Marathon on April 15th, 2013 killing and wounding several people. During an interview on CBC with Peter Mansbridge, Justin Trudeau, the leader of the Liberal Party, was asked how he would respond to the Boston bombing if he were the Prime Minister. Mr Trudeau stated that he would begin by offering his condolences to those affected by the bombing and then he would begin by looking for the root

causes of terrorism because until one dealt with root causes one could not deal with the question of why individuals
become involved in terrorist activities. Prime Minister
Stephen Harper quickly attacked Mr Trudeau's comment
and stated:

> Our security agencies work with each other and with
> others around the globe to track people who are threats
> to Canada and to watch threats that evolve. *I think
> though, this is not a time to commit sociology.* Global
> terrorist attacks, people who have agendas of violence
> that are deep and abiding, are a threat to all the values
> that our society stands for and I don't think we want to
> convey any view to the Canadian public other than
> condemnation of this kind of violence, contemplation
> of this violence and our utter determination through our
> laws and through our activities to do everything we can
> to prevent it (Cohen, 2013, emphasis added).

In order to consider how we, as academics, could engage
the public in our work as a means of countering the pervasive climate of anti-intellectualism, we developed a public
criminology course at our university with the aim of
bringing important social, political and personal matters in
discussion with multiple publics[3] (Sanders & Eisler,
2014).

In our minds, public criminology is about the "construction of and participation in more and more public
spaces of critical intervention"…as Castree (2006: 408)
puts it, "Lots of small contributions matter as much as a
few big ones." (Oslender, 2007: 112). By engaging multiple publics in dialogues on important social and criminological issues, we hoped to counter what Oslender refers
to as the "all pervasive, penetrating power of 24/7 media"

---

[3] We are indebted to Dr. Christopher Schneider (included in this
issue) for providing his public sociology course as a guide for the
creation and implementation of our public criminology colloquium.

and its use by political actors to construct social problems and create social and criminal justice policies based on ideological foundations and not methodologically solid research (2007: 101). The articles and commentaries included in this special issue were part of our departmental engagement in public criminology. These readings showcase the work of a number of scholars whose empirical research provides critical evidence that is vital to a better understanding of criminals, crime and its control.

BIBLIOGRAPHY

Barak, Gregg. 2007. "Doing newsmaking criminology from within the academy." *Theoretical Criminology* 11: 191-207.

Becker, Howard S. 1967. "Whose side are we on?" *Social Problems,* 14: 239-247.

Burawoy, Michael 2012. "Forward" pp. x-xi in Nyden, Philip, Hossfeld, Leslie, and Nyden, Gwendoly (Eds.) *Public Sociology: Research, Action, and Change.* Sage publications: London.

Burawoy, Michael. 2004a. "For Public Sociology" *American Sociological Review* 70(1): 4-28.

Burawoy, Michael. 2004b. "Public Sociologies: Contradictions, Dilemmas, and Possibilities" *Social Forces* 82(4): 1603-1618.

Burawoy, Michael, William Gamson, Charlotte Ryan, Stephen Pfohl, Diane Vaughan, Charles Derber, and Juliet Schor. 2004. "Public sociologies: A symposium from Boston College" *Social Problems,* 51: 103-130.

Carlen, Pat. 1996. *Jigsaw: A Political Criminology of Youth Homelessness*. Buckingham: Open University Press.

Castrie, Noel. 2006. "Geography's New Public Intellectuals?" *Antipode*, 38(2): 396-412.

Cohen, Toby. 2013. "String of Terror Incidents No Reason to 'Commit Sociology'." *National Post*, April 25.

Currie, Elliott. 2007. "Against Marginality: Arguments for a public criminology." *Theoretical Criminology* 11(2): 175-190.

Garland, David. 2001. *The Culture of Control.* Chicago, IL: The University of Chicago Press.

Loader, I. and Sparks, R. 2011. *Public Criminology?* London: Routledge.

Mills, C. Wright. 1959. *The Sociological Imagination.* Oxford: Oxford University Press.

Oslender, Ulrich. 2007. "The Resurfacing of the Public Intellectual: Towards the Proliferation of Public Spaces of Critical Intervention." *ACME: An International E-Journal for Critical Geographies*, 6(1), 98-123.

Sanders, C. B. and Eisler, L. 2014. "The Public Would Rather Watch Hockey: The promises and challenges of *doing* public criminology within the academy" *Radical Criminology* (4): 37-66.

Uggen, Christopher and Michelle Inderbitzin. 2010. "Public criminologies" *American Society of Criminology* 9(4): 725-749.

Young, J. 2012. *The Criminological Imagination* Cambridge: Polity Press.

PUBLIC CRIMINOLOGY AND THE 2011 VANCOUVER RIOT: PUBLIC PERCEPTIONS OF CRIME AND JUSTICE IN THE 21ST CENTURY

CHRISTOPHER J. SCHNEIDER[1]

F acilitating public dialogue is at the core of doing public criminology. Advancements in technology, in the form of social media platforms, briefly outlined below, allow criminologists to survey the broad landscape of public opinions, particularly those related to matters of crime. Empirically investigating how online users respond to criminal events like riots (in the form of user-generated posts) can provide some insight into how criminologists might respond to crime. This process, I suggest, can directly inform the public criminologist about public debates over such matters even as they occur in real time.

The need for public criminologists to pay more attention to public debates in conjunction with the role of public shaming related to crime and punishment, as it now unfolds online, is becoming an important area of scholarly investigation. This paper explores this process. The paper draws from, and builds upon, previous research (Altheide and Schneider 2013;Schneider and Trottier 2012; Schnei-

---

[1] Christopher J. Schneider, PhD, Department of Sociology, Brandon University. <schneiderc@brandonu.ca>. For more about the author, see page 42.

der and Trottier 2013; Schneider 2015) related to the 2011 Vancouver riot. Other research related to the 2011 Vancouver riot has examined restorative justice issues (Arvanitidis 2013) and collective apology narratives (Lavoie, Eaton, Sanders, and Smith 2014). I use Qualitative Media Analysis as a methodological approach to deal with materials gathered from social media as a guide for other criminologists to engage in similar forms of public criminology. The questions that guide the direction of this paper include: (1) what can the online response to the 2011 Vancouver riot tell us about the public perception of crime and crime control?; (2): how might these responses shape subsequent online perceptions of the riot? And, (3): how then might public criminologists best serve publics, including the growth of online publics that respond to riots and other criminal events? The first two questions help to provide a more informed sense of the public debate about the riot, a process that elucidates an approach to the third question in the manner that online media serve as a point of entrée for the public criminologist.

I first provide a brief overview of the 2011 Vancouver riot and the role of social media in drawing increased awareness to the riot. I then outline how to deal methodologically with materials gathered from social media. Next, I develop some basic user-generated themes relating to crime. Lastly, I conclude with a discussion for how this might contribute to a public criminology, and offer some suggestions for how one might generate public debate.

THE 2011 VANCOUVER RIOT AND SOCIAL MEDIA

There was a riot on the streets of downtown Vancouver, British Columbia on the evening of June 15, 2011. Riots are complex social events that involve people and violence. These disturbances can emerge from within a

framework of social contexts such as underlying economic, political, or cultural factors. Examples might include
race riots (Bergeson and Herman 1998), sports riots
(Rosenfeld 1997), or the 2008 riots in Greece. The catalyst
of the latter riots was attributed to the police shooting of
an unarmed teenager (similarly, the 2011 riots in England
followed the shooting of an unarmed black man). However, to deny the influence of any number of diverse "political and economic epiphenomena" factors that contributed
to the 2008 riots in Greece (Karamichas 2009), or even
other similar disturbances (e.g. 1992 Los Angeles riots),
would indeed be a serious oversimplification.

A common thread between these disturbances is the la-
beling of these events as "riots" by state agents (most usually police) and the conceptual treatment in response to
the label by government officials, media journalists, and
citizens. A recent development includes this process as it
can now develop online on social media, as explored in
this paper. Despite the various underlying factors that may
contribute to the classification of an event as a riot, the
contextual process, and conceptual treatment, nevertheless, is usually attributed to the legal classification of a riot
as a criminal disturbance (i.e., a riot as a crime).

A disturbance of this sort can refer to a great deal of
matters even while no universally agreed upon definition
of what exactly constitutes a criminal disturbance exists.
Riots share two characteristics: (1) the naming of the
event as a riot and (2) the presence and involvement of police and other state agents. Thus, to label a social gather-
ing a "riot" remains a political designation. To avoid confusion, the term riot will be used herein in reference to the
unrest on the streets of downtown Vancouver in 2011 and
1994.

A similar riot occurred in Vancouver seventeen years
earlier on June 14, 1994. Each riot in Vancouver (i.e.,

1994 and 2011) followed a decisive Game 7 of the National Hockey League (NHL) Stanley Cup Finals. British Columbia's only NHL team, the Vancouver Canucks, lost each contest. Following both losses in 1994 and 2011, some of those who had gathered downtown overturned cars, smashed windows, set fires, and looted retail establishments. In both instances, police swooped in to disperse the crowds and, in the process, arrested suspected rioters. In 1994, police requested (and later confiscated) materials from local news media, that included, raw television footage, film and negatives seized from the Canadian Broadcasting Corporation (CBC), and from the *Vancouver Sun* and the *Province* newspapers, among other news media.

Following the 1994 Vancouver riot, police presented the public with edited news media footage to help identify suspected rioters (Doyle 2003). Media materials used to identify these suspects were collected (seized), and organized (edited), by police, and *then* presented to citizens to aid with identification. In 2011, we see the inverse occur, where the collection and organization of media materials (i.e. evidence for the identification of suspected rioters) were almost entirely conducted by those *not* affiliated with law enforcement (Schneider and Trottier2012).

While Canada has seen other "Stanley Cup riots"—in Montreal in 1993 and in Vancouver 1994—the 2011 riot was the first of these events where social media played an active and prominent role in documenting the event, and also shaping the outcome, i.e., how the riot was interpreted and defined in news media and by police and public users online (Altheide and Schneider 2013; Schneider and Trottier 2012; Schneider and Trottier 2013; Schneider 2015). Social media are a hybrid of media and interaction (Altheide and Schneider 2013). The phrase "social media" is quite often used interchangeably with "social networking,[2]" yet the two are distinct. Social media are the dissemination platform (like television) and social networking usually refers to the interactive component, where online users can access and publish information. To avoid confusion, "social media" is used in reference to both.

The 2011 Vancouver riot is one of the most documented riots in human history. What makes this criminal event especially unique is that *members of the public generated almost all of this documentation*, much of it also provided to police. The proliferation of smart phones, and other communication and information devices equipped with recording technologies, along with social media, contributed to the wellspring of citizen-recorded-distributed data. These materials, believed by many users as evidence of criminal activity (e.g. pictures or videos of the riot in progress), were then submitted to the Vancouver Police Department (VPD) (who also solicited the public to provide this information). The VPD received documentation of the riot from the public even as the riot was in progress. As the riot was contained, documentation provided to police increased with dramatic frequency. According to police, there were so many people that "forwarded information to the VPD for their investigation within hours of the riot [that] the VPD's website crashed for several hours" (VPD Stanley Cup Riot Review 2011, 14). In just four days following the riot more than one million photographs were reportedly sent to police (CBC News 2011a).

On July 20, 2011, the VPD reported that they "had received 4,300 e-mail tips, 1,500 hours of video, and 15,000 images *as a result of the public's assistance*" (VPD Stanley Cup Riot Review 2011, 75, *my emphasis*). In less than five months following the riot, the VPD claimed to have

---

[2] See boyd and Ellison (2007) for a definition and history of social networking.

processed the "equivalent to 7,500 DVDs or 45,000 CDs" worth of data. These data included "over 5,000 hours of video" documenting more than "15,000 criminal acts." The sheer volume of data provided to police is astounding considering that "the riot was controlled in approximately three hours" (VPD Stanley Cup Riot Review 2011, 7). Some of this public documentation was also circulated on-line, along with vast amounts of public commentary. Much of these data are then readily available for collection and analysis.

METHODOLOGY

Qualitative Media Analysis (QMA) is a suitable methodology for collecting and examining meanings in media documents, like user posts made to social media sites in response to the 2011 Vancouver riot. The 2011 Vancouver riot provides a useful case study to collect and examine public opinions pertaining to the riot. There were a handful of social media sites dedicated to the 2011 Vancouver riot, however, according to news media reports, the "Vancouver Riot Pics: Post Your Photos" Facebook group page[3] was the "largest Facebook group... dedicated solely to posting pictures of rioters" (CBC 2011b). More than 70,000 people "liked" (i.e. endorsed) the page in less than 24 hours after it was created. In total, 12,587 posts were made to the main wall of the Facebook group page in just two-weeks following the riot. During this time the page was "liked" 102,784 times. After this two-week period, for reasons unknown, interest and user activity on the page declined. For instance, over the next four weeks (June 29-August 28, 2011) there were only 350 posts made to the main wall (a decrease of 97.22%), and the page was "un-liked" by 1,967 users. These observations indicate the

---

[3] https://www.facebook.com/VancouverUp.datesandnews?fref=ts

two-week time frame following the riot as best suited for data collection and analysis (Altheide and Schneider 2013).

In total, 12,587 posts were collected between June 15, 2011 (the evening of the riot) until June 29, 2011 from the "Vancouver Riot Pics: Post Your Photos" Facebook group page. These data were captured and stored in chronological order[4] using Adobe Acrobat Pro. The dataset consists of one 2,118-page PDF document. Saturation sampling was utilized. Selected search terms that were initially entered into the dataset included: crime, law, and punishment. The three terms combined appeared a total of 636 times across the 12,587 user posts and netted 45 pages of aggregated data. These data were then reviewed for recurring terms that helped to locate additional search terms, including "police," "justice," "jail[5]" and related terms, "criminal justice," "justice system," and "legal," to list a few. These terms and phrases produced additional searches of the original data. This procedure was repeated until no new posts surfaced. These data were then reviewed for basic user-generated themes posted by users in response to the 2011 Vancouver riot in British Columbia. The *production of evidence* and *punishment* emerged as two basic themes. These are discussed in further detail below.

---

[4] A much more thorough discussion of this process can be found in Qualitative Media Analysis (Altheide and Schneider 2013, pp. 103-114).

[5] "Jail" (which appeared 309 times) was the preferred term among Facebook users in reference to some form of "incarceration" (which appeared 2 times) for offenders. Other terms like "prison" (which appeared 64 times) or "correctional facility" (which only appeared 1 time) were much less frequent. For this reason "jail" will be used herein in reference to all forms of correctional service.

ANALYSIS AND FINDINGS

In the sections that follow, I present two basic themes that emerged from user posts featured on the "Vancouver Riot Pics: Post Your Photos" Facebook page. The first theme pertains to the production of evidence and the second theme to punishment. The two thematic findings below indicate that many online users of the examined data were much in favour of immediate sanctions against the accused in response to the user-production of evidence (theme #1) where public shaming emerges as a dominant alternative punishment to jail (theme #2). Online "punishment" spared taxpayers the financial costs associated with the incarceration of offenders and amended the perceived inadequacy and unhurried speed of the justice system. A basic argument then is that the real time format of social media (i.e., the immediate circulation of evidence of crimes in progress) further promotes the desire among users for the immediacy of punishment while simultaneously exacerbating the perceived weakness of the justice system. This paper serves as a reminder for the importance of due process in a time when immediacy seems to undermine this very basic principle of justice.

THEME #1: USER-PRODUCTION OF EVIDENCE

The initial stated purpose of the "Vancouver Riot Pics: Post Your Photos" Facebook group page was to identify riot suspects, or in the words of the page creator, to "put a label on those losers that made this city look so bad" (June 15, 10:19pm). Following this first post made as the riot was still in progress, a commonly shared sentiment that quickly emerged across user posts was some derivation of the old adage "do the crime, do the time." Many insisted that they were providing aid to authorities[6] by providing what was believed to be evidence in the form of documentation (e.g., pictures and videos) in order to identify accused rioters to bring them to justice, as noted by one user: "LET'S ALL ASSIST and HELP BRING EACH and EVERY FRICKEN IDIOT TO JUSTICE on HERE! IF YOU DO THE CRIME...YOU PAY WITH TIME!" (June 15, 11:40pm). Time was in reference to jail, as expressed by many other users, and for some, this even meant life behind bars.

For instance, a user post made the morning following the riot read: "Rioting Can carry a Life Sentence, Under Sections 67-68 of the Criminal Code of Canada... Put them All Away for Life for Destroying Our City!!!" (June 16, 7:22am). A handful of posts that followed this one included citations and various excerpts from the *Criminal Code of Canada* in support of calls for life imprisonment. Whereas other posts were intended to remind users of the "crime" that brought them together on the Facebook page in the first place (when discussions might have moved off topic).

> Focus people.. opinions and editoials [sic] are for blogs this page is for IDing the criminals .. and in case you forgot here's the crime commited.. [sic] from section 64 of the criminal code: An "unlawful assembly" occurs when 3 or more persons with intent to carry out any common purpose assemble in such a manner... (June 17, 10:21am).

In many circumstances, but especially in response to the user circulation of evidence of what was *believed* to be documentation of crime (e.g., photographs and videos),

---

[6] Elsewhere we refer to this as "'crowd-sourced policing' to refer to the utilization by social media users of narratives consistent with criminal justice discourse" (Schneider and Trottier 2012, 62).

the presumed guilt of those accused was taken for granted, outside of the principles of fundamental justice (i.e., due process). Evidence was a dominant theme of the examined data. On the "Vancouver Riot Pics: Post Your Photos" Facebook group page much of the discussion (i.e., posts) concerned circulating "real evidence" in reference to "pictures that you think will actually help the cops" (June 16, 2:01am).

The user-generated production (and circulation) of evidence on sites like Facebook also served as a basic source for news media. As the riot unfolded, various social media sites (e.g., Facebook) quickly became a basic part of the news media riot narrative that directed increased attention to dedicated social media riot sites. To help illustrate the point, let us briefly consider an exceptional, but iconic example drawn from social media. A variety of iconic images emerged from the riot, some to the great amusement of the public, such as the "kissing couple" photograph taken by Richard Lam. The photograph was named "Photo of the Year 2011" by *Esquire Magazine* and dubbed "the kiss" in the December 26, 2011 issue of *Sports Illustrated Magazine* which called the picture "the most compelling sports image of the year."[7]

If the iconic *positive*, as it were, was the kissing photo, then the iconic *negative* was a Facebook post made by a person called "Brock Anton." A screen shot (see caption below) of the post quickly went viral and generated immediate and universal condemnation.

---

[7] Due to the aggressive copyright lawyers at GETTY, we cannot reprint this photo (despite having the photographer's permission!) If you would like to check it out on-line, see: http://bfy.tw/1RjI

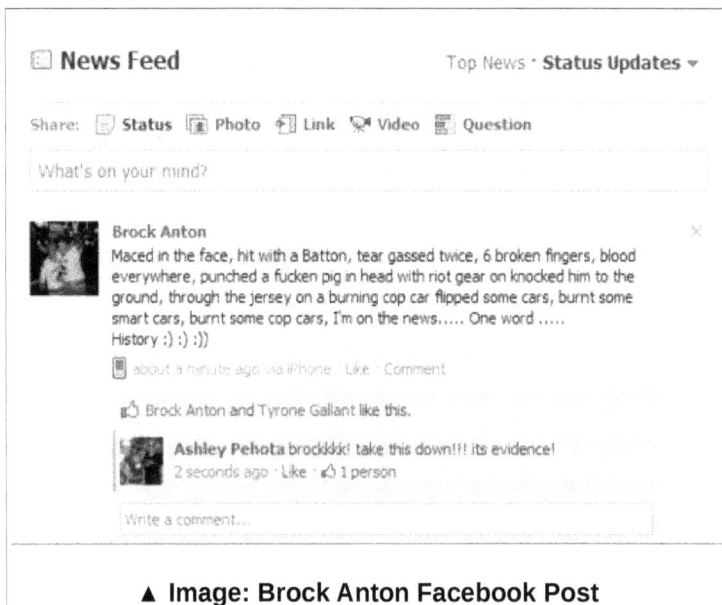

News Feed — Top News · Status Updates ▾

Share: Status Photo Link Video Question

What's on your mind?

Brock Anton
Maced in the face, hit with a Batton, tear gassed twice, 6 broken fingers, blood everywhere, punched a fucken pig in head with riot gear on knocked him to the ground, through the jersey on a burning cop car flipped some cars, burnt some smart cars, burnt some cop cars, I'm on the news..... One word .....
History :) :) :))

about a minute ago via iPhone · Like · Comment

Brock Anton and Tyrone Gallant like this.

Ashley Pehota brockkkk! take this down!!! its evidence!
2 seconds ago · Like · 1 person

Write a comment...

▲ Image: Brock Anton Facebook Post

Excerpts of the post made national headlines and ignited an online firestorm that included the "Brock Anton Sucks Dick" Facebook page, the tagline of which read: "Title = Prediction of Brock's future activities with his new cellmate." More than 3,000 people "liked" the page. Immediate calls for his capture and swift punishment were made on the "Vancouver Riot Pics: Post Your Photos" Facebook page. One user referred to Brock Anton as "everyone's favorite RIOT Coverboy" (June 17, 1:39pm).

Few if any users questioned his implied guilt because he "admitted on his facebook [sic] that he partook in the riot" (June 16, 12:22am). Another user wrote: "WOW posting what you did on FB was an awesome idea Brock Anton, Hope you think jail is just as fun" (June 16, 8:57am). Demands to "get this loser behind bars" (June 16, 9:31am), and questions of the status of his impending arrest followed: "So, 12 hours later, is BROCK ANTON in custody yet or what??????????" (June 16, 11:58am).

More than fifteen months later, a *Globe and Mail* report absolved Brock Anton of any wrongdoing in connection with the post. The headline of the report read: "Riot 'lightning rod' goes uncharged; Number of accused now 156, police say, but believe man who boasted on Facebook actually not as involved as he claimed." In reference to Brock Anton's post a VPD spokesperson, Constable Brian Montague, noted:

> [We] have investigated him extensively and if we found him doing the things he said he did, there's no doubt in my mind that we would be requesting charges on him[8]. You kind of have to read between the lines there. He was obviously down there that night. But he's not doing the things he says he is (Dhillon 2012).

Brock Anton might have been an exception, but the example illustrates the fervor of the public response to the riot, on the one hand, and raises questions about taken for granted notions of guilt, on the other hand, even while not all users outright accepted the guilt of those accused online. The point to highlight is that users had to make sense of what the evidence meant, i.e. what constituted a depiction of what was thought to be a crime (stupidity, for instance, while not a recognized criminal offence, was another central theme of user posts, see Schneider and Trottier 2012).

Often "real evidence" was understood as recorded documentation of a disruption of the norm. A garbage can on fire, for instance, is not necessarily out of the ordinary in some urban spaces, whereas, this is certainly always the case with burning police cars. Pictures of people standing (or posing) in front of burning police cars, an image irri-

---

[8] In the province of British Columbia police recommend charges and Crown Counsel makes the decision whether or not to lay charges based on the likelihood of conviction.

tating to many, was not believed to constitute a criminal act for many users.

> I'd like to point out something EXTREMELY obvious. For everyone posting pictures of people just standing around, or posing for pictures in front of a fire, give it a rest. Unless you have some other evidence proving these people committed a felony[9], stop flooding the photo's section and leave room for the real criminals (June 17, 1:02pm).

I now turn my attention to the second theme, user discussions of punishment on the "Vancouver Riot Pics: Post Your Photos" Facebook page. It is worth repeating here that this paper is a reminder for the necessity of the principles of fundamental justice for the accused. This is becoming increasingly important in order to counter public assumptions of guilty until proven innocent, a perspective no doubt driven by the immediacy that social media offers. The danger here is that immediacy can be understood to threaten some of the basic principles of justice, including punishment without process.

THEME #2: PUNISHMENT OF THE ACCUSED

What remained consistent across user posts was the expressed *need* to punish those guilty of participating in the riot. How to punish these offenders and what exact "punishment fit the crime" was hotly contested. A small handful of users were in support of draconian measures of punishment even before any charges had been laid (e.g., flagellation, public lashings, life imprisonment, forced labour, and in a few circumstances, even the death penalty).

---

[9] Felony is a United States legal term and is not a recognized legal term in Canada. The user is very likely referring to an indictable offence (see Schneider 2012 for a discussion about the influence of American crime media in Canada).

While others called for restraint, public shaming online was viewed by many as an acceptable and just response. Public shaming was understood as both a form of punishment as well as a suitable deterrent mechanism. The riot was a large-scale social event in which many people were believed to have actively participated in the chaos (one user put this figure at "10,000 people"[10]). Because of the sheer magnitude of the riot (and damages) it was widely understood by users that it was not possible to "put everyone in jail" (June 20, 2:18pm). "So many idiots... so few jail cells!" another noted (June 17, 1:20pm). All users did not universally share this belief. Statements such as "ALL the guys in this video[11] need to go to jail" (June 18, 7:52am) appeared. Consider the following:

> Jail time should be on the table for all involved... However, our liberal brain-dead judges will most likely give them a slap on the wrist and tell them not to do it again (June 18, 8:02am).

The need to shame those involved emerged in response to the limited capacity of jail, but was more directly attributed to the belief that the "candy-ass justice system" will just let rioters "off the hook with a slap and a tickle" (June 16, 3:04pm). In this regard, many users expressed deep frustrations with the correctional institution.

Indeed, it was widely believed that "social shaming may be the only justice that these clowns see" (June 20, 1:58pm). According to another user: "If we can't send them to jail then lets [sic] shame them and publicly hold

---

[10] As of February 2013 police have recommended charges against 315 suspected rioters.

[11] Users seemed to collectively agree that video constituted the best form of evidence. See Schneider (2015) for further discussion of this matter.

them accountable instead!" (June 17, 5:20pm). Yet another post read: "public shaming is social justice" (June 18, 7:09am). Few users recognized the realizable harm of this process (only two posts observed the possibility of stigmatization). A few others noted that public shaming would lead to an increased burden on society, and subsequently, the justice system, and would therefore be a counterintuitive form of punishment.

> The consequence of public shaming on the internet is lifelong. However, not giving these people a chance to reintegrate into society will only make them a continued burden to society. At an extreme: No job →welfare →theft → life long crime →lifelong commitment of tax dollars. That is not something I want to continue paying for...(June 18, 9:34am).

Funding was a major point of contention. Punishment in all its forms (under the correctional apparatus) is funded by tax money, and users were very much aware of this fact. On the "Vancouver Riot Pics: Post Your Photos" Facebook group page, punishment was framed in terms of cost-benefit analysis. As such, discussions of cost effective alternatives were debated, posts such as: "ALOT of community service" (June 17, 1:12am), and restitution, like garnishing wages "to help pay back the costs" (June 16, 8:48pm) were frequent. Those costs included riot related expenses incurred by the city of Vancouver, the VPD, and local stores and businesses that were looted and vandalized. The accompanying belief of forthcoming insurance rate increases and, above all, the cost for the cleanup of the city were the most pressing concerns for those users. Consistent throughout these posts was the belief that the rioters were to *pay* financially for their crimes. This issue, however, was complicated by the assumed class status of those that participated in the rioting.

Many of the accused were assumed to be members of lower class, such as those on welfare, *and without jobs*, and therefore, for instance, unable to participate in wage restitution as an alternative form of punishment. One user post read: "no job? well they can take half your welfare cheque" (June 16, 6:46pm). The irony here of course is that taxpayer funds (i.e., welfare) in such a scenario would still be used to pay for riot related damages. The imagined status of the rioters was twofold: either users were too poor to afford to pay for the damages they caused because they were unemployed, or they were young (i.e., teenagers, one user noted that "75%" of the rioters "seem to be kids"), or both. Young riot participants, however, were assumed as "spoiled kids," and not necessarily of a lower class, but, nevertheless, still unable to pay for the damages.

> OK everyone stop calling these idiots people ! i [sic] watched it all night and they were all KIDS...who have no respect, do not pay taxes and still live at home with parents they had nothing better to do it is disgusting but to them its something to do and just plain fun...a rush a thrill excitement [sic] THEY WERE ALL DUMB KIDS, PEOPLE pls separate [sic] the words from PEO-PLE to KIDS (June 16, 9:42am).

Perhaps not surprisingly, many blamed parents and urged them to turn in their kids[12]. Consistent with cost-benefit analysis others suggested that parents pay for damages caused by their children. One post read: "Is there legal precedent for charging parents for damage caused by their asshat kids downtown? Hope so." (June 15, 11:56pm). Such measures were believed to reduce costs associated with the riot. Reducing the cost burden on citizens re-

---

[12] Evidence suggests this actually occurred, e.g., consider the headline of one CBC news report that read "Alleged Vancouver looter turned in by parents" (June 17, 2011).

mained a consistent theme across posts that discussed punishment.

Incarceration was understood as a prohibitively expensive burden to place upon the public. One user noted that rioters should "build houses for the homeless" to "save us some tax dollars… don't just send them to jail" (June 19, 9:35am). Jail was viewed as too expensive. According to another: "*if they just go to jail*, we the tax payers will have to pick up the tab" (June 17, 8:25pm, *my emphasis*), to pay for "their lax jail time" (June 16, 10:42am). In fact, jail, for many users, was getting off too easy, a "soft punishment" that is "handed out" (June 16, 9:27am). For these users, jail was recognized as a place for "feeding and housing" rioters (June 20, 8:40pm), a place to "party" with others (June 16, 9:50pm) or "watch TV" (June 17, 11:46pm), and in some circumstances, a resort: "I don't know if I believe jail time is good for these goofs, (I reckon it's a free pass to play golf, not pay rent and get pizza delivery [to] *mission prison[13]*)" (June 18, 7:47am). Another remarked: "I don't want these people going to jail. I think there is no point in *providing them with shelter and food* on the tax payer's dollar" and suggested that "severe fines" and "community service" serve as punishment options (June 17, 12:55am, *my emphasis*). Other suggestions, such as serving in the military unpaid for a year were also offered. Above all, the most popular punishment option remained public shaming, which was believed would do real justice:

> I think pointing out their [i.e., rioters] lack of moral character, and exposing them, and the shame they brought on the people of Vancouver is more justice

---

[13] Mission Institution is a medium-security facility for male offenders located in the central Fraser Valley, British Columbia.

than any law enforcement [sic] could ever bring (June
17, 10:14am).

The above data reveal that as users produce evidence of
crime (i.e., riot) a growing dissatisfaction with the correctional institution seems to coincide with this process
specifically in dealing promptly with accused rioters. Alternatives to standard forms of punishment (i.e. incarceration) are offered. This occurs because the production of
documentation (i.e., evidence—pictures and videos) vali-
dates user beliefs that the accused do not deserve the "soft
punishment" of jail. The evidence is also believed to reveal that the majority of the accused because of their perceived relative age would not be able to pay back the costs
associated with the cleanup. This process furthers tensions
to punish immediately and in a cost effective manner and
public shaming online meets these criteria. A basic argument of this paper is that the immediate circulation of evidence of crime promotes an increasing desire among online users for swift punishment while advancing beliefs of
the perceived weakness of the justice system. This paper
serves as a reminder for the necessity of due process in an
era when immediacy threatens one of the most basic principles of justice.

Discussion and Conclusion

Let us now briefly return to the first question posed at the
outset of this paper. What can these online responses to
the riot tell us about the public perception of crime and
crime control? Riots are multi-faceted events that now un-
fold online (e.g., recent riots across the Middle East and
the August 2011 riots that rocked England). These social
relations create new conditions for how crime now comes
to be known, and is then interpreted by publics. In these
spaces, publics can offer immediate responses to crime,
such as punishment sanctions in the form of public sham-

ing. This form of punishment emerged as a suitable alternative for various reasons, including, the perception that offenders were either of a particular socio-economic status, young, or both, but above all, unable to pay for the nature of their crimes.

The perception of the 2011 Vancouver riot was also believed by users to be much larger than was actually the case. This was evident in the discussions about the believed number of rioters, versus the number of those recommended for charges. More importantly, however, this belief (i.e., magnitude of the riot), in part, was also a justification for sparing rioters jail sentences. This was not because it was viewed as a more humane way of treating offenders, but rather, these alternatives to jail were suggested to spare the tax paying public the unnecessary financial burden of paying for the mess. While community service was viewed as a possible alternative, it was also believed that additional punishment, in the form of public shaming and humiliation, should accompany community service.

Let us now briefly turn to the second question posed earlier. How might these responses shape subsequent online perceptions of the riot? The Brock Anton post and responses to this post serve as an illustrative example. This post made news headlines across Canada and drew national ire. The post elicited strong responses from online users condemning the perceived flagrant and callous disregard for law and order. The public understanding, as expressed in the examined Facebook data, in response to Brock Anton (and other suspected rioters), was for immediate and swift sanctions in the form of arrests, charges, and punishment, and in the case of Brock Anton, even without due process. On the one hand, the disregard for law and order (expressed in his post) was immediate; on the other hand, the consequences (i.e., punishment) were not. This disjuncture further promoted the expressed need to punish, and exacerbated the belief among users of the weakness of the justice system (i.e. slow to respond, softened or short sentences, etc.).

The basic task of public criminology is to encourage public debate on the topic of crime. This can include a great many issues, debates concerning crime control and reduction, the likelihood of recidivism, certain policies and laws, and, making the topic of harm central to these matters by spotlighting the possible ills that might emerge for victims of crime, offenders, and publics (e.g., public safety). Public debates, as the above data indicate, can now emerge even during the commission of a criminal event. Posts on the examined Facebook page began to appear while the riot was in progress. In this case, the frame of the debates that followed were set by the parameters of the Facebook page, which outlines what can, and will, be discussed, up to, and including, user-generated commentary, and the circulation of the names of suspected rioters, pictures, and videos. This can lead to the unnecessary harm and stigmatization of persons with little or no involvement, but also, against accused suspects, as was the case with Ms. Camille Cacnio.

Ms. Cacnio was identified online as a rioter and later charged. Because of the online notoriety of her actions that emerged from just a few seconds of video, coupled with her online public apology[14], it was reported that she dropped out of university and was terminated from three different jobs (CBC 2012c). In his ruling of her case, sentencing judge, British Columbia Provincial court Judge Joseph Galati noted: "Ms. Cacnio, to some degree, has been unjustly persecuted by the would-be pundits of the social media" (CBC 2012c). The above user-generated empirical data indicates public shaming as a popular and acceptable contemporary measure of justice and judicial consideration of public shaming on social media illustrates

[14] http://therealcamille.wordpress.com/2011/06/20/dear-vancouver-i-am-sorry/

the increasing significance of this type of public reaction. The need then for public criminologists to pay more attention to public debates in conjunction with the explicit role of public shaming (i.e., harm) related to crime and punishment, as it unfolds online, is becoming an increasingly important area of scholarly investigation.

Because of the immediacy of social media, the public criminologist might be notably absent from such debates, as was the case in the above data (not one post appeared to be made directly by a criminologist or criminal justice professional). What then is the role of the public criminologist under such circumstances? How should we best serve publics relating to such crime debates online? I suggest that it first makes sense to understand the debate, including, what issues are under debate, which leads us to ask other questions, including the *why* and *how* of the issues. Examining online data in the form of user-authored posts allows for a more reflexive approach when understanding the matters important to the very publics that we serve.

Let us now finally return to our third question posed at the beginning of this paper. How then might public criminologists best serve publics, including the growth of online publics that respond to riots and other criminal events? One approach might be to actively situate oneself in the debates that emerge online in direct response to criminal events. In such spaces, the public criminologist could get sense of the topic at hand (i.e., survey posts), and publish (i.e., post) responses through interaction with various online publics. I refer to this form of public engagement elsewhere as *e-public sociology* (Schneider2014a), or what we might call here *e-public criminology*. *E-public criminology* consists of a third distinguishable category situated between Burawoy's (2005) *traditional* and *organic* forms of public sociology. The traditional form consists of publications written with a public audience in mind whereas the organic form involves directly interacting with publics. Social media platforms enable scholars interested in public engagement to now do both simultaneously. Such engagement permits the injection of our "criminological products" directly into real time public debates. Given that police agencies now use social media for similar purposes (Schneider 2014b) it seems that public criminologists should do the same. The hope is that this will help contribute to both increased public understandings, but also, in the words of Loader and Sparks (2011), a "better politics of crime."

Empirically investigating public opinions offered online in response to crime can better contribute to a more informed sense of various public understandings about crime. Online materials like Facebook posts can help criminologists to better situate themselves in debates that emerge in response to crime and provide evidence informed commentary because doing criminology produces scientific explanations for crime, *and also* its potential consequences (e.g. shaming). By understanding where public perceptions come from, and by directly contributing our scientific explanations to online public debates, criminologists can now provide insights to publics in direct ways not possible in the recent past. These "interventions" in public life may then contribute to harm reduction among the very publics that we serve. Future work in public criminology might develop strategies for entering public debates online, and perhaps test the effectiveness of such approaches.

ACKNOWLEDGMENTS

I am grateful to colleagues Lauren Eisler, Ariane Hanemaayer, and Carrie Sanders for their helpful feedback on early versions of this manuscript. Comments provided by the anonymous peer reviewers were also especially helpful.

ABOUT THE AUTHOR

Christopher J. Schneider (PhD Arizona State University) is an Associate Professor of Sociology at Brandon University. He has published three books and numerous articles and chapters. His most recent books include, *The Public Sociology Debate: Ethics and Engagement* (co-edited with Ariane Hanemaayer, UBC Press, 2014) and *Qualitative Media Analysis* (2/ed) (co-authored with David Altheide, Sage, 2013). His recent research and publications focus on information technology (e.g., social media) and related changes to police work in Canada. Dr. Schneider has received award recognition for his teaching, research, and service. In 2013 he was the recipient of a Distinguished Academics Award awarded by the Confederation of University Faculty Associations of British Columbia. His research and commentary have been featured in hundreds of news reports across North America including *The New York Times*, among others.

REFERENCES

Altheide, David L. and Christopher J. Schneider. 2013. *Qualitative Media Analysis* (2nd ed). CA: Sage.

Arvanitidis, Tania. 2013. *From Revenge to Restoration: Evaluating General Deterrence as a Primary Sentencing Purpose for Rioters in Vancouver, British Columbia.* (Unpublished master's thesis). School of Criminology, Simon Fraser University, Burnaby. Retrieved January 27, 2014: http://summit.sfu.ca/item/13584

Bergeson, Albert and Max Herman. 1998. "Immigration, Race and Riot: The 1992 Los Angeles Uprising." *American Sociological Review* 63(1): 39-54.

boyd, danah m. and Nicole B. Ellison. 2007. "Social Network
    Sites: Definition, History, and Scholarship." *Journal of
    Computer-Mediated Communication* 13(1).

Burawoy, Michael. 2005. "2004 Presidential Address: For
    Public Sociology." *American Sociological Review* 70:4-28.

Canadian Broadcasting Corporation (2011, June 19a). 1 Million
    Riot Photos Sent to Police.
    http://www.cbc.ca/news/canada/british-
    columbia/story/2011/06/19/bc-stanley-cup-riot-charges.html

Canadian Broadcasting Corporation. (2011, June 21b). Public
    Shaming. *The Current*. Retrieved from
    http://www.cbc.ca/thecurrent/episode/2011/06/21/public-
    shaming/

Canadian Broadcasting Corporation (2012, September 8c).
    Stanley Cup Riot Looter Spared Jail Sentence.
    http://www.cbc.ca/news/canada/british-
    columbia/story/2012/09/07/bc-rioter-cacnio-sentenced.html

Dhillon, Sunny (2012, September 25). Stanley Cup 'Lightning
    Rod' Goes Uncharged. *Globe and Mail*. Retrieved
    from:http://www.theglobeandmail.com/news/britishcolumbi
    a/stanley-cup-riot-lightning-rod-goes-
    uncharged/article4568504/

Doyle, Aaron. 2003. *Arresting Images: Crime and Policing in
    Front of the Television Camera*. Toronto, ON: University of
    Toronto Press.

Karamichas, John. 2009. "The December 2008 Riots in
    Greece." *Social Movement Studies* 8(3): 289-293.

Lavoie, Jennifer A. A., Judy Eaton, Carrie B. Sanders, and
    Matthew Smith. 2014. "'The Wall is the City': A Narrative
    Analysis of Vancouver's Post-Riot Apology Wall," (pp. 203-
    222) in Mark D. Johns, Shing-Ling S. Chen, Laura A. Terlip
    (ed). *Symbolic Interaction and New Social Media* (*Studies in
    Symbolic Interaction*, Vol. 43). Emerald Group Publishing.

Loader, Ian and Richard Sparks. 2011. *Public Criminology?* New York, NY: Routledge.

Rosenfeld, Michael J. 1997. "Celebration, Politics, Selective Looting and Riots: A Micro Level Study of the Bulls Riot of 1992 in Chicago." *Social Problems* 44(4): 483-502.

Schneider, Christopher J. 2012. "American Crime Media in Canada: Law & Order and the Definition of the Situation" (pp. 155-166) in A. Salvini, D. Altheide, and C. Nuti, (eds), *Present and Future of Symbolic Interactionism.* Pisa University Press.

Schneider, Christopher J. 2014a. "Social Media and *e-Public Sociology*" (pp. 205-224) in *The Public Sociology Debate: Ethics and Engagement*, edited by Ariane Hanemaayer and Christopher J. Schneider. University of British Columbia Press.

Schneider, Christopher J. 2014b. "Police Presentational Strategies on Twitter in Canada" *Policing & Society: An International Journal of Research and Policy,* 1-19.

Schneider, Christopher J., and Trottier, Daniel. 2012. "The 2011 Vancouver Riot and the Role of Facebook in Crowd-Sourced Policing." *BC Studies*, no. 175, Autumn: 57-72.

Schneider, Christopher J. and Daniel Trottier. 2013. "Social and the 2011 Vancouver Riot." *Studies in Symbolic Interaction*, Vol. 40: 335-362.

Schneider, Christopher J. 2015. "Meaning making online: Vancouver's 2011 Stanley Cup riot" (pp. 81-102) in *Kleine Geheimnisse: Alltagssoziologische Einsichten* (trans: *Little Secrets:Everyday Sociological Insights*) edited by Michael Dellwing, Scott Grills, and Heinz Bude. Springer Germany.

Vancouver Police Department—2011 Stanley Cup Riot Review, September 6, 2011. http://vancouver.ca/police/assets/pdf/reports-policies/vpd-riot-review.pdf

THE SAVED AND THE DAMNED: RACIALIZED MEDIA CONSTRUCTIONS OF FEMALE DRUG OFFENDERS*

PAULINE K. BRENNAN[1], MEDA CHESNEY-LIND,[1]
ABBY L. VANDENBERG[1], TIMBRE WULF-LUDDEN[1]

I n 2012, more arrests were made for drug offenses than for any other single offense category. Over 1.5 million drug arrests were made that year, and 211,020 of those ar-

---

* This research was supported by three grants provided by the University of Nebraska Omaha—a grant from the University Committee for Research and Creative Activity and two summer research stipends from the University's School of Criminology and Criminal Justice. Points of view or opinions stated in this paper are those of the authors and do not necessarily represent the official positions or policies of the University of Nebraska Omaha or Kearney, the University of Hawaii at Manoa, or the Nebraska Department of Correctional Services. An earlier version of this paper was presented at the 2011 Annual Meeting of the American Society of Criminology in Washington, DC. Please address correspondence to Pauline K. Brennan, University of Nebraska Omaha, School of Criminology and Criminal Justice, CPACS 218, 6001 Dodge Street, Omaha, NE 68182-0149, via e-mail pkbrennan@unomaha.edu, or by phone (402) 554-2205 or fax (402) 554-2326.

[1] For author biographies, please see "About the Authors" 1-4 respectively, on page 88.

rests were for female offenders (Federal Bureau of Investigation [FBI] 2013a, 2013b). Of women in state prisons, more than 25 percent were incarcerated for a drug offense at yearend 2012 (Carson & Golinelli 2013, 10); several decades earlier (in 1979, for example), the proportion of women serving time for drug offenses stood at roughly 10 percent (Chesney-Lind & Pasko 2004), which suggests that the "drug war," with its emphasis on street-level sweeps of those engaged in the drug trade and harsh mandatory sentencing policies, has taken a particular toll on women. A Report prepared by the Women's Prison Project in 2006, for example, noted that the number of women serving sentences of more than a year grew by more than 700 percent between 1977 and 2004, which is twice the rate of growth in the male prison population over the same time period (Greene, Pranis, & Frost 2006). It is important to emphasize that female prison populations have risen more quickly than male populations in all 50 states (Greene et al., 2006).

But, the "war" has affected some women more than others. To elaborate, with U.S. Census data and data provided from 34 states that participated in the National Corrections Reporting Program in 2003, statisticians for the Human Rights Watch estimated that the national rate of imprisonment for black women convicted of drug offenses was 44 per 100,000 population, compared to a rate of less than 10 per 100,000 white women (Human Rights Watch [HRW] 2008, 19, Table 13). On average, across the country in 2003 black women were incarcerated for drug offenses at a rate that was 4.8 times higher than the rate for white women (HRW 2008, 19, Table 13).

We believe that media constructions of white and minority female drug offenders may contribute to the differential treatment experienced by women of color who enter the criminal justice system. A fair amount of research has been conducted on media reports of crime, but the overwhelming majority of these studies has focused on accounts of male offenders. A general conclusion that seems to underlie such studies is that the typical offender in crime stories is a young, minority male (Barak 1994; Barlow 1998; Chermak 1994; Chiricos & Eschholz 2002; Graber 1980; Humphries 1981; Madriz 1997; Surette 1992). Because individuals come to "perceive things the way the media portray them" (Surette 1992, 76), most people are inclined to conclude that the typical offender is an African-American or Hispanic male (Walker, Spohn, & DeLone 2012). Therefore, "the media contribution [to assumptions about criminal activity] is one of both linking blacks to the issue of crime and, moreover, rendering stereotypes of blacks more negative" (Hurwitz & Peffley 1997, 376; see also Entman 1990, 1992, 1994, 1997).

Importantly, notions of who is likely to offend are often coupled with ideas about who is likely to be rehabilitated and, therefore, who may deserve more lenient treatment by the criminal justice system. Consistent with that notion, Chiricos and Eschholz (2002) noted that the dominant perception of crime as a minority phenomenon likely influenced "the dramatic escalation of punitiveness toward criminals in the past 20 years, with incarceration rates tripling despite stagnant... crime rates" (p.401). They further stated that the ways in which minorities are portrayed by the media reinforce the notion that these groups "constitute a 'social threat'" that warrants a punitive response by the criminal justice system (Chiricos & Eschholz 2002, 416). In short, the extant literature indicates that news stories about crime are likely to provide descriptions of minority males who deserve harsh treatment.

But, women also commit crime and their stories also appear in the news. Despite this reality, few examinations of how female offenders are depicted in crime stories and whether such portrayals vary for females of different races/ethnicities exist. To date, only five studies have examined how media portrayals differ for minority women relative to white women offenders (Bond-Maupin 1998; Brennan & Vandenberg 2009; Farr 1999, 2000; Huckerby 2003). In all five of these studies, depictions of minority women were more negative than depictions of white women. However, in none of the investigations did the researchers consider how crime narratives or overall story tones may have been influenced by the type of offense a woman was alleged to have committed. In short, no study has yet examined whether an offender's race/ethnicity affects how stories are constructed for females accused or alleged of having committed a drug offense. To address this void, we examined stories that appeared on the front pages of 17 nationally-available newspapers from different regions of the United States to determine whether narrative themes and overall story tones differed for white and minority women. We expected that stories about minority female drug offenders would be more negative than stories about their white counterparts, and that differences would be most evident in stories about illicit-drug crimes.

Our exploratory study began with a literature review, which contains a discussion of the black feminist perspective and Goffman's frame analysis; both of these theoretical perspectives guided our analyses of the stories we encountered. In addition, while reviewing stories, we also considered previous research on depictions of female offenders as well as Sykes and Matza's (1957) discussion of justifications of untoward behavior, but applied our own thinking with regard to the degree to which similar accounts materialized in stories about female drug offenders, whether other themes emerged, how the themes we encountered were differentially applied in stories about white and minority women, and whether overall story tones differed depending on the race/ethnicity of the female drug offender. Our research methodology follows Altheide's (1996) approach to qualitative document analysis. In following this approach, we first examined basic descriptive statistics related to offender race/ethnicity and the drug focus of the stories we found. From there, we ascertained the extent to which various mitigating and exacerbating themes materialized, and determined whether a story's overall tone was favorable/neutral or unfavorable. We then examined differences by race/ethnicity, with attention paid to stories about women who committed illicit-drug offenses. We conclude our study with a discussion of the implications of our findings.

LITERATURE REVIEW

The primary theoretical perspective that guided this study is critical race feminism, sometimes called black feminist criminology (Potter 2008; Belknap 2014). Black feminist scholars direct our attention to racist ideologies that affect perceptions of minority women and how they are treated. Such scholars argue that the perceptions and experiences of white women are quite distinct from those for black or Hispanic women. Whereas white women may suffer primarily from the effects of sexism, minority women experience "double and multiple marginality" where "racism and sexism are combined with each other" to influence perceptions and treatment by others (Belknap 2014; Chesney-Lind & Morash 2011). More than sexual oppression is involved for minority women because color is an added stigma and a devaluating factor that makes them vulnerable to more intense forms of marginalized treatment (Higginbotham 1983).

> Black, brown, yellow, and red people have to live within the boundaries defined by others because of their

> color. Racism […] operates to promote the tolerance of
> inequities on the part of members of society. Historical-
> ly, and to this day, racism is institutionalized in the
> United States and has a daily impact on the lives of
> racial ethnic people. (Higginbotham 1983, 200-201)

Thus, when compared with white women, minority wom-
en can never be regarded as similarly oppressed or as
equal to white women because they live under additional
restrictions and pressures (Higginbotham 1983, 212; see
also Healey 1997). In short, as black feminist theorists
would argue, researchers must consider a person's
race/ethnicity *and* gender (in tandem) in any attempt to
understand how females may be treated (Collins 2000;
Davis 1981; hooks 1981).

Indeed, some have found that criminal justice officials
rely on gender and racial/ethnic stereotypes when attempting to categorize others (Steen, Engen, & Gainey 2005). In
their most basic form, stereotypes are cognitive techniques
that operate like "mental filing cabinets that allow the individual to group like objects together in the mind" (Entman 1997, 29). In this way, stereotypes provide useful
mental shortcuts that allow one to make sense of information with relatively little cognitive effort (Entman 1997;
Fairchild & Cozens 1981; Gladwell 2005; Hurwitz & Peffley 1997; Willemsen & van Schie 1989). Although racial
and ethnic stereotypes are not inherently negative, individuals may develop prejudices toward members of other
racial/ethnic groups when repeatedly exposed to information that fits into negative categories (Entman 1997).

Researchers acknowledge that minority women have
consistently been stereotyped more negatively than white
women (Brennan 2002, 2006; Castro 1998; Farr 2000;
Healey 1997; Landrine 1985; Madriz 1997; Portillos
1999; Young 1986). Landrine (1985), for example, found
that white women were more likely to be stereotyped as

"competent, dependent, emotional, intelligent, passive…
and warm" (p.72), whereas black women were more likely
to be stereotyped as "dirty, hostile, and superstitious" (p.
71-72). Furthermore, black women are often depicted as
aggressive or dangerous (Brennan 2002, 2006; Irwin &
Chesney-Lind 2008; Farr 1997; Madriz 1997, Young
1986). And, there is a tendency for minority females, in
general, to be stereotyped as "hyper sexed" (Farr 2000,
55; see also Madriz 1997; Young 1986) and as "welfare
queens" (Hurwitz & Peffley 1997, 393). In short, "[w]hite
women fit more closely the gendered, racist, classist conception of 'femininity' [put forth by Klein (1973)]"
(Madriz 1997, 343). Such notions of femininity affect how
women are treated by the criminal justice system. Rafter
(1990), for example, has documented the harsh treatment
of women slaves in the United States and explained that
such women were viewed as quite distinct from their
white counterparts and, hence, not "worthy" of chivalrous
treatment.

The above discussion is interesting when one considers
that women are not expected to commit crime (Berrington
& Honkatukia 2002; Willemsen & van Schie 1989).
Willemsen and van Schie (1989) found that "stereotypes
about criminal behavior were very pronounced and pre-
dominantly masculine" (p.635). They also noted that these
"stereotypes influence[d] the interpretation of behavior"
(Willemsen & van Schie 1989, 625). Therefore, when females commit crime, they have not only broken the law,
but have also "transgressed the norms and expectations associated with appropriate feminine behaviour [sic]"
(Berrington & Honkatukia 2002, 50). Because minority
women are viewed more negatively than white women
and are more likely to be stereotyped as "masculine," one
may expect that they would be more likely to be associated with criminal behavior and harsh treatment by the

criminal justice system than white women in news media outlets.

With regard to depictions of women in the news, Goffman's frame analysis (1974) provides a useful starting point for a discussion of the ways in which feminists might explore media narratives about female offenders. Goffman coined the term "frame" to describe the way individuals and collectivities construct borders around events and issues, situating them to make sense of their world. With regard to women, Goffman believed the corporate media, particularly through the use of advertisements, tended to distill the social world in a way that clearly disadvantaged women. In his work *Gender Advertisements,* Goffman (1979) explored notions of "gender display," and then explained how depictions of women in advertisements tended to ratify male power and privilege over women. We would expand this notion, though, and argue that media depictions of women may also enforce notions of good and bad femininity in ways that may align with the "whore/madonna" dichotomy (Chesney-Lind 1999). Such categorizations are particularly important in discussions about female offenders, as well as in discussions regarding the treatment of minority women.

Few researchers, however, have examined how female offenders are depicted in crime stories and whether such portrayals vary for females of different races/ethnicities. To date, only five studies have been published regarding differences in media portrayals of minority women versus white women, with attention largely focused on media accounts of atypical women who committed murder (Bond-Maupin 1998; Brennan & Vandenberg 2009; Farr 1997,

2000; Huckerby 2003).[2] Farr (1997), for example, analyzed stories for women on death row and found that such
women could be classified as falling into one of five categories, depending on their personal characteristics and the
circumstances surrounding their crimes. Women of color
fell disproportionately into two categories—the "Explosive Avengers" and "Robber-Predators" (Farr 1997, 267,
268). The Explosive Avengers "often were described as
manlike or lesbian" and, therefore, "poly-deviant," with
crimes that resembled those committed by men (Farr
1997, 268). In a later study, Farr (2000, 56) examined only
lesbians on death row. She found that for 14 of the 35 cases in her sample, the "representations [of the women] were
masculinized. [...] All but one of them were [about] wom-
en of color."[3]

Bond-Maupin's (1998) examination of depictions of female offenders on the television program *America's Most
Wanted* also revealed that a woman's race/ethnicity influenced depictions of her femininity. Specifically, she observed that

> Dominant notions of femininity are widely used....
> One pervasive image associated with dominant inter-

---

[2] In another study, Chesney-Lind (1999) examined how female
offenders, in general, were demonized by the media. She did not,
however, examine differential racial/ethnic portrayals. In a later
study, Chesney-Lind and Eliason (2006) examined media
constructions of women of color and lesbian offenders, and found
that girls of color were routinely masculinized in the coverage of the
gang crisis and that lesbian women were disproportionately overrepresented among the few women sentenced to death in the United
States (e.g., Eileen Wurnos).

[3] While it is expected that all of the women on death row would be
depicted negatively, given the extreme nature of their offenses and
their extreme punishment, Farr (1997, 2000) found that the severity
of the negative depictions did vary by race/ethnicity.

pretations of femininity is sexuality. This television
sexuality is manipulative and bestows power on wom-
en that men cannot resist. [...] Ethnicity makes manipulative sexuality exotic. It also establishes a social distance between White fugitives and women of color. Although viewers are warned that White fugitives are
dangerous, the most ruthless [because of their exotic
sexuality] are Russian or Asian. (Bond-Maupin 1998,
43)

Huckerby (2003) arrived at a similar conclusion upon examining the print media's portrayal of Khoua Her, a 24-
year-old Hmong immigrant from Thailand convicted of
killing her children. Overall, Huckerby found that Her's
femininity was diminished because of her "outsider
status" (2003, 153) and perceived sexual deviance, which
suggested that "not all criminal mothers [were] subject to
the same treatment by the criminal justice system or media" (2003, 152). Khoua Her was held accountable, in
part, because of negative ethnic stereotypes.

More recently, Brennan and Vandenberg (2009) examined all calendar year 2006 front-page news stories about
female offenders from the *Los Angeles Times* and the *New
York Times*. The examined stories were about women who
committed a wide array of offenses (e.g., violent, white-
collar, drug, fraud, immigration, and other offenses).
About an equal number of stories were found for white
and minority women, but the stories about white women
were more likely to contain excuses or justifications for
their alleged or actual offenses. For example, a higher percentage of the stories about white women discussed how
forces beyond the woman's control (e.g., mental illness, a
weather-related disaster) excused her behavior. A higher
percentage of the stories about white women also contained discussions of how a crime was committed for the
benefit of others (e.g., for the sake of a corporation), why
decisions to mount an investigation or file charges by au-

thorities were unfounded, and/or minimized the harm done. The presence of such narratives worked to slant crime stories in a favorable direction. Overall, Brennan and Vandenberg (2009) found that nearly three times as many stories about white women were favorable when compared to the stories about minority women.

Brennan and Vandenberg (2009) used Skyes and Matza's (1957) discussion of "Techniques of Neutralization" to guide their analyses because they believed that newspaper reporters were inclined to use similar rationalizations when writing stories about certain types of offenders. Unlike Brennan and Vandenberg, however, Skyes and Matza (1957) were not interested in newspaper accounts of offenders. Rather, they believed that most delinquents felt the need to rationalize or justify their behavior in order to minimize their feelings of shame and the likely negative reactions from others. Sykes and Matza (1957) identified and discussed five major types of rationalizations, which they termed "Techniques of Neutralization."

The first technique of neutralization identified by Sykes and Matza (1957) was the "denial or responsibility" (p. 667). If using this technique, a delinquent will explain that his behavior was due to forces beyond his control (e.g., unloving parents, bad companions, poor living conditions) (p.667). In other words, the offender portrays himself as "more acted upon than acting" (p.667). Delinquents may also deny or downplay the harm they caused. Instead, and for example, they may define auto theft as temporarily "borrowing" a vehicle and vandalism as a simple act of mischief that a homeowner may easily address (p.667). Third, delinquents may deny that anyone was victimized. "The injury, it may be claimed, is not really an injury; rather, it is a form of rightful retaliation or punishment" (Sykes and Matza 1957, 668). For example, a delinquent may explain that a "crooked" store owner deserved to have items stolen from his store (p.668). A fourth technique, which Skyes and Matza label "condemnation of the condemners," may be used by delinquents to shift attention away from themselves to those pointing the blame. In other words, those who blame the delinquent may be construed as "hypocrites, deviants in disguise, or impelled by personal spite" (p.668). Such constructions serve to minimize or neutralize any wrongdoing on the part of the offender. The final technique of neutralization identified by Sykes and Matza (1957) was an "appeal to higher loyalties" (p.669). When using such a technique, a delinquent may state that she violated the law for the benefit of another person (e.g., a brother or a sister) or group (e.g., a friendship clique). The delinquent may, for example, state "I didn't do it for myself" (Sykes and Matza 1957, 669). In short, techniques of neutralization are situational narratives that serve to excuse or justify criminal behavior. These techniques are not used solely by those who come into contact with the criminal justice system; such justifications are used by individuals throughout society to explain an array of untoward behaviors (Sykes and Matza 1957, 669).

We believe that crime story narratives are likely to contain similar justifications for some offenders. While this is our expectation, we also believe that other excuses and justifications will materialize in the stories about female drug offenders. Moreover, we predict that media accounts will be more favorable for white women than for minority women; white women will be more likely to have their drug offenses excused or justified in some manner.

METHODOLOGY

ALTHEIDE'S (1996) QUALITATIVE DOCUMENT ANALYSIS

Our research method follows Altheide's (1996) approach to qualitative document analysis. According to Altheide (1996), qualitative document analysis "follows a recursive and reflective movement" between concept development, sampling, data collection, data coding, analysis, an interpretation (p.16). As with quantitative content analysis, qualitative document analysis begins with the coding of certain variables identified by past researchers as important. But, unlike a quantitative content analysis, which tests specific hypotheses with predefined variables, qualitative document analysis emphasizes the importance of having researchers add new, emergent themes to a coding scheme (or data file) over time. "The aim is to be systematic and analytical, but not rigid; categories of variables initially guide the study, but others are allowed and expected to emerge throughout the study" (Altheide 1996, 16). This means that researchers engage in a process of constant discovery and constant comparison of documents. And, in the process, basic numeric findings (i.e., as they relate to pre-identified and emergent concepts) are important and so too are narrative descriptions of specific cases. In short, researchers who engage in qualitative document analysis extensively read, sort, and search through materials, make comparisons within categories, code, identify and code new concepts, and then write mini-summaries about what they discover (Altheide 1996, 41).[4] When presenting findings from a qualitative document analysis, a researcher will first provide a numeric summary of their findings and then explain these findings with a discussion that includes specific illustrative examples.

Following Altheide (1996) articulated approach, we coded whether the crime story narratives we encountered provided justifications or excuses similar to those identified by Sykes and Matza (1957) as typical among delinquents: denial of responsibility, denial of injury, denial of victim, condemnation of the condemners, and appeals to a higher loyalty.[5] But, we did not limit our study solely to the coding of these neutralizing themes. Instead, our coding and evaluation of crime story narratives was a continuous process, which meant that we evaluated and reevaluated the contents of a crime story several times throughout the data-coding process and added the additional themes we uncovered.

When conducting our analysis, it became clear that journalists constructed crime narratives in ways that resembled the "neutralizers" identified by Sykes and Matza (1957) in their research on the ways in which juvenile offenders justified or excused their delinquent behavior. We found that journalists tended to rely on similar justifica-

---

[4] It is important to add that a qualitative document analysis differs in emphasis and approach from grounded theory. Altheide (1996) explains that "grounded theory stresses more the systematic coding of field notes," whereas qualitative document analysis "is more oriented to concept development, data collection, ... reflection, and protocol refinement" (p. 17).

[5] To be clear, we do not intend to test the perspective put forth by Sykes and Matza (1957). Rather, we have simply borrowed their terminology and concepts to examine potential ways journalists may create favorable or unfavorable impressions of female offenders.

tions when writing about certain female offenders. At the same time, however, we also encountered at least two themes that appeared to be more gendered and raced: "hope of reformation" (for further discussion, see Brennan & Vandenberg 2009) and "character praise." These themes, in particular, tended to mitigate the effects of the woman's drug use, which would normally classify her as a bad or flawed woman.

We also considered whether a story had negative elements or qualities. In other words, our qualitative document analysis also considered whether any exacerbating factors were present. Such factors serve to paint an unfavorable depiction of the offender. Stories with negative thematic elements either ascribed guilt to the offender, mentioned real injury to a real victim, praised accusers, indicated a self-interested motivation on the part of the offender, suggested that the offender could not be reformed, and/or attacked the offender's character. By considering the emphasis that a particular story gave to elements that either neutralized or exacerbated the offender's alleged or actual drug offense, we were able to assess each story's overall tone. Our assessment produced an overall story tone (OST) variable that rated our impressions of the female offenders after considering "what was portrayed, reported, suggested, or implied in the context" of the stories about women who violated the law (Grabe 1999, 38; see also Pollak & Kurbin 2007, 66). [6]

---

[6] Inter-rater reliability for the variable that measured overall story tone (OST) was approximately 94% among three coders. In cases of discrepancy, coders discussed their rationales until at least two coders were in agreement. According to Altheide (1996), "the best way to achieve investigator agreement is to work together to not only record the same documents but also to discuss meanings and interpretations of categories and codes" (p. 41).

Selection of Newspaper Stories

Given the exploratory nature of this study, it was difficult for us to anticipate the types of stories we would encounter at the start of our research. Therefore, we followed Altheide's (1996, 33) approach to qualitative document analysis and assembled a purposive sample of news stories.[7] Our research explores the narrative content of front-page newspaper articles that featured female drug offenders. The newspapers that were analyzed included 17 widely available U.S. newspapers from the 2006 calendar year, and included the *Arizona Republic, Atlanta Journal-Constitution, Boston Globe, Charlotte Observer, Chicago Tribune, Denver Post, Detroit Free Press, Houston Chronicle, Los Angeles Times, Miami Herald, Minneapolis Star Tribune, New York Times, Omaha World Herald, Philadelphia Inquirer, Seattle Times, Washington Post,* and *USA Today.* These newspapers were selected because they provide a geographically diverse sample of news reporting in the United States. In addition, all were based in cities with large (or relatively large) minority populations and were among the top 100 most widely-circulated newspapers in the United States in 2006, as ranked by a nationally reputable media monitoring service (BurrellesLuce 2006).[8] These last two purposive aspects were important because they assured the wide-readership of news stories, and therefore the dissemination of the messages contained within the stories.

---

[7] Quantitative content analysis, in contrast, relies on random or stratified samples (Altheide, 1996, p. 15).

[8] Although we would have preferred to examine the top 17 most widely distributed newspapers in our study, this was impossible to do while still maintaining a geographically purposive sample. Therefore, we selected the highest-ranked newspaper within each geographic region of interest.

We scanned through reels of microfilm in order to find stories about female offenders that appeared on the front pages of the 17 selected newspapers. We used microfilm because it provided access to photographic images that would not have been available had we searched for articles via Lexis-Nexis or other similar databases. We focused specifically on front-page stories because previous scholars have determined that newspaper editors place stories on the front page when they deem them important and/or when they desire to attract the greatest number of readers (Buckler & Travis 2005; Budd 1964; Chermak 1998; Chermak & Chapman 2007; Lundman 2003; Mawby & Brown 1984). In addition, even if individuals do not subscribe to a newspaper service, they will likely see front-page articles, at least in passing, during their daily routines. In other words, those passing by or skimming the front page are likely to be exposed to its content on some level.

A total of 95 crime stories about female drug offenders were found in the 17 newspapers from across the country[9]; 64 of these included indications of the offender's race/ethnicity. The types of drug offenses varied across the stories. Some of the stories were about women who had engaged

---

[9] We determined that articles were crime stories when the narrative mentioned a woman's actual or alleged criminality. Actual criminality meant the reporter noted the woman's formal contact with the criminal justice system (e.g., an arrest, charges filed, a sentence). Stories with alleged criminality either indicated that a female was under investigation by criminal justice authorities, although no formal contact with the system had yet occurred, or were written in such a way as to insinuate that the woman's actions had an underlying criminal component. Drug stories were considered to be any crime story in which references to street drugs, alcohol, and/or prescription drugs were included in descriptions of the woman's actual or alleged offense (e.g., possession, drug use, sale, distribution, trafficking).

in illicit-drug offenses (e.g., possession, use, or sale). Other stories were about alcohol-related offenses (e.g., driving while impaired, underage drinking) or offenses related to pharmaceuticals (e.g., forged/altered prescriptions, illegal distribution of medications).

Our analysis begins with a presentation of descriptive statistics that provide information on the number of drug stories for white and for minority women and the number of stories about illicit drugs (street) and non-street drugs. From there, our analyses zero-in on newspaper accounts of white and minority women alleged or accused of having committed illicit-drug crimes, given that the "war on drugs" has emphasized street-level drug sweeps. Our findings below show how story themes and overall tones differed in the stories about white when compared to the stories about minority women. As we will show and explain with narrative descriptions of specific cases, these differences were largely the product of the emphasis that news reporters placed on a given offender's degree of guilt, harm to another person, and reform potential.

FINDINGS

OFFENDER RACE/ETHNICITY AND TYPE OF DRUG

Table 1 denotes how many of the stories were about white versus minority women. The table presents a dichotomous measure that classified offenders as either "white" or "minority," which is the measure we used in the analyses that follow. As Table 1 indicates, the number of stories gathered for both groups was nearly equal; 48.4 percent of stories were about a white female offender and 51.6 percent featured a minority female offender. Of the stories for minority women, stories about black women were the most common.

TABLE 1. OFFENDER RACE/ETHNICITY and TYPE of DRUG (N=64)[a]		
Variable	**N**	**%**
Race/ethnicity		
White	31	48.4
Combined Minority Group [b]	33	51.6
Black	25	39.1
Latina	3	4.7
Native American	3	4.7
Multiple Minority [c]	2	3.1
Type of Drug		
Illicit ("street") Drug [d]	31	58.5
Non-Street Drug	22	41.5
Alcohol	10	18.9
Pharmaceuticals [e]	12	22.6

[a] The type of drug was not specified in 11 newspaper stories.

[b] All minority women were grouped together. This grouping includes stories about black, Latina, and Native-American women. It also includes stories with multiple female offenders of different racial/ethnic backgrounds who were given equal coverage in a given article.

[c] Two stories included multiple female offenders of different racial/ethnic minority backgrounds. The race/ethnicity of the women in these stories, therefore, was coded as "multiple."

[d] Illicit (or "street") drugs include marijuana, crack, cocaine, methamphetamine, heroin, PCP, and khat.

[e] Pharmaceuticals include steroids, Oxycontin, Oxycodone, Xanax, Percocet, Vicodin, Erythropoietin, and other prescription medications.

Table 1 further shows variation in the type of drug mentioned in these stories. About 60 percent of the stories were about illicit-drug offenses. The other stories focused on either alcohol-related offenses (18.9%) or offenses involving pharmaceuticals (22.6%). If a story noted both street and non-street drugs, only the street drug was coded because such an offense generally carries a more severe penalty (e.g., punishments for cocaine possession are typically more serious than penalties for driving while intoxicated or forging a prescription). About two-thirds (64%) of the stories for minority women were about illicit drugs; by comparison, street-drug offenses were featured in slightly more than half (53.6%) of the stories for white women (table not shown). Given the racial/ethnic disparities that exist in the media coverage of female offenders, generally, and in the incarceration rates for female drug offenders, specifically (HRW 2008, 19, Table 13), one might expect to find that newspaper accounts of white women who commit street-drug offenses may differ from portrayals of similarly-situated minority women. We examine this possibility in later sections of this paper.

Narrative Elements of Crime Stories and Overall Story Tones

Some stories depicted the female offender in a positive light. In these stories, the offender's negative behavior was excused or justified and/or her positive characteristics were emphasized. In order to determine whether a female offender was portrayed favorably, we considered seven different neutralizing themes that we encountered throughout the course of our study— denial of responsibility, denial of injury, denial of victim, condemnation of the condemners, appeals to a higher loyalty, hope of reformation, and character praise. These themes appeared to varying degrees (e.g., were emphasized as opposed to being merely mentioned) in the stories we read.[10]

Variable	%
TABLE 2. OVERALL STORY TONE and NEUTRALIZING THEMES (N=64)	
Overall Favorable or Neutral Tone	51.6
Denial of Responsibility (DR)	48.4
Denial of Injury (DI)	1.6
Denial of Victim (DV)	1.6
Appeal to Higher Loyalty (AL)	7.8
Condemnation of the Condemners (CC)	25.0
Hope of Reformation (HR)	28.1
Character Praise (CP)	34.4

First, as indicated by Table 2, 48.4 percent of the stories minimized the female offender's culpability for her drug offense. A fair percentage (25.0%) of the accounts also criticized law enforcement or other social agency tactics, a technique that Sykes and Matza (1957) referred to as "condemnation of the condemners." In addition to this known technique of neutralization, we also found that some reporters described how certain female offenders

---

[10] It is important to note that the neutralizing (or mitigating) and the exacerbating (or aggravating) themes are not mutually exclusive. Thus, a reporter could work a number of neutralizing and exacerbating narratives into the same story. Therefore, the percentages presented in this paper only refer to the presence or absence of a particular narrative theme in a story. Furthermore, the overall story tone (OST) is based on the relative weight given to neutralizing and/or exacerbating narratives in the story, as a whole; OST cannot be determined from merely the presence or absence of a specific narrative theme.

successfully completed or were likely to complete drug rehabilitation, thereby reforming their lives; close to 30 percent of the stories contained such an element. Finally, about a third of the stories (34.4%) mentioned praise for the offender's character. Some of these accounts included references to a woman's compliance to traditional aspects of femininity and described the offenders as good wives, good mothers, attractive, and so on (for further discussions, see Armstrong 1999; Chesney-Lind 1999; Madriz 1997).

While the aforementioned neutralizing elements appeared in a fair number of the stories we encountered, only 7.8 percent of the stories explained that the female offender committed her crime for the benefit of others (i.e., an "appeal to a higher loyalty"). Furthermore, very few of the stories denied that injury occurred or insinuated that no one was harmed. When these neutralizing aspects were assessed for their overall emphasis in each crime story, we concluded that 51.6 percent of all the stories had overall neutral or positive tones.[11]

By comparison, Table 3 indicates that 48.4 percent of the stories conveyed an overall negative message because of their overwhelming focus on one or more exacerbating (or aggravating) elements. Negative narrative elements appeared to varying degrees in the stories we analyzed.

---

[11] Approximately 31.3 percent (n=20) of the stories had an overall favorable tone. Twenty percent (20.3%) of stories (n=13) had an overall neutral tone; neutral stories were balanced in terms of the extent to which various neutralizing and exacerbating narrative themes were used.

TABLE 3. OVERALL STORY TONE and EXACERBATING THEMES (N=64)	
Variable	%
Overall Unfavorable or Tone	48.4
Attribution of Responsibility (AR)	95.3
Real Injury (RI)	20.3
Real Victim (RV)	20.3
Self Interest (SI)	42.2
Praise for the Condemners (PC)	31.3
Beyond Reformation (BR)	40.6
Character Assassination (CA)	45.3

Over 95 percent of the stories attributed some level of guilt to the accused woman. Twenty percent of the stories discussed the extent of injury that occurred, and the same percentage of stories included remarks about a specific victim or victims. A motive of self-interest was present in 42.2 percent of the stories, and police or other agency work was praised in 31.3 percent of the stories. Table 3 also indicates that about 40 percent of the stories depicted the female offender as beyond reformation. For example, such stories mentioned repeated relapses, failed treatment, and/or that the female offender had "returned to her old ways." Furthermore, 45.3 percent included attacks on the female offender's character. For example, some stories described female offenders as unfit mothers, filthy, unattractive, and sexually promiscuous.

OVERALL STORY TONES AND THEMES FOR WHITE AND MINORITY FEMALES

The black feminist perspective provided an overall framework for our study, and a central purpose of this paper was to determine the extent to which media portrayals of white female drug offenders differed from portrayals of their minority counterparts. In this section we present the results of our exploratory analysis based on a relatively small sample of crime stories. Although there is not enough statistical power in our sample for us to report levels of statistical significance, nor would such reports be warranted in an exploratory study, our results are important because they are the first of their kind.

We were first interested in determining whether overall story tones differed for white and for minority female drug offenders, in general. We found that a similar percentage of stories for white and minority women had overall negative tones (51.6 % of the stories for white women and 51.5% of the stories for minority women). We then considered whether the type of drug impacted story tones for white and for minority women.

When we focused solely on stories about women who committed illicit- (or street-) drug offenses (who are arguably the focus of the "war on drug" efforts), we found that two-thirds of the stories about white women who engaged in illicit- (or street-) drug crimes had neutral or positive overall tones, compared with one-third of the stories about minority women who engaged in illicit-drug offenses. Given these differences in overall story tones, we decided to more closely examine differences in the degree to which neutralizing (or mitigating) and exacerbating (or aggravating) thematic elements were present in the stories we read.

Figure 1 (on page 70) presents a visual summary of the differences in the presence of neutralizing/mitigating story elements for white and minority females alleged or accused of having committed offenses involving illicit (or street) drugs. Figure 2, which follows, presents a visual summary of the differences in the presence of exacerbating/aggravating story elements by race/ethnicity. These figures are best examined in tandem as their elements should be simultaneously considered in order for one to determine a story's overall tone.

Among the illicit-drug stories we examined, all women, regardless of their race/ethnicity, had some level of guilt attributed to them for the street-level drug offenses they committed (see Figure 2). While that was true, Figure 1 shows that the stories about white women were more likely to contain elements that served to minimize their culpability. Both figures further suggest that a discussion of victims was not common. This was expected, given that most drug offenses are considered to be "victimless crimes" (i.e., they involve only the offender and no other party is directly affected). Nonetheless, a higher percentage of the stories about minority women discussed victims who had suffered injury as a result of the offender's actions (Figure 2).

We could find no clear racial/ethnic pattern with regard to the offender's motivation for the crime. While Figure 1 suggested that white women may have been more inclined to commit a drug offense for someone else's benefit (e.g., at a boyfriend's request), Figure 2 indicated that a higher percentage of the stories about white women provided narratives of self-interested motives (e.g., would do anything to get high, wanted to earn fast money). The figures also showed that both praise for, and condemnation of, law enforcement tactics were more likely to be found in the stories about minority women, which meant that there was no clear pattern in the use of these opposing narratives by race/ethnicity. It was also interesting to discover that a higher percentage of the stories about white women offered both positive (Figure 1) and negative (Figure 2) character narratives than the stories about minority women. In other words, both character praise and character attacks were more common in the stories about white women.

While some of the aforementioned findings are inconclusive with regard to racial and ethnic disparities (i.e., those related to offense motivation, law enforcement tactics, and statements about the offender's character), an examination of Figure 1 and Figure 2 produced a consistent conclusion about the manner in which "Hope of Reformation" and "Beyond Reformation" appeared in the narratives of stories about street-drug offenders. To elaborate, a higher percentage of the stories about white women (46.7%) documented their successful drug treatment (compared with 31.3% of the stories for minority women). The opposite occurred in the stories about minority women: a higher percentage of these stories (50%) provided accounts of their failed drug treatment (compared with 33.3% of the stories for white women).

FIGURE 1. DIFFERENCES in the USE of NEUTRALIZING/MITIGATING THEMES by OFFENDER RACE/ETHNICITY

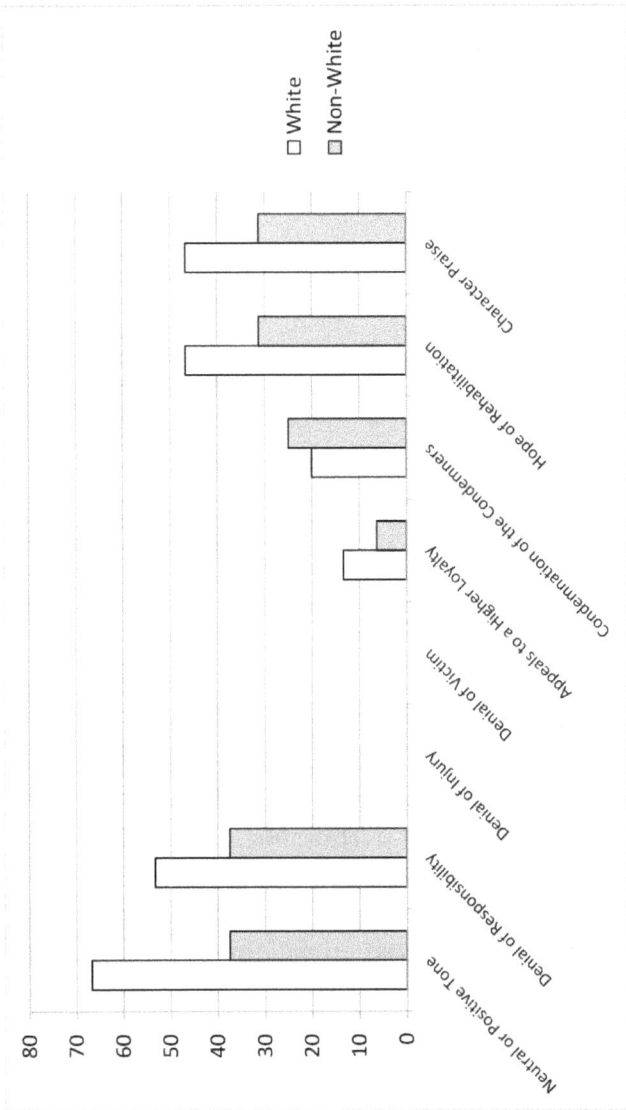

FIGURE 2. DIFFERENCES in the USE of
EXACERBATING/AGGRAVATING THEMES
by OFFENDER RACE/ETHNICITY

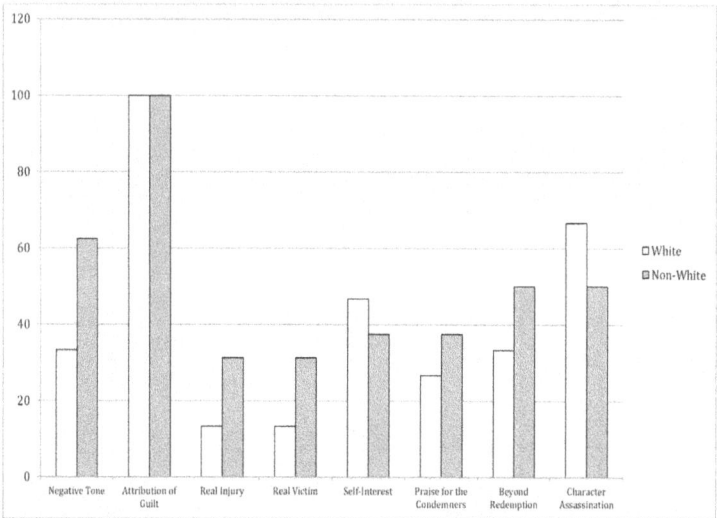

The discussion that follows more fully explains how newspaper story tones differed for female offenders of varying races/ethnicities due to the emphasis placed on an offender's degree of guilt, harm to another person, and potential for reform. While a story's emphasis on culpability or harm influenced its overall tone, discussions of the capacity to be saved or reformed seemed to differ most markedly for white women versus minority women. As such, much of the discussion that follows will focus on the differential use of two opposing themes—"Hope of Reformation" versus "Beyond Reformation."

DENIAL OF RESPONSIBILITY VERSUS ATTRIBUTION OF GUILT

Some of the stories indicated that an accused woman was not fully responsible for her actions due to some external circumstance or force beyond her control; stories with this element were coded for "denial of responsibility". This measure is consistent with previous references to "mad" or "sad" women (see, for example, Armstrong 1999; Chesney-Lind 1999). Our exploratory analysis of the stories about females who committed offenses that involved illicit (or street) drugs suggested that culpability was minimized in 53.3 percent of stories about white women and in 37.5 percent of stories about minority women (Figure 1). One example of the use of this neutralizing or mitigating theme comes from a story that appeared in the *Omaha World Herald* about Kathleen E. Adey, a 20-year-old white woman from Omaha arrested for possession of crack cocaine.

The story focused on Adey's much older boyfriend, John E. Hubbard, 61. Hubbard was depicted as a corrupt and deceptive ex-attorney who manipulated Adey. He was described as very rich and influential; he lived in a "6,000-square-foot stucco home, designed to suggest a 16th-century Mediterranean villa" and was the lead attorney in several high-profile lawsuits (Dejka, 2006, p. 2). Adey, in contrast, was depicted as a young woman in danger of being led to a life of immorality by Hubbard.

The reporter further suggested that Adey needed protection, not punishment. The "hero" of the story was Adey's father who "took drastic action to keep his 20-year-old daughter away from the wrong man" (Dejka 2006, 1). Jefferey Adey, who worried that his daughter had been led astray by Hubbard, tracked the couple to a motel room. He then forced his way in and "held Hubbard until deputies arrived" (Dejka 2006, 2). Although the police arrested both Hubbard and the young Adey after finding crack cocaine and two crack pipes, Kathleen Adey was not portrayed as an equal participant in the crime. Indeed, the headline for the story was "Dad's worries lead to lawyer's arrest." Guilt was firmly attributed to Hubbard, thus minimizing Adey's culpability. Readers were left with the impression that Adey was a manipulated young woman, in need of her father's protection.

Stories that attributed guilt to a female offender, in contrast, indicated that the crime was committed freely with no extraneous causes. Our assessments of attributions of guilt are consistent with references to "bad" women made by previous scholars (see, for example, Wilczynski 1991). As an example, a *Washington Post* story, "Somalia Drug Trade," attributed guilt to Somalian women who sold the narcotic, khat (Wax 2006, A11). The reporter specifically focused on Maryann Ali, an ex-school teacher and mother of ten. According to the reporter, khat is a drug habitually ingested by many Somalian men, and that "opponents [of the drug] call the habit a national epidemic and say men who use the drug neglect their families by spending huge amounts of cash and time on it [the narcotic]" (Wax 2006, p. A11). Ali did not deny selling khat or the negative consequences of the drug. Instead, Ali emphasized that she, and other female dealers like her, "took 'any job we could find, and khat was it. And it seemed better than becoming a fighter or taking food handouts. I was an educated woman; I couldn't do that'" (Wax 2006, A13). In short, Ali was depicted as a woman who rationally decided to sell narcotics, without concern for addicted users. Such an account led to the conclusion that Ali was fully culpable for her criminal actions.

REAL INJURY, REAL VICTIM

Reporters may also emphasize the amount of harm done to a specific victim (or victims). Recall that 31.3 percent of the stories about minority women included such exacerbating/aggravating themes (see Figure 2). In comparison, only 13.3 percent of the stories about white women mentioned either the degree of harm done or a specific victim (see Figure 2).

A story in the *USA Today* highlighted how a female drug offender's actions resulted in real injury to real victims. In this story, the reporter profiled a corrupt Chicago police officer who assisted a local gang in "distributing a potent form of heroin that...killed more than 130 people in recent weeks" (Leinwand 2006, 2A). Readers learned that police officer Tashika Sledge, a black woman, befriended one of the leaders of the Mickey Cobras gang. She subsequently offered her personal vehicle to gang's leader so that he could "deliver 2 pounds of marijuana to a customer in Gary, Indiana" and used her position of authority to "[tip] him off to police surveillance" (Leinwand 2006, 2A). Moreover, she helped the gang sell and traffic heroin laced with the drug, fentanyl: a combination whose strength was often unknown to users. As a result, this narcotic was noted to be "particularly potent and deadly" (Leinwand 2006, 2A) and individuals were likely to overdose when they used it. In fact, "police and health officials... said the potent heroin was one of the most dangerous drug combinations to hit the streets in years" (Leinwand 2006, 2A).

While the reporter of this story did not focus on any specific victim, she did place a great deal of emphasis on the overall impact of the drug that Sledge helped traffic. The drug was distributed over a very large geographical area. Specifically, it affected communities in Chicago,

"Detroit, St. Louis, Philadelphia, Harrisburg, Pa., Camden, N.J., and Wilmington, Delaware" (Leinwand 2006, 2A). Moreover, this heroin-fentanyl cocktail "was linked to 53 deaths and 362 non-fatal overdoses in Chicago from April 13 to May 16. At least 54 deaths in Detroit and 31 in Philadelphia have been linked" to the drug, as well (Leinwand, 2006, p. 2A). Aside from the drug users who were affected, innocent residents in these areas were also victimized. These residents stated that their "lives have been made more dangerous by drug dealing at the [Dearborn Homes public housing] complex" and that "the gang has been linked to several shootings" there (Leinwand 2006, 2A). When these residents learned that Sledge and 29 other people connected to the Mickey Cobras gang had been taken off the street, they expressed relief.

To summarize, this article portrayed Sledge as a dangerous individual. She posed a lethal threat to residents of her own community, as well as to others from areas beyond her jurisdiction. Her actions are antithetical to the oath she took to "protect and serve" her community. Instead of helping law-abiding citizens, she aided and abetted members of a notorious gang in trafficking deadly narcotics. In doing so, she destroyed the lives of many.

HOPE OF REFORMATION VERSUS BEYOND REFORMATION

As mentioned earlier, the neutralizing/mitigating themes we identified served to produce more neutral or favorable overall story tones. "Hope of Reformation" appeared when reporters discussed a female offender's rehabilitative progress, which suggested that sympathy was warranted and that the female was not likely to pose a continued threat to society.

While not all women had their criminal behavior minimized in this manner, it is important to note that a higher percentage of stories about white females who were alleged or accused of having committed an illicit drug offense contained this neutralizer (see Figure 1). This neutralizer, for example, appeared in a *Chicago Tribune* story, "Court gives meth addicts way out" (Casillas 2006, 1). This story focused on Janice Sidwell, a 39-year-old white woman and mother of two. Sidwell had a history of selling and using methamphetamine. The reporter described how Sidwell and Rick Cantwell, the father of her children, were fortunate enough to have been sent to the drug court, rather than to prison. The reporter detailed how the "[drug] court offers a chance to avoid prison time and provides a much fuller safety net, directing addicts to drug counseling, mental health treatment, even parenting classes" (Casillas 2006, 16). Sidwell's success and determination to stay clean were highlighted throughout the story. The reporter pointed out that "Sidwell entered drug court in 2004 and has been clean since" (Casillas 2006, 16). Sidwell's resolve to strengthen her family was another theme throughout the article. The reporter noted that Sidwell recently regained custody of her son and daughter, and was determined to make up for lost time. Additionally, Sidwell and Cantwell made plans to get married, and Sidwell was quoted as saying "Drug court saved our family" (Casillas 2006, 16). The strong focus on Sidwell's success in drug court left the reader with the impression that she will now lead a law-abiding life, thanks to the intervention.

Another example of hope of reformation comes from a story in the *Minneapolis Star Tribune*: "A Past Officially Forgiven" (Blake 2006, 1). In this story, the *Star* reporter described the impressive transformation of Karen Edmonson, a white woman, who was depicted smiling in a photograph on the front page of the paper. The reporter began the story by noting that Edmonson started abusing drugs at age 11, dropped out of high school by 10th grade, and was convicted and sentenced for dealing methamphetamine at age 21. "Twenty years later, Edmonson, 49, … has a master's degree, a successful business, and her health—a phenomenal life… especially considering that even when drug abusers get clean, they often lead marginal lives" (Blake 2006, 1). The reader soon learned that there is nothing marginal about Edmonson's current life.

> She has been clean for 20 years, … is a licensed psychologist, social worker, and alcohol and drug counselor. She ran a program at the University of Minnesota focused on people with multiple addictions in the late 1980s and 1990s and has traveled around the country giving speeches and selling drug treatment manuals. (Blake, 2006, p. A14).

Moreover, she and her husband run a business that helps others get required certifications so that they may offer medical and mental health classes. In other words, for the past 20 years, Edmonson has worked to helped others in their recovery from addiction.

Given her successful rehabilitation and positive contributions to society, "President Bush tacked on one more achievement [by] granting Edmonson a pardon and officially forgiving her crime 28 years ago" (Blake 2006, 1). The article ended with a narrative from Edmonson's husband who said the pardon was appropriately given to a "remarkable person" and that it is "'truly recognition of how she's been living her life'" (Blake 2006, A14).

The *Atlanta Journal-Constitution* also featured a story about a white woman who overcame her addition to drugs. A paragraph in the story recounted how Ashley Smith became addicted to crystal methamphetamine after she tried it for the first time. She then gave up custody of her daughter, quickly dropped to 90 pounds, and began hearing voices (Rockwell 2006, A12). Despite the presence of this negative information, the story focused on Smith's testimony before the U.S. Congress about the dangers of methamphetamine. Therefore, this article placed the most emphasis on Smith's mental resolve and her ability to overcome addiction.

This front-page story also included a photograph of Smith, who appeared happy and focused. Readers learned that her unlikely road to recovery began after she was held hostage in her apartment by an individual who was on the run after shooting a judge, a federal agent, and two others in the Fulton County [Atlanta] Courthouse (Rockwell 2006, A12). During her captivity, Smith persuaded her captor to leave, then called the police. For her actions, she received a $70,000 reward, and the ordeal provided the impetus for Smith to "kick the habit" (Rockwell 2006, A12). Smith later published a book entitled "Unlikely Angel: The Untold Story of the Atlanta Hostage Hero" (Rockwell 2006, A12).

When appearing before Congress, the "soft-spoken Smith" was "calm and poised" (Rockwell 2006, A12). She explained how she came to the realization that she had to stop using methamphetamine and prevent others from ever using the drug. During her testimony, Smith urged lawmakers to support television campaigns that depicted the negative effects of methamphetamine, because she never would have used the drug had she known of its dangers.

While some of the stories we reviewed indicated that women are capable of turning their lives around, other stories profiled women who were beyond reformation. As noted, this technique of exacerbation was applied in a racially disparate manner (see Figure 2). Whereas a third of the stories about white female street-drug offenders described them as unlikely to change, 50 percent of the stories about their minority counterparts noted their inability to reform.

With regard to minority women, a *New York Times* story about Debra Harris and a *Los Angeles Times* story about Bertha Cuestas both provided explanations of how reformation was not likely or possible. What is interesting about these two stories is that the format was exactly the same, despite the fact that the articles were written about two completely different women, in two different newspapers, and at two different times of the year.

The *Los Angeles Times* story about Cuestas, a Latina offender, described how she had repeatedly been arrested for drug offenses and prostitution; she "had been arrested 21 times" and "knew the drill" (Garvey & Leonard 2006, A1). Police officers added that she had been arrested "too many times" (Garvey & Leonard 2006, A1). Other law enforcement officials were quoted as saying that laws "give longtime chronic offenders like Cuestas too many chances to reoffend with little consequences" (Garvey & Leonard 2006, A22).

The story from the *New York Times* described how Harris, an African-American female, was recently arrested because she provided a dirty urine sample during a final visit with her parole officer. Before this parole violation, "she had been imprisoned three times over the years" (Eckholm 2006, A12). After acquainting the reader with Cuestas and Harris, reporters from both papers then discussed minority males who had also been arrested for drug offenses. These men, like Cuestas and Harris, were no strangers to the criminal justice system. After drawing a parallel between the men and women, the reporters ended with ominous predictions of each woman's future criminality. The *New York Times* article concluded with the following quote from Harris: "'In some ways, I feel like I'm back in the same old spot. [House arrest] keeps my life structured for now. It's crazy out there'" (Eckholm 2006, A12). The implication is that without oversight from the criminal justice system, she will be unable to resist the temptations of crime. The ending of the story from the *Los Angeles Times* was more dramatic because it contained the following: "Postscript: [by the time this article was finished and ready for the press] Cuestas was rearrested for failing to appear in court" (Garvey & Leonard 2006, A22).

Another story about an offender's inability to reform and consequent demise was about a black woman named Hazel Brewer. This article, which appeared in the *Chicago Tribune*, explained how Brewer died of a drug overdose. Brewer was described by *Tribune* reporters as a chronic drug offender who willfully bought and used the drugs that killed her only hours after she left a detox program. Brewer's extensive history of drug use was detailed in the story. Her brother explained how she progressed from using cigarettes and marijuana as a teen to using crack and heroin as an adult. The reporter explained that although Brewer often promised her family that she would "get clean," she was rarely sober (Rozas 2006, 22). Brewer's brother further explained that his sister would often binge on drugs, "check in to treatment programs, and then go back to drugs again" (Rozas 2006, 22). Brewer's extensive history of drug use and disregard for the help offered by many drug treatment providers left the reader believing that Brewer would have continued to use heroin had she lived; reformation was not possible for her.

DISCUSSION

Few scholars have examined the impact that a female offender's race/ethnicity has on a news story written about her crime. To date, only five studies have systematically examined how media portrayals differ for minority women relative to white women offenders (Bond-Maupin 1998; Brennan & Vandenberg 2009; Farr 1999, 2000; Huckerby 2003). In all of these studies, researchers concluded that stories written about the crimes committed by minority women were more negative in tone than the stories written about white women. While this conclusion was consistent across the five studies, in none of the investigations did the researchers consider how crime narratives or overall story tones may have been influenced by the type of offense a woman was alleged to have committed. Furthermore, almost all previous studies focused exclusively on women who committed violent crimes (Berrington & Honkatukia 2002; Bond-Maupin 1998; Farr 1997, 2000).

We conducted the current study because we believe that examinations of female criminality should move beyond an exclusive focus on violent women. In particular, we were interested in media depictions of female drug offenders, given the significance of current policies for such offenses in the United States. In 2012, more individuals were arrested for drug offenses than for any other crime, and women accounted for over 200,000 of these arrests (FBI 2013a, 2013b). With regard to changes in correctional populations, 25 percent of women incarcerated in state prisons are held for drug offenses (Carson & Golinelli 2013, 10), but the rate of incarceration for black female drug offenders is substantially higher than the rate for white women (HRW 2008, 19, Table 13). We believe that differences in media constructions of white and minority female drug offenders may provide a possible explanation for the differential treatment experienced by women of color who enter the criminal justice system. Indeed, researchers find that ideas about crime and criminals are based, in large part, on the stories that individuals learn about from the media

(Autunes & Hurley 1977; Chermak 1994; Chiricos & Eschholz 2002; Fishman & Weimann 1985; Garofalo 1981; Gilliam & Iyengar 2000; Surette 1992).

When we placed our focus solely on the stories about illicit- (or street-) drug offenders (who are arguably the focus of the "war on drugs" efforts), we found that a greater proportion of the stories about white women had neutral or positive overall tones because more of their narrative focus contained neutralizing (or mitigating) thematic elements. Specifically, two-thirds of the stories about white women who engaged in street-drug offenses had neutral or favorable overall tones, but this was true for only one-third of the stories about minority women accused or alleged to have committed illicit-drug offenses. These findings are consistent with the black feminist perspective, which maintains that minority women are perceived and, therefore, treated more negatively than white women.

The overall tones of newspaper stories differed for females of varying races/ethnicities due to differences in the emphasis placed on an offender's degree of guilt, the harm she caused to another person, and her potential for reform. A higher percentage of the stories about white women contained narrative elements that served to minimize their culpability and/or provided presentations of successful drug treatment or some other indication that their lives were now moving in a positive direction. Our findings are consistent with the contention that beliefs about the culpability of offenders are rooted largely in negative racial and ethnic stereotypes (Barlow 1998; Chiricos & Eschholz 2002; Entman 1990, 1992, 1994, 1997; Gilliam & Iyengar 2000; Lundman 2003; Lundman, Douglass, & Hanson 2004; Peffley, Shields, & Williams 1996; Welch 2007), and that the media play a prominent role in the maintenance of these stereotypes (Welch, Fenwick, & Roberts 1998).

Within the criminal sentencing literature, focal concerns theorists argue that offenders who are viewed as culpable for their actions and/or incapable of reform receive more punitive sanctions (Steffensmeier, Ulmer, & Kramer 1998). Consistent with this notion, Hurwitz and Peffley (1997) argued that negative depictions of black drug users influenced public support for the harsh punishment of offenders, rather than rehabilitation. In the current study, discussions of reform potential differed markedly for white women versus minority women. A higher percentage of the stories about white women documented their successful drug treatment, whereas a higher percentage of the stories about minority women provided accounts of their failed drug treatment, relapse, and/or re-arrest.

Negative portrayals influence not only the opinions of the general public, but also the opinions of actors in the criminal justice system including police, prosecutors, judges, juries, probation officers, and prison administrators. Legal decision making is "complex, repetitive, and often constrained by information, time, and resources in ways that may produce considerable ambiguity or uncertainty for arriving at a 'satisfactory decision'" (Demuth 2003, 880). Criminal justice agents, therefore, use "perceptual shorthand" (Steffensmeier et al. 1998; see also Bridges & Steen 1998; Demuth 2003) based on stereotypes to efficiently make decisions. The use of cognitive shortcuts, however, may lead judges to:

> project behavioral expectations about such things as offenders' risk of recidivism or danger to the community. Once in place and continuously reinforced, such patterned thinking and acting are resistant to change and may result in the inclusion of racial and ethnic biases in criminal case processing. (Demuth 2003, 880-881)

The results presented in this paper, then, are important because they point to media frames of the crime problem and criminals that might well provide an explanation for the dramatic and persistent racial/ethnic disparities that pervade our criminal justice system.

While the results of this study are consistent with the black feminist perspective and are in-line with discussions about negative stereotypes that pervade our society and the disproportionate confinement of minority women in U.S. prisons, there are some limitations that must be noted. First, our sample size is small. This limited our ability to conduct a more in-depth investigation. Researchers who gather a greater number of stories, for example, may be able to examine whether differences emerge in stories *among* minority female criminals. To elaborate, these scholars may be able to determine how portrayals of African-American female offenders differ from the depictions of Latinas and/or Native American women. Similarly, due to our study's relatively small sample size, our analyses were limited to comparisons of narratives for broadly-defined drug categories (i.e., illicit-drug offenses versus alcohol-related and pharmaceutical offenses). With more stories, future researchers may be able to conduct more in-depth examinations of how race/ethnicity impacts the presentation of stories about specific types of street-drug offenses (e.g., stories about crack cocaine or methamphetamine). Moreover, it may also be possible that a woman's social class may be an important determinant of the overall tone of a story and the thematic elements that are contained within a story. However, the concept of social class is a very difficult one to measure based on the types of information generally available within newspaper crime stories. To be clear, we attempted to measure a woman's social class based on indications of her occupation, level of educational attainment, income, and place of residence or living conditions (e.g., whether she was noted to live in an affluent area or in poverty). We found that more than half of the crime stories provided no indication of a woman's social class. And, in the stories that contained some indication of social class, the vast majority of the stories were about lower class women. Thus, data were either missing for the social class variable or suggested that there was little variation in social class for the stories we encountered.

Aside from these limitations, the results gleaned from our exploratory study are important because they have direct implications for how people may develop stereotypes about criminal events and offenders—and ones that would sustain harsh treatment, even of women, if the person in question were African American, Latina, Native American, Pacific Islander, or some other person of color. It has long been established that minority offenders are overrepresented at every stage of criminal justice processing (for a detailed discussion see Walker et al. 2012). What is less clear, however, is why this happens. A number of scholars have posited that this phenomenon is related to negative racial/ethnic stereotypes that are prevalent in American society (Chiricos & Eschholz 2002; Gilliam & Iyengar 2000). Moreover, many have argued that the media play a key role in perpetuating stereotypes, including notions about who is likely to be guilty and, thus, who deserves harsh punishment (Chiricos & Eschholz 2002; Entman 1990, 1992, 1994, 1997; Madriz 1997). Because everyone is exposed to messages from the news media, it is unlikely that anyone will be immune from its influence. Furthermore, public support for harsh responses to criminal behavior, particularly for members of minority groups, gives politicians and policy makers a license to continue to pursue incarceration rather than drug treatment in response to the problem of drug addiction, despite the fact that the former is arguably far more costly and less effective.

ABOUT THE AUTHORS

1. Pauline K. Brennan received her Ph.D. in Criminal Justice from the University at Albany, SUNY, and is an Associate Professor and the Doctoral Program Chair for the School of Criminology and Criminal Justice at the University of Nebraska Omaha. Her areas of research include inequity in court processing, corrections policy, and issues related to adult-female offenders and victims. She has published papers on the combined effects of race/ethnicity and sex on court processing outcomes, media depictions of offenders, correctional policies for male and female offenders, and the challenges of service delivery for immigrant victims of domestic violence.

2. Meda Chesney-Lind, Ph.D., is Professor of Women's Studies at the University of Hawaii at Manoa. Nationally recognized for her work on women and crime, her books include *Girls, Delinquency and Juvenile Justice* (Wadsworth, 1992), *The Female Offender* (Sage, 1997), *Female Gangs in America* (Lakeview Press, 1999), *Invisible Punishment* (New Press, 2002), *Girls, Women and Crime* (Sage, 2004), and *Beyond Bad Girls* (Routledge, 2008). She recently finished two edited collections—one on trends in girls' violence, entitled *Fighting for Girls* (SUNY, 2010) and a collection of international essays entitled *Feminist Theories of Crime* (Ashgate, 2011).

3. Abby L. Vandenberg received her Ph.D. from the School of Criminology and Criminal Justice at the

University of Nebraska Omaha in 2013. Her research interests include media accounts of crime, correctional policy, and criminal justice processing. In 2011, she received the Elton S. Carter Award for Excellence in a Master's Thesis for her work on media portrayals of female offenders. She currently serves as Research Manager for the Nebraska Department of Correctional Services.

4. Timbre Wulf-Ludden received her Ph.D. from the School of Criminology and Criminal Justice at the University of Nebraska Omaha in 2013. Her research interests are varied but her primary focus has been in the field of corrections. She has studied prison violence, interpersonal relationships among incarcerated men and women, as well as programming for female offenders. She is currently an Assistant Professor of Criminal Justice at the University of Nebraska Kearney.

References

Altheide, D.L. 1996. *Qualitative media analysis*. Thousand Oaks, CA: Sage Publications.

Antunes, G. E., & Hurley, P. A. 1977. "The representation of criminal events in Houston's two daily newspapers." *Journalism Quarterly*, 54(4): 756-760.

Armstrong, I. 1999. "Women and their 'uncontrollable impulses': The Medicalization of women's crime and differential gender sentencing." *Psychiatry, Psychology, and Law*, 6(1): 67-77.

Barak, G. 1994. "Between the waves: Mass-mediated themes of crime and justice." *Berkeley Journal of Sociology*, 21(3): 133-147.

Barlow, M. H. 1998. "Race and the problem of crime in "Time" and "Newsweek" cover stories, 1946 to 1995." *Social Justice,* 25(2): 149-183.

Belknap, J. 2014. *Invisible women: Gender, crime, and justice (4th edition).* Stamford, Connecticut: Cengage Learning.

Berrington, E., & P. Honkatukia. 2002. "An evil monster and a poor thing: Female violence in the media." *Journal of Scandinavian Studies in Criminology and Crime Prevention,* 3(1): 50-72.

Blake, A. 2006, April 20. "A past officially forgiven." *Minneapolis Star Tribune*, pp. A1, A14.

Bond-Maupin, L. 1998. "'That wasn't even me they showed': Women as criminals on *America's Most Wanted.*" *Violence Against Women,* 4(1): 30-44.

Brennan, P. K. 2002. *Women sentenced to jail in New York City.* New York, NY: LFB Scholarly Publishing.

Brennan, P. K. 2006. "Sentencing female misdemeanants: An examination of the direct and indirect effects of race/ethnicity." *Justice Quarterly,* 23(1): 60-95.

Brennan, P. K., & A. L. Vandenberg. 2009. "Depictions of female offenders in front-page newspaper stories: The importance of race/ethnicity." *International Journal of Social Inquiry,* 2(2): 141-175.

Bridges, S., & S. Steen. 1998. "Racial disparities in official assessments of juvenile offenders: Attributional stereotypes as mediating mechanisms." *American Sociological Review,* 63(4): 554-570.

Buckler, K., & L. Travis. 2005. "Assessing the newsworthiness of homicide events: An analysis of coverage in the *Houston Chronicle.*" *Journal of Criminal Justice and Popular Culture,* 12(1): 1-25.

Budd, R. W. 1964. "Attention score: A device for measuring news' play." *Journalism Quarterly,* 41(2): 259-262.

BurrellesLuce. 2006. "Top 100 daily newspapers in the U.S. by circulation: 2006." Retrieved http://www.burrellesluce.com/top100/2006_Top_100List.pdf (February 3, 2010).

Carson, E.A., & D. Golinelli. 2013. *Prisoners in 2012: Advance counts.* Washington, DC: Bureau of Justice Statistics.

Casillas, O. 2006, February 27. "Court gives meth addicts way out." *Chicago Tribune,* pp. 1, 16.

Castro, D. O. 1998. "'Hot blood and easy virtue': Mass media and the making of racist Latino/a stereotypes." In *Images of color, images of crime,* edited by C. R. Mann & M. S. Zatz, (pp. 134-144). Los Angeles, CA: Roxbury Publishing Company.

Chermak, S. 1994. "Body count news: How crime is presented in the news media." *Justice Quarterly,* 11(4): 561-582.

Chermak, S. 1998. "Predicting crime story salience: The effects of crime, victim, and defendant characteristics." *Journal of Criminal Justice,* 26(1): 61-70.

Chermak, S., & N.M. Chapman. 2007. "Predicting crime story salience: A replication." *Journal of Criminal Justice,* 35(4): 351-363.

Chesney-Lind, M. 1999. "Media misogyny: Demonizing 'violent' girls and women." In *Making trouble: Cultural constructions of crime, deviance and control,* edited by J. Ferrell & N. Websdale, (pp. 115-140). New York, NY: Walter de Gruyter, Inc.

Chesney-Lind, M., & M. Eliason. 2006. "From invisible to incorrigible: The demonization of marginalized women and girls." *Crime, Media and Culture,* 2(1), 29-48.

Chesney-Lind, & M. Morash. 2011. *Feminist theories of crime.* Surrey, UK: Ashgate Publishing Limited.

Chesney-Lind, M., & L. Pasko. 2004. *The female offender: Girls, women and crime* (2nd Ed.). Thousand Oaks, CA: Sage Publications, Inc.

Chiricos, T., & S. Eschholz. 2002. "The racial and ethnic typification of crime and the criminal typification of race and ethnicity in local television news." *Journal of Research in Crime and Delinquency,* 39(4): 400-420.

Collins, P. H. 2000. *Black feminist thought: Knowledge, consciousness, and the politics of empowerment.* New York, NY: Routledge.

Davis, A.Y. 1981. *Women, race, & class.* New York, NY: Random House.

Dejka, J. 2006, September 17. Dad's worries lead to lawyer's arrest. *Omaha World Herald,* pp. 1, 2.

Demuth, S. 2003. Racial and ethnic differences in pretrial release decisions and outcomes: A comparison of Hispanic, black, and white felony arrestees. *Criminology,* 41(3): 873-907.

Eckholm, E. 2006, August 12. Help for the hardest part of prison: Staying out. *New York Times,* pp. A1, A12.

Entman, R. 1990. Modern racism and the images of blacks in local television news. *Critical Studies in Mass Communication,* 7(4): 332-345.

Entman, R. 1992. Blacks in the news: Television, modern racism and cultural change. *Journalism Quarterly,* 69(2): 341-361.

Entman, R. 1994. Representation and reality in the portrayal of blacks on network television news. *Journalism Quarterly,* 71(3): 509-520.

Entman, R. 1997. African Americans according to TV news. Eds. E. E. Dennis & E. C. Pease, *The media in black and white* (pp. 29-36). New Brunswick, NJ: Transaction Publishers.

Fairchild, H. H., & Cozens, J. A. 1981. Chicano, Hispanic, or Mexican American: What's in a name? *Hispanic Journal of Behavioral Sciences,* 3(2): 191-198.

Farr, K. A. 1997. Aggravating and differentiating factors in the cases of white and minority women on death row. *Crime & Delinquency,* 43(3): 260-278.

Farr, K. A. 2000. Defeminizing and dehumanizing female murderers: Depictions of lesbians on death row. *Women & Criminal Justice,* 11(1): 49-66.

Federal Bureau of Investigation [FBI]. 2013a. *Crime in the United States, 2012.* Washington, DC: United States Department of Justice. http://www.fbi.gov/about-us/cjis/ucr/crime-in-the-u.s/2012/crime-in-the-u.s.-2012/tables/29tabledatadecpdf (January 26, 2015).

Federal Bureau of Investigation [FBI]. 2013b. *Crime in the United States, 2012.* Washington, DC: United States Department of Justice. http://www.fbi.gov/about-us/cjis/ucr/crime-in-the-u.s/2012/crime-in-the-u.s.-2012/tables/33tabledatadecoverviewpdf (January 26, 2015).

Fishman, G., & Weimann, G. 1985. Presenting the victim: Sex-based bias in press reports on crime. *Justice Quarterly,* 2(4): 491-503.

Garofalo, J. 1981. Crime and the mass media: A selective review of research. *Journal of Research in Crime and Delinquency,* 18(2): 319-350.

Garvey, M., & Leonard, J. 2006, December 26. Why L.A. jail cells have revolving doors. *Los Angeles Times*, pp. A1, A22.

Gilliam, F. D., & Iyengar, S. 2000. Prime suspects: The influence of local television news on the viewing public. *American Journal of Political Science,* 44(3): 560-573.

Gladwell, M. 2005. *Blink: The power of thinking without thinking.* New York, NY: Little, Brown and Company.

Goffman, E. 1974. *Frame analysis: An essay on the organization of experience.* Cambridge, MA: Harvard University Press.

Goffman, E. 1979. *Gender advertisements.* New York, NY: Harper & Row.

Grabe, M. E. 1999. Television news magazine crime stories: A functionalist perspective. *Critical Studies in Mass Communication,* 16(2): 155-171.

Graber, D. A. 1980. *Crime news and the public.* New York, NY: Praeger Publishers.

Greene, J., Pranis, K., & Frost, N.A. 2006. *Hard hit: The growth in the imprisonment of women, 1977-2004.* New York, NY: Women's Prison Association.

Healey, J. F. 1997. *Race, ethnicity, and gender in the United States: Inequality, group conflict, and power.* Thousand Oaks, CA: Pine Forge Press.

hooks, b. 1981. Ain't I a woman? Black women and feminism. Boston, MA: South End Press.

Higginbotham, E. 1983. Laid bare by the system: Work and survival for black and Hispanic women. Eds. A. Swerdlow & H. Lessinger, *Class, race, and sex: The dynamics of control* (pp. 200-215). Boston, Massachusetts: G.K. Hall and Company.

Huckerby, J. 2003. Women who kill their children: Case study and conclusions concerning the differences in the fall from maternal grace by Khoua Her and Andrea Yates. *Duke Journal of Gender Law & Policy,* 10: 149-172.

Human Rights Watch [HRW]. 2008. *Targeting blacks: Drug law enforcement and race in the United States.* New York, NY: Human Rights Watch.

Humphries, D. 1981. Serious crime, news coverage, and ideology: A content analysis of crime coverage in a metropolitan newspaper. *Crime & Delinquency*, 27(2): 191-205.

Hurwitz, J., & Peffley, M. 1997. Public perceptions of race and crime: The role of racial stereotypes. *American Journal of Political Science*, 41(2): 375-401.

Irwin, K., & Chesney-Lind, M. 2008. Girls' violence: Beyond dangerous masculinity. *Sociology Compass*, 2/3: 837-855.

Klein, D. 1973. The etiology of female crime: A review of the literature. *Issues in Criminology*, 8(2): 3-30.

Landrine, H. 1985. Race x class stereotypes of women. *Sex Roles*, 13(1/2): 65-75.

Leinwand, D. 2006, June 22. Chicago drug ring arrests: Raids target gang ring behind deadly heroin. *USA Today*, pp. 1A-2A.

Lundman, R. J. 2003. The newsworthiness and selection bias in news about murder: Comparative and relative effects of novelty and race and gender typifications on newspaper coverage of homicide. *Sociological Forum*, 18(3): 357-386.

Lundman, R. J., Douglass, O. M., & Hanson, J. M. 2004. News about murder in an African American newspaper: Effects of relative frequency and race and gender typifications. *The Sociological Quarterly*, 45(2): 249-272.

Madriz, E. 1997. Images of criminals and victims: A study on women's fear and social control. *Gender & Society*, 11(3): 342-356.

Mawby, R. I., & Brown, J. 1984. Newspaper images of the victim: A British study. *Victimology: An International Journal*, 9(1): 82-94.

Peffley, M., Shields, T., & Williams, B. 1996. The intersection of race and crime in television news stories: An experimental study. *Political Communication*, 13: 309-327.

Pollak, J. M., & Kurbin, C. E. 2007. Crime in the news: How crimes, offenders and victims and portrayed in the media.

Journal of Criminal Justice and Popular Culture, 14(1): 59-83.

Portillos, E. L. 1999. The social construction of gender in the barrio. Eds. M. Chesney-Lind & J. Hagedom, *Female gangs in America* (pp. 232-244). Chicago, IL: Lake View Press.

Potter. H. 2006. An argument for black feminist criminology. *Feminist Criminology*, 1(2): 106-124.

Rafter, N. H. 1990. *Partial justice: Women, prisons, and social control.* New Brunswick, NJ: Transaction Publishers

Rockwell, L. 2006, January 24. Smith gets own captive audience. *Atlanta Journal-Constitution*, pp. A1, A12.

Rozas, A. 2006, June 8. Hazel Brewer of Lombard, mother of 4. *Chicago Tribune*, pp. 1- back page.

Sherrill, R. 2001, January 8. Death Trip: The American way of execution. *The Nation*, p. 1B.

Steen, S., Engen, R. L., & Gainey, R. R. 2005. Images of danger and culpability: Racial stereotyping, case processing, and criminal sentencing. *Criminology,* 43(2), 435-468.

Steffensmeier, D., Ulmer, J. & Kramer, J. 1998. The interaction of race, gender, and age in criminal sentencing: The punishment cost of being young, Black, and male. *Criminology,* 36(4), 763-798.

Surette, R. 1992. *Media, crime, and criminal justice: Images and realities.* Pacific Grove, CA: Brooks/Cole.

Sykes, G. M., & Matza, D. 1957. Techniques of neutralization: A theory of deviance. *American Sociological Review,* 22(6): 667-670.

Walker, S., Spohn, C, & DeLone, M. 2012. *The Color of Justice: Race, Ethnicity, and Crime in America* (5th Ed.). Belmont, CA: Wadsworth.

Wax, E. 2006. April 16. Somalia drug trade. *Washington Post,* pp. A1, A11, A13.

Welch, K. 2007. Black criminal stereotypes and racial profiling. *Journal of Contemporary Criminal Justice,* 23(3): 276-288.

Welch, M., Fenwick, M., & Roberts, M. 1998. State managers, intellectuals, and the media: A content analysis of ideology in experts' quotes in feature newspaper articles on crime. *Justice Quarterly,* 15(2): 219-241.

Wilczynski, A. 1991. Images of women who kill their infants: The mad and the bad. *Women &Criminal Justice,* 2(2): 71-88.

Willemsen, T. M., & van Schie, E. C. M. 1989. Sex stereotypes and responses to juvenile delinquency. *Sex Roles,* 20(11/12): 623-638.

Young, V. D. 1986. Gender expectations and their impact on black female offenders and victims. *Justice Quarterly,* 3(3): 305-327.

THE PLIGHT OF CHILDREN AND YOUTH: A HUMAN RIGHTS STUDY

BERNARD SCHISSEL[1]

The paradigm of human rights that is the cornerstone of the United Nations Universal Declaration of Human Rights focuses on the autonomous individual's inherent rights to freedom, justice and peace. Such a rights paradigm invokes the notion of the right to protect free will and its many manifestations in a "democratic," western political framework. And, indeed, for non-colonized societies which are now in the throes of affluence, such a rights paradigm would seem logical and moral. However, the idea of a western-based human rights program as the standard upon which universal rights, including children's rights, should be seen is under mounting scrutiny. The critiques are clear. First, many societies adhere to a collective rights paradigm in which the rights of the individual do not necessarily take precedence over the rights of the collective. Second, and most importantly, an individual-rights paradigm works only within a context in which individuals already have access to a minimum standard of quality of life, a society in which people can "afford" to be free. Kwame Nkrumah of Ghana and Julius Nyerere of Kenya

---

[1] Program Head, Doctor of Social Sciences, Office of Interdisciplinary Studies, Royal Roads University

were devoted to the principles of economic statism that dictated that "freedom from want, from hunger, and from economic deprivation necessitated limiting political liberties that could destroy the party or state in its initial stages." (Pollis and Schwab 2006) In their eyes, the solution to the problems faced by countries in Africa, countries that had experienced centuries of colonial domination, lay not within a libertarian political philosophy but within political strategies that enforced at least a minimum level of economic prosperity, strategies often at odds with individual rights.

Apologists for a western-based human rights model argue that globalization has created the context in which the world itself is becoming more standardized and that the rights embodied in the United Nations Universal Declaration of Human Rights and the United Nations Convention on the Rights of the Child (CRC) are contemporary to all societies and, in many traditional societies, drawn from the pastoral rights of the individual (Drydyk 2006). The argument is compelling: if we are opening up the world to economic innovation and dispersal, then we need a rights-based doctrine to ensure that individuals are not treated as mere commodities, especially with respect to labour and consumption. On the other hand, the oftentimes seemingly insurmountable plight of the majority of the world's children does not seem to be ameliorated by doctrinal legal paradigms, because, at a very basic level, such paradigms are based on adult conceptions, adult ways of knowing— or adult sensibilities. In the liberal democratic tradition, these adult ways of knowing would include the need to protect the child as an especially vulnerable, incompletely-developed citizen. In this tradition, the three r's of child protection become risk, resilience and reconciliation, all elements of child care that are foundational. The problem arises, however—and it is the problem that I confront in this article—is that the three r's are based on a type of medical/therapeutic approach that may be important in the short term, but often fails as a framework for a protracted healing program. The response to the social problems of the young is typically modernist, typically corrective and juridical in its reactive focus, and delinquent in its failure to envision proactive measures for child empowerment that may be the only source for real change.

I draw on the compelling work of Skott-Myhre and Tarulli (2008) to help form the argument that child rights need to reconsidered and envisioned within the day to day reality of children throughout the world and not just in the context of liberal democratic values that assume a minimum standard of socio-economic and political care. Rights, in this new paradigm, are not given but produced by the subjects who are traditionally the targets of endowed rights:

> The codes and regulations of the juridical form are always secondary to the courageous acts of children who resist with their bodies the unwarranted incursion of adults into their lives. In other words, it is the bodies of children and their activities that produce children's rights, both through their overt acts of resistance, but perhaps even more through their creative capacities to produce the world. (Skott-Myhre and Tarulli 2008, 71).

The problem for those of us who have been trained and socialized within a juridical paradigm based on western democratic principles is that we have several philosophical blinders that we may need to shed. Firstly, we have been steeped in a cultural belief that the legal status of a child is tied to that child's cognitive abilities that result from developmental maturity. Rights accrue to children and youth on the basis of a science-determined taxonomy based on age. The problem is that such a normative way of producing and universalizing the "legal citizen" is devoid

of all considerations of context and history and, most importantly, devoid of a conception of rights as the result of
"immanent potential—rights as daily life are composed
out of the activities of lived experiences of multiple bodies
creating the world through their activities and actions"
(Skott-Myhre and Tarulli, 2008: 70-71). Secondly, our intellectual training has laden us with a bifurcated world-
view that sees the child and the adult as separate entities
and disallows us from conceiving of development as a
process of living as a child and an adult simultaneously.
Thus, children, in our traditional ontology, are always "citizens in waiting…potential bearers of rights…not ends in
themselves but rather creatures in the process of development" (Arneil 2002, 71). Thirdly, it is so difficult for the
modern, juridical-trained mind to conceive of free will as
anything other than embedded in the control of the individual. To conceive of the ownership of individual thought
as something beyond the individual takes a leap-of-faith
that few of us are prepared to make. Moreover, it is difficult to conceive of how thought is a collective production
and how we would, for example, give over to children—
and not to justice bureaucracies—the will to collectively
produce rights.

One of the problems for child policy both within and
without Canada is that our understanding of young people
is based on antiquated "modernist" paradigms of what it
means to be young, especially in a 21st century context
characterized by globalization, shifting population demo-
graphics, proliferating information and communication
technologies (ICTs), climate change, and the rise of funda-
mentalist movements (Lynch 2010). One modernist
paradigm is scientifically paternalistic, based on the developmental presumption of the "vulnerable child": young
people are vulnerable because of chronological (biological
difference) and need to be protected from the physical and

emotional dangers of the adult world. Another modernist paradigm stands in opposition to the idea of vulnerable child: children, especially as they approach teenage years, are volatile and incompletely socialized and, as a result, pose a security threat. Such a belief system argues for methods of control that include "heavy-handed," punishment-based responses to non-conventional behaviour. Many of the societal reactions to children and youth that I describe in this article stem from a belief that punishment is appropriate as a first response to bad behaviour in young people.

Both paradigms stem from the same biological understanding of young people and result, in many instances, in child policy based on the assumption that children and adults need to have separate rights. As a consequence, many of the rights that apply to adults are denied to children due to the very western, scientific ethos that age primarily determines capability and culpability (Skott-Myhre & Tarulli 2008). Ironically, such beliefs foster and grow in a socio-political environment in which the "competent child" is the ideal. Institutions like the family and the school strive to foster independence and competency and the ideological framework for such institutions is that children are our greatest natural resource and that they need to be protected and nurtured.

One of the ways for criminologists, as public intellectuals, to approach issues of childhood injustice is to take an epistemological position that acknowledges and incorporates young people's "ways of knowing." This focus on hearing the voices of the young is the foundation for research that starts with children and youth and ends with policies that are first and foremost derived from the knowledge and insights that young people provide. This rather democratic approach to the ontology of children and youth is built upon a social inclusion paradigm, the presumption being that young people are productive members of society and have the right to have input into the development and administration of their society and their place in it (Hache et al 2010; Watson 2008; Luxton 2005). The African Charter on the Rights and Welfare of the Child, 1999 (Kaime 2009) states that the child has a right and a responsibility to contribute to the sustainability of the community and nation. This is in contrast to an historical reality of almost universal exclusion of children and youth from politics and social policy development (Boyle et al., 2007). The inclusion focus is based on a human rights model that invests young people with the same rights and privileges (including self-determination) that accrue to adults.

Embarking on a social inclusion approach for young people demands that criminologists, as advocates for children's rights, need often stand against developmental presumptions that young people's rights and prohibitions need to be bestowed upon them on the basis of chronological (biological) difference—that they need to be protected from the adult world and that the adult world needs to be protected from them. Instead, a criminologist advocate would argue that the legal rights of a child or youth need to be constituted by them and not by the adult world around them; i.e. children must act with agency to create their world, and their rights are the result of their ontological reality. For many public advocates, this is a rather revolutionary position and sometimes hard to defend. This is where sound research, based on young people's epistemology, needs to be in place. In the end, it would be naïve to assume that all young people, even the very youngest, have the intellectual capacities to decide their futures. However, a child-based epistemology does not need to be absolute—nor does any epistemology. Epistemological approaches are complex and cannot be definitive, but they can be intuitive and informative. I hope to illustrate this in the forthcoming discussions.

The question for those interested in issues of justice is why we philosophically treasure young people while creating conditions under which their civil liberties are often submerged. How would the world of rights and justice look otherwise than the way we currently understand it.

The arguments and information in this paper culminate in a new way of understanding the plight of the child in the global world and of fostering ways that make better the world of children by drawing on a foundational assumption that children have wisdom and knowledge that needs to be heard and used. The human rights framework of that way of seeing the world of children is based on the notion of the collective right of children to be heard, their right to make a difference.

The State of Children and Youth: A Rights Abuse Analysis

At the end of this paper, I explore what a new human rights agenda for young people would look like. But before I do so, I want to illustrate, within a rights framework, why we so badly need a new paradigm for enfranchising a significant part of the world community. As we will come to see, leaving young people out of the global conversation places them at unusual risk. My focus here is primarily on Canada, a country that we would expect, given its wealth and democratic history, to have a relatively exemplary approach to the place of children and youth in society.

The explorations that follow are a barometer of how Canada, in the context of a global world, treats children and youth. I present the information within a framework of human rights that I would hope that any caring global citizen would consider inviolable. The first of those rights, the right to protection from privation, is central to everyone's well-being but is arguably most important for young people because we know that early exposure to poverty has lifelong consequences. The right to be protected from poverty is also an issue that is so closely connected to all other dimensions of human rights that it, in itself, may be the central global problem the world faces; certainly it is the main problem for most of the world's children.

CHILD POVERTY AND THE RIGHT TO A DECENT STANDARD OF LIVING

A growing body of evidence shows that the plight of the young worldwide is not improving, is often related to adult-generated conflicts, and is fundamentally related to issues of poverty and exploitation (Cockburn & Kobubo-Mariara 2010; Borer et al. 2006). And as we know from decades of good criminological research, poverty is so closely related to how young people are treated in all systems of social control, especially the justice system. Yet one of the greatest challenges for policy makers working with children and youth is poverty reduction at least and the elimination of poverty at best (Bastos & Machado 2009; Aber et al. 2007). Children represent nearly 34% of the world's population, they are proportionately poorer than their adult counterparts, and are often absent from political theory and discourse, and policy development. As a result, their rights to a decent living standard are persistently under threat. While we may think that child poverty is mostly a phenomenon of the developing world, the following figure is a barometer of how Canada stands as a rich nation.

FIGURE 1. THE PERCENTAGE OF CHILDREN LIVING BELOW POVERTY LINES, 2013

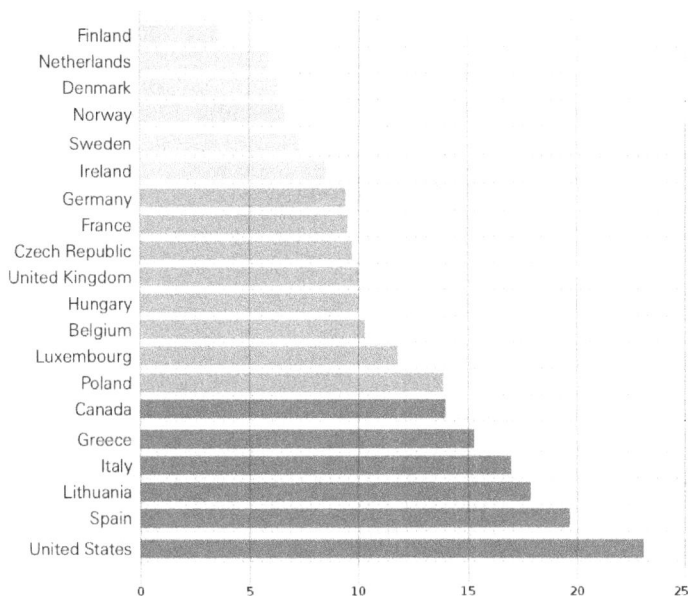

Figure 1. Source: Unicef, 2013 *Child Well-being in Rich Countries: A Comparative Overview*. Innocenti Report Card 11: Unicef Office of Research, Florence Excerpt from Table 1.1a, Relative Child Poverty Rates (page 7) | http://www.unicef-irc.org/publications/pdf/rc11_eng.pdf

It is evident that child poverty is a fundamental problem for Canadian society, but it is also evident that the elimination of child poverty is possible—industrialized countries like Finland and the Netherlands have come close to eliminating the poverty of the young. The Canadian Report Card on Child and Family Poverty shows quite clearly that child poverty rates decrease as transfer payments from federal and provincial governments to helping agencies increase (Campaign 2000 2008). The question remains why countries like Canada and the United States, countries of considerable wealth, have not used policies as straightforward as transfer payments to poor regions to address such a foundational human rights issue.

Poverty is a human rights violation for many reasons but mostly because it has such traumatic effect on its victims. Figure 2 illustrates the geographic distribution of child poverty in Canada and this spatial rendering tells us much about poverty and its effects.

FIGURE 2: CHILD POVERTY RATES BY PROVINCE, 2011

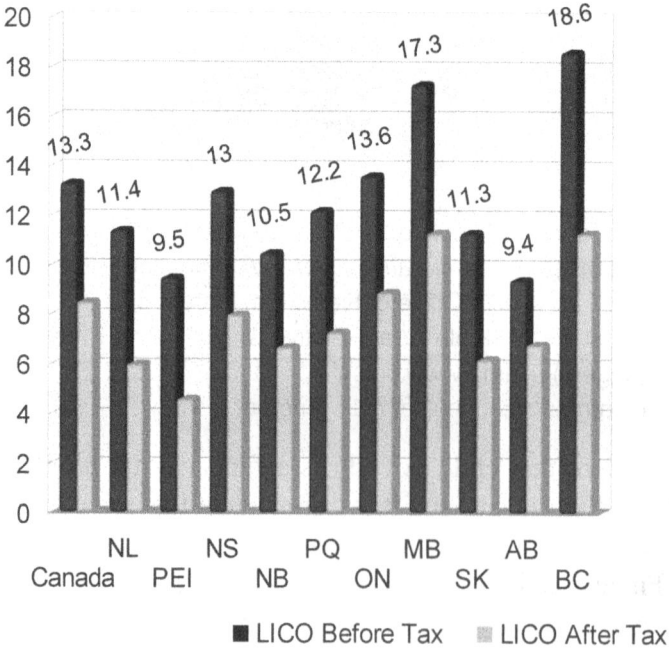

Figure 2. Source: Statistics Canada. *Table 202-0802 – Persons under 18 in low income families, 2011,* CANSIM (database). [Low Income Cut-Off (1992 Base)]

Clearly, poverty is associated with area; the territories and the provinces with northern, isolated communities show the highest rates. In addition, it is not necessarily the "have not" provinces that have the highest rates of child poverty. British Columbia, Saskatchewan, Ontario, and Quebec, relatively wealthy provinces, have failed to distribute their wealth to those geographic sectors that are in extreme need. Geoffrey York (1991) in his significant work from years ago entitled *The Dispossessed: Life and Death in Native Canada*, showed quite clearly how rapid resource development in northern Canada sent many First Nations communities into a downward spiral in which displaced communities were left with diminished access to food, increased exposure to toxic environments, and diminishing access to ways of making a living, in spite of industrial promises for increased standards of living with resource development. His work explains one of the sources of geographically-determined child poverty in Canada: community and social disruption that accompanies the forced displacement of people.

The following figure helps us look beyond geography to explore the social reality of poverty.

Figure 3: The Social Face of Poverty in Canada: 2006 Poverty Rates for Children 0-14 Years, Selected Groups

All Children	18%
Aboriginal children	36%
Racialized Groups	33%
With Disability	27%
Immigrant children	41%
Recent Immigrants	48%

31% of all families living below the poverty line are Single Parent Female-headed families

Figure 3. Source: Campaign 2000 Report Card on Child and Family Poverty in Canada – 2011. *Revisiting Family Security in Secure Times: 2011 Report Card of Child and Family Poverty in Canada. (pg 7).*
http://ywcacanada.ca/data/research_docs/00000223.pdf

Poverty attacks certain categories of children more than others. While 18% of children in Canada live below the poverty line, children of Aboriginal ancestry, visible minority children and immigrant children are especially disadvantaged. In addition, 31% of all families living in poverty are female-headed single parent families. The Campaign 2000 (2011) concludes that there is a working segment of Canadian society that is poor; families in this "working-poor" segment are unable to maintain an adequate standard of living despite one or two parents/guardians who are working full time, and who supplement their wages with trips to the food bank, especially when children are involved. Forty percent of all Canadian children are supported in part by food banks every year. To put all this in perspective, in 2010, 5% of single parent families in Sweden and 8% in Denmark lived below the poverty line. Clearly, child and family poverty is not inevitable; it is not the result of laziness or lack of initiative. Poverty is not the cost of "doing business" in a dynamic economy. It is the result of a constellation of historical and political forces that result in a fundamental violation of the human rights of children and youth, the right to a decent standard of living. For anyone who takes the role of the public intellectual advocating on behalf of children and youth, the starting point for advocacy is the effect that the income gradient has on the well-being of all kinds. As we will come to see, poverty has extremely harsh effects on young people to the extent that it often permanently alters their life chances, in direct violation of the Canadian Charter of Rights and Freedoms and the United Nations Convention on the Rights of the Child.

CHILD HEALTH AND THE FREEDOM FROM ILL HEALTH

The social gradient probably has its most severe effect on health, especially with respect to children. While a human rights agenda for children should include the right to live safely, immune from social and physical harm, and should include the rights to access health care, the following discussions will show that for Canada, where universal health care is foundational, children do not do very well, especially in certain social and geographical sectors. Figure 4 illustrates the infant mortality rates for selected countries. Infant mortality reflects not only child and maternal health care, but also the social and economic conditions that contribute to poor health and substandard maternal care.

FIGURE 4. SELECTED COUNTRIES' INFANT MORTALITY RATES, DEATHS PER 1000 LIVE BIRTHS (2014)

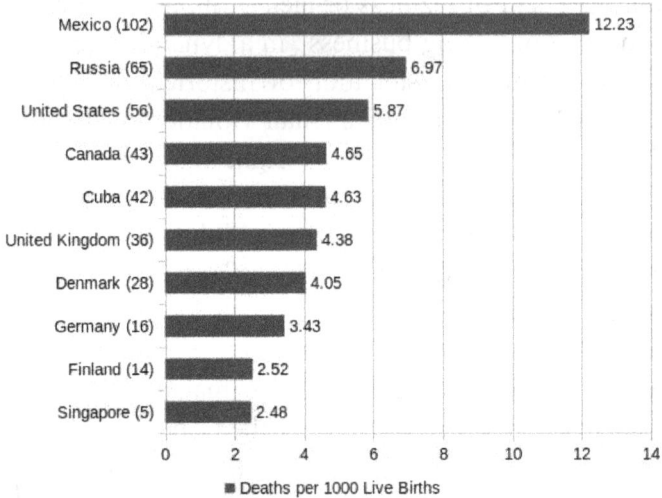

Figure 4. **Source:** US-CIA World Factbook (2014)
https://www.cia.gov/library/publications/the-world-factbook/fields/2091.html
Note: Numbers after each country indicated world rankings

In 2014, Canada ranked 43th in the world in the prevention of infant mortality despite the reality that we are one of the richest nations in the world. In 1990, Canada ranked sixth in the world. The obvious question is what happened? In a 20-25 year period, our ability to maintain the health of newborn children plummeted to levels that put Canada on the edge of the developing world, at least in regard to infant mortality. It is interesting that in that interim, the Canadian government declared in three successive periods (2000, 2005, and 2010) that child poverty would be eliminated.

Figure 5 illustrates that child and family health is very much related to geography. Within Canada, the northern territories (especially Nunavut) have high rates of infant mortality but so do provinces like Saskatchewan, Manitoba, Alberta and Newfoundland/Labrador. All of these jurisdictions are characterized by relatively large populations living in northern areas of Canada, areas that are often cut-off from mainstream Canada to their disadvantage.

FIGURE 5: INFANT MORTALITY BY PROVINCE IN CANADA, 2011

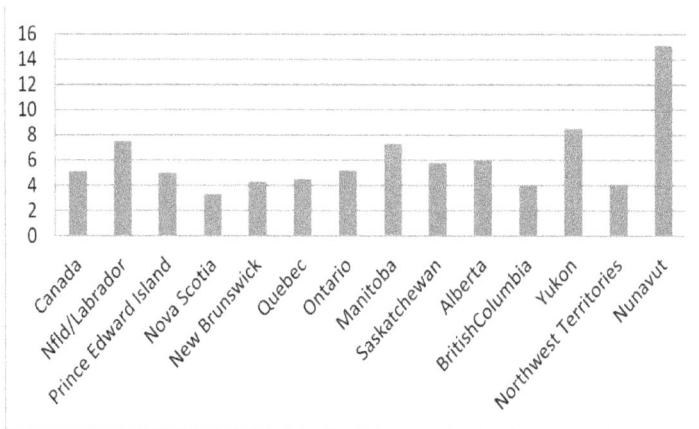

Figure 5. Source: Statistics Canada. *Infant Mortality Rates by Province and Territory.* http://www.statcan.gc.ca/tables-tableaux/sum-som/l01/cst01/health21a-eng.htm

Figure 6 is both puzzling and revealing. It presents hospitalization rates for asthma for young people under 20 in selected cities in Canada, cities that span the geographical continuum from west to east.

FIGURE 6. HOSPITALIZATION RATES FOR ASTHMA IN CHILDREN (UNDER 20 YEARS OF AGE/100,000 PEOPLE), 2006

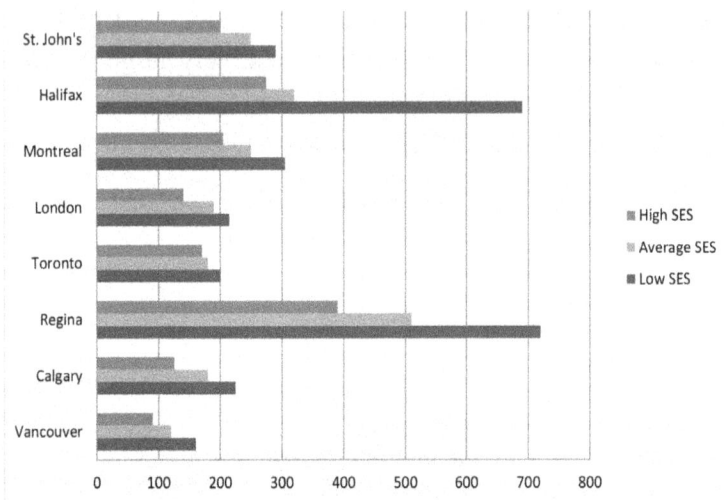

Figure 6. Source: *Reducing Gaps in Health: A Focus on Socio-Economic Status in Urban Canada, 2008.* The above table is based on information in a series of tables identified as Tables D.16, D.15, D.13, D.9, D.11, D.7, D.4, & D.3 (pgs.121-134) Ottawa: Canadian Institute for Health Information/Institut Canadien d'Information sur la Sante, https://secure.cihi.ca/free_products/Reducing_Gaps_in_ Health_Report_EN_081009.pdf

The information is somewhat perplexing because it shows that two cities, Halifax and Regina, have inordinately high rates of child/youth hospitalization for asthma. What is it about these two relatively affluent cities that determines such a high demand for hospital care for kids? The table is also very revealing because it shows that children and youth from the lowest socio-economic category have the highest rates of hospitalization for asthma, double the rates for high socio-economic status children.

As we try to work through the disparities in health that are evident in the above tables, there are certain realities about children and health that stand out. Clearly, being poor disposes kids to being at greater health jeopardy than their wealthier counterparts. Often poor kids live in isolated northern areas of Canada and in inner cities, typified by Regina and Halifax. In both areas, the realities are that good food is difficult to obtain and expensive when it is available. Darcy Frey (2004) has an invaluable book on inner city kids entitled *The Last Shot: City Streets, Basketball Dreams* in which he describes a New York inner-city community that is poor, isolated from the privileges of mainstream society, and whose kids depend on the dream of an NBA career as their only perceived means of escape from poverty. What he shows in addition, however, is that typically poor, inner city communities have very few of the amenities that one would expect in a sustainable, livable community, especially grocery stores with fresh food that is not overpriced. The Coney Island projects community does not have grocery stores within the community; parents have to commute miles by train or bus to access fresh food. There are, however, fast food stores sprinkled throughout the projects that become the primary food source for the community. We know that fast food consumption is one of the root causes of health issues in children in North America, especially issues of obesity and childhood diabetes (Thompson 2012).

Neighbourhoods that typically do not have access to healthy, fresh food have come to be known as "food deserts," communities in which adults and children have to "commute out" to find decent grocery stores. People in these communities do not have food security, something which people outside poor communities take for granted.

> For residents who live in Toronto's inner suburbs and Priority Neighbourhoods, access to good quality and affordable food is a growing challenge. Today, many grocery stores are located either next to new commer-

cial developments in the inner city or alongside large, retail developments in the outer suburbs. As a result, they are often a considerable distance away from those who live in these inner suburbs and Priority Neighbourhoods, making them difficult, time consuming and costly to access without a car. The importance of nearby grocery stores in the inner suburbs and Priority Neighbourhoods is that they provide easy access to a range of healthy food options, including fresh fruits and vegetables, meats, dairy and bread... Unable to easily access good quality food, those living in many inner suburbs are served instead by an army of corner, convenience and fast food outlets that offer an assortment of unhealthy foods high in fats, sugars and salts...

Toronto, however, is not alone in its struggle to improve access to healthy food options and eliminate the existence of food deserts. Cities of all sizes across North America face similar challenges to those in Toronto. [2]

It is important to realize, as well, that food insecurity is not restricted to inner cities. The northern communities in Canada suffer many of the same food ills that are suffered by inner city communities. Fresh food is expensive and hard to come by and fast food is cheap and easy to access. The Canadian Medical Association in 2010 published the results of a study that indicated that 70 per cent of Inuit families in Northern Canada have reported not having enough food; two-thirds of parents reported that they ran out of food at times (CMA 2010). A study conducted specifically in the Northwest Territories showed that 44% of the calories ingested by the people came from soda and bottled juices and that childhood diabetes was epidemic in the north (Thompson 2012).

---

[2] Excerpted from: "Food Deserts and Priority Neighbourhoods in Toronto," *Martin Prosperity Insights*, The Rothman School of Management, University of Toronto, June 15, 2010.

The other issue regarding child health and poor communities that warrants our concern is victimization. The reality of inner city street life is that young people are vulnerable to high rates of sexual and physical exploitation. A Winnipeg Free Press article offers an example:

> Jane Runner has spent the past 21 years talking to sexually exploited teens and women about their experiences on the street. She offered some sobering statistics to the court on Monday. Runner, who heads programming at New Directions in Winnipeg, said there are "hundreds" of teen and pre-teen girls working the streets, with an even greater number abused by adults behind closed doors. The youngest she has heard of was eight, and the average age is about 13. She told court that 80 per cent of child prostitution occurs in gang houses and "trick pads." Runner estimated that 70 per cent of the girls are aboriginal, more than 70 per cent are wards of Child and Family Services, and more than 80 per cent get involved after running away from their placements. Runner said a majority of the kids in prostitution have already been victims of sexual abuse. Other common precursors include fetal alcohol syndrome and physical abuse at home. "Unfortunately, we're seeing a lot more of the generations, where maybe the mother or the older sister have been previously involved in the sex trade before they get involved," Runner said.[3]

The issue of sexual exploitation has clear implications for criminology and justice studies. The arguments by the police and the courts that it is difficult to bring the exploiters of children to justice because of evidentiary issues and issue of credible child testimony seem unfair and counterproductive. At a very basic level, the problem is that as long as we treat exploitation of kids as a "crime control"

---

[3] Excerpt from: McIntyre, Mike. 2007. "Hundreds of kids in sex trade; Testimony jolts inquest; police say hands tied" Feb 20, *Winnipeg Free Press*

issue, and not an issue of community health, the impotency of the law will continue. And, of course, the language of the sex "trade" compounds the problem of legal and public perception because it implies the market of exchange for sexual favours for money. The issue at hand is the undeniable exploitation of children by sexual predators. Importantly, the term prostitution, because it itself implies mutual consent and mutual benefit, tends to hide the predatory reality of the sex trade. The discourse of prostitution condemns children for their complicity. As we, as criminologist and legal scholars, work through issue of crime, justice, and law, it is important to consider that the use of the law, as the place in which real justice can occur, may not be the most appropriate vehicle for promoting child rights and child security. The task may best rest with agencies that focus on individual and community healing and community enhancement.

FREEDOM FROM LABOUR EXPLOITATION AND THE RIGHT TO WORK

Most people who have a sense of the global world understand that child labour is a persistent child and youth rights issue which we often discuss only in the context of the developing world. We know that children as young as five work in factories in developing countries to provide cheap consumer goods for the global economy. Rarely do we think about child labour as a problem for North America and yet the following figures illustrate that, indeed, children and youth do work, they contribute to the family economy and the economy of the country and, they do so in the context of very little labour rights protection. The discussions herein are not framed around the moral debates about children and youth in the work place, but rather about what a "right to work" child/youth rights framework might look like when we consider that kids have the right to work, they have the right to organize, and they have the right to be protected from labour exploitation. In fact, they should have the same rights that accrue to adults.

Figure 7 shows the percentages of children and youth who work by provincial jurisdictions.

FIGURE 7. PROPORTION OF STUDENTS WORKING, AGES 15-19 (APRIL 2007 AND APRIL 2015)

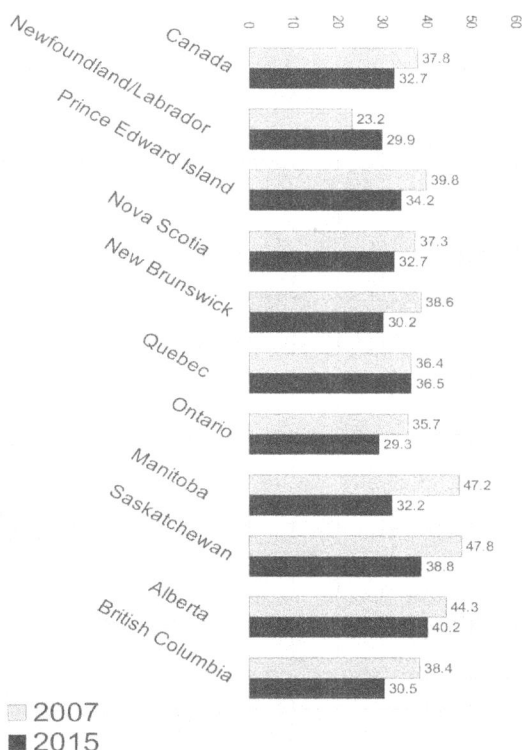

2007
2015

Figure 7. Source: *Canadian Labour Force Survey, 2007.* Statistics Canada. Table 282-0005 - Labour force survey estimates (LFS), Employment rate by province, by full- and part-time students during school months, CANSIM (database). http://www5.statcan.gc.ca/cansim/a26? lang=eng&id=2820005

Young people, particularly in resource rich provinces like Alberta and Saskatchewan work more so than youth in other provinces, in part because the opportunities for work are numerous. While the data for the above table cover 15-19 year olds, it is important to realize that many kids under 15 also work. For example, in 2005, Alberta reduced the legal age for young people to work from 14 to 12 to accommodate the labour requirements generated by the resource extraction sector, in particular the labour requirements of the fast food industry. British Columbia did the same in 2002.

The degree that young people work across Canada is compounded by the following: young people are much more likely to be injured on the job than adults; they are especially in danger if they are working illegally compared to adults; and they are most likely to be hurt working in the fast food and agricultural sectors, the sectors in which kids typically find work. (Raykov and Taylor 2013).

Clearly, children have few labour rights protection. They most often work for minimum wage or below. They most often receive very little mentoring or on-the-job training, specifically with regards to safety and especially with regards to their labour rights. They are poorly paid, poorly protected, non-secured labour is compounded by retail employers who encourage their young employees to spend money at their places of employment, on price-reduced food in the fast food sector, or on brand-name clothes in the retail clothing sector (Schissel 2011; Schlosser 2005). In many ways, their labour is free as they give back some of their earnings to buy lunch and dinner, or to dress in clothes dictated by the employer for work.

If we make the assumption that some children and youth have to work, or even just choose to work, then there is no reason to expect that they would not receive the same rights, privileges and protections that accrue to adults. That is generally not the case, and the question remains why. One of most enduring arguments as to why we persist in exploiting young labour is that we are embedded in an historical legacy that believes that hard work is character-building. With the inception of the system of public education in Canada, led by education reformer Egerton Ryerson (1844-1876), Canadian public policy spawned a type of "puritan work ethic" that equated hard work with moral development. Despite the positive education reforms that Ryerson and others implemented, including the introduction of standardized public education, Canada became a country in which children could be forced to work because work was an elemental moral activity. The darkest legacy of the "work-education" movement indeed was the development of residential schools to "isolate and reprogram" First Nations kids through hard work, discipline, and severe punishment (Milloy 2000). As we observe children and youth still working in Canada without the protection of labour rights, it is clear that the puritanical position that children's moral development is incomplete is still with us. That is precisely why Manfred Liebel and others have called for a new human rights manifesto that embeds the fundamental right to work for children and youth within a framework of safe, secure, and well-paid work (Liebel, 2010). He also calls for labour policy to be driven by young people themselves.

THE RIGHT TO EDUCATION AND TRAINING

I include education as one of the fundamental rights for children and youth for two reasons. Firstly, as the following discussions will show, how well young people do in our formal system of education has immediate and long-term implications for all forms of well-being including mental and physical health and exposure to the criminal justice system. Secondly, studies that track the life histories of young people in conflict with the law show most often that the spiral into the justice system often starts with problems in school. The implication is clear: if school is meaningful, then young people have a reasonable chance at a good life.

Figures 8 and 9 show just how important success in school is. Figure 8 is a simple but clear illustration that the starting point for success is wealth.

FIGURE 8. CANADIAN CHILDREN, BY INCOME, AGE 9, "DOING WELL IN SCHOOL" (2006-2007)

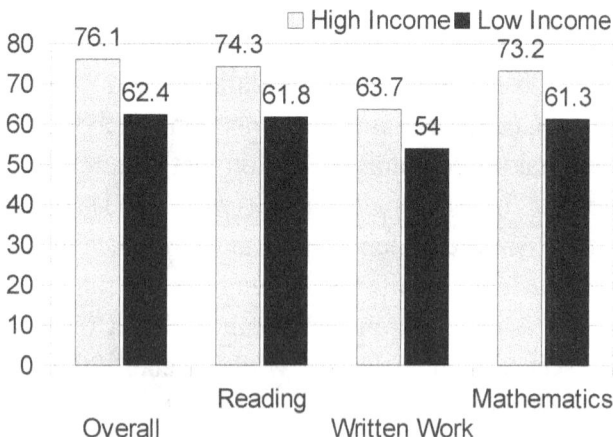

Figure 8. Source: Statistics Canada: *National Longitudinal Survey of Children and Youth 2006/2007.*
http://www.statcan.gc.ca/pub/89-599-m/2009006/t003-eng.htm

Simply put, grade point average in all basic subject areas is associated with wealth. This finding defies, in principle, the presumption of public education that all children have access to equal and standard education. Figure 9 tells us more about the role that school success plays in a young person's life.

FIGURE 9. ADOLESCENT HEALTH STATUS AND BEHAVIOURS BY SCHOOL ENGAGEMENT, AGES 12-15 YEARS (2006-2007)

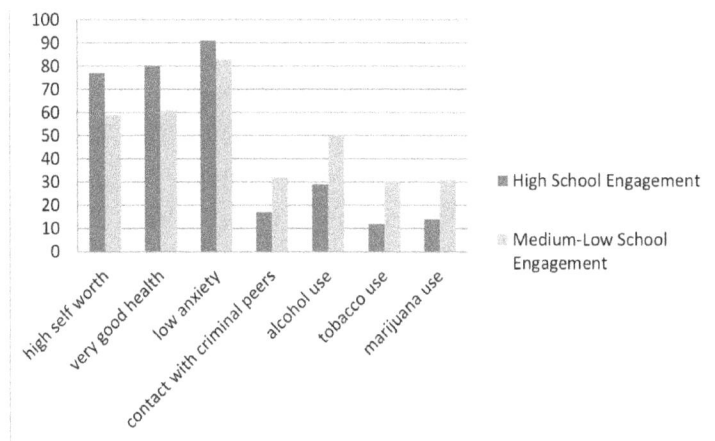

Figure 9. Source: Canadian Population Health Initiative, *Youth Health Outcomes and Behaviours in Relation to Developmental Assets.* (2009) Ottawa: the Canadian Institute for Health Information/nstitut Canadien d'Information sur la Sante. Excerpt from Table 3, Percentage of Youth (12-15) Reporting Health Outcomes in Relationship to School Engagement (page 6). https://secure.cihi.ca/free_products/cphi_youth_health_outcomes_aib_e.pdf

School is the one public space that young people are allowed to occupy during the day. It is the equivalent of their work place, so it is not a mystery why being connected to school has such positive benefits for kids. High levels of school engagement result in kids that have high self-esteem, good health, low levels of anxiety and relative immunity from contact with the criminal justice system and substance abuse. It is not difficult to understand that if kids cannot adjust to school, or more fundamentally if schools cannot welcome and nourish all kinds of young people, then school can become a risk. Unfortunately, our common sense cultural presumption is that school failure is about student failure. Some very good research, although not widely publicized, has shown that this presumption is misleading. The alternative and community school movements have illustrated very clearly that when schools adopt an inclusive framework that welcomes difference and does not punish failure, kids flourish. For many kids at risk, they not only flourish but become advocates and mentors for other kids at risk (Robertson 2013; Schissel 2011).

A human rights approach that incorporates education needs to be built on the principles firstly that education is not a drain on the economy or public revenue. Secondly, an education manifesto would need to reframe educational administration to include young people directly in the administration and management of schools. Thirdly, the ideal school would need to be based on the assumption that the institution is a public place for young people and that it needs to be, in part, under their jurisdiction. School is so important in the current and future lives of the young that it can no longer warehouse students in overcrowded classes just because it is fiscally prudent to do so. Education is too important to well-being.

FREEDOM FROM LEGAL DISCRIMINATION AND THE RIGHT TO JUSTICE

The last focus of our discussions is probably the most significant in relation to the role of public criminology for two very important reasons. First, all of the issues we have discussed herein are related to youth crime and justice; the disadvantages that some children and youth experience in the Canadian socio-political economy predispose young people to interaction with the justice system. Interaction with the justice system predisposes them to protracted disadvantage most of their lives. Second, many of the young people who come into contact with the justice system and who ultimately end up in custody are identifiable by poor health. They often suffer from skin problems and poor dentition, conditions that are often indicative of poor nutrition and a lack of health care. In fact, in many ways, the problems of youth in trouble with the law are often problems of health and not of crime. We have, I argue, created a problem of crime from what would be more rightly conceived of as a problem of collective and individual health.

A rights paradigm for young people in contact with the criminal justice system would surely need to be based on a series of inviolable legal rights: the right to legal protection, including the right to *adequate* legal counsel; the absolute right to non-discrimination by the law, including the right to be dealt with under the principles of the best interests of the child/youth; and the "right to accuse your accuser," including the right to actively defend themselves in courts of law. The foundational question that encompasses the above rights is whether all of these rights that accrue to adults within the justice system are the same rights that young people experience.

Figure 10 gives us a fairly stark indication that the Canadian youth justice system uses an inordinately severe, "crime and punishment" approach to youth in trouble with the law. Children's legal rights do not appear to be well-served in this country.

FIGURE 10. YOUTH AS A PERCENTAGE OF TOTAL PRISON POPULATION, SELECTED COUNTRIES, 2014-2015

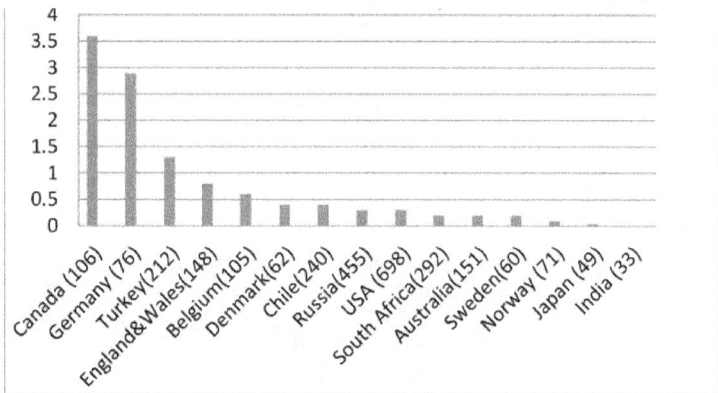

Figure 10. Source: International Centre for Prison Studies. World Prison Brief. http://www.prisonstudies.org/country/*** (where *** stands for the country. The number in brackets beside each state is their overall rate of incarceration / 100,000 of their population.)

Historically, Canada locks up more kids per capita than most other industrialized nations. In fact, in 2012, Canada incarcerated young offenders at a rate twice that of the United States. Interestingly, for adults in Canada and the USA, this trend is reversed. Countries like Japan and Norway lock up almost no young offenders, choosing instead, to use other, community-based methods to help young people in trouble with the law. For some reason or other, Canada has gotten into the habit of dealing with young offenders through imprisonment, a likely characteristic of the state paternalism that has characterized Canada's history in relation to children and youth. Importantly, despite Canada's reputation for being tough on young people, the current government is pursuing youth justice reform that would actually toughen the law and is coming under considerable international criticism (Paperny 2011).

Figure 11 illustrates the disparities in incarceration of young people across the country.

FIGURE 11: YOUTH INCARCERATION RATES IN CANADA, BY PROVINCE FOR 2006 AND 2007

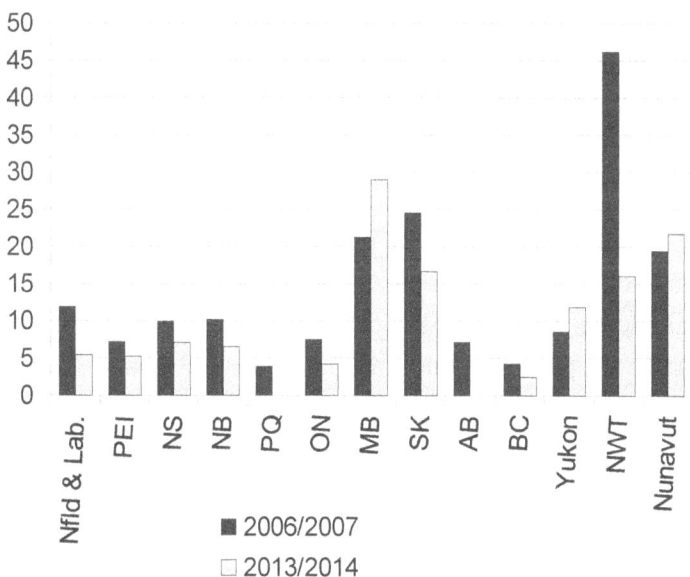

Figure 11. SOURCE: Statistics Canada Table 251-008 - Incarceration rates per 10,000 young persons in provincial and territorial correctional services, annual, Comparing 2006/2007 with 2013/2014. Note: Data is suppressed for Quebec and Alberta in 2013/14. | CANSIM database: http://www5.statcan.gc.ca/cansim/a26?lang=eng&retrLang=eng&id=2510008

Provinces like Saskatchewan and Manitoba choose to use jail to "treat" young offenders much more so than the other provinces. The same trends are also evident in the Northwest Territories and Nunavut; in these isolated jurisdictions, services for youth are few and far between and the courts are often compelled to use custody as a form of default treatment centre. For Saskatchewan and Manitoba, it is much more confounding as to why the courts use custody in cities like Regina, Saskatoon, and Winnipeg. Provinces like Quebec and British Columbia have found a better way and that better way includes community services and schools to help young people to restore their lives. The disparities in justice within Canada regarding the treatment of children and youth are tied historically and contemporarily to race relations, racism, education and residential schools, immigration and migration and resource development. The race dimension of this complex problem is represented in Figure 12.

The following figure is based on rather dated data. I have included this table because it is the last evidence available comparing all the provinces in Canada. Statistics Canada did publish some information on Aborginal youth incarceration for 2011[4] but the table excludes Nova Scotia, Quebec, Saskatchewan, British Columbia and Nunavut. Interestingly the results for the provinces that are included in both time periods (2004 and 2011) are much the same. Therefore, I have included this somewhat dated table because it includes comparisons for all provinces.

---

[4] "Aboriginal youth admissions to correctional services, by province and territory, 2010/2011." Statistics Canada, Canadian Centre for Justice Statistics, Youth Custody and Community Services Survey. http://www.statcan.gc.ca/pub/85-002-x/2012001/article/11716-eng.htm#r2

FIGURE 12. INCARCERATION RATES FOR ABORIGINAL AND NON-ABORIGINAL YOUTH IN CANADA

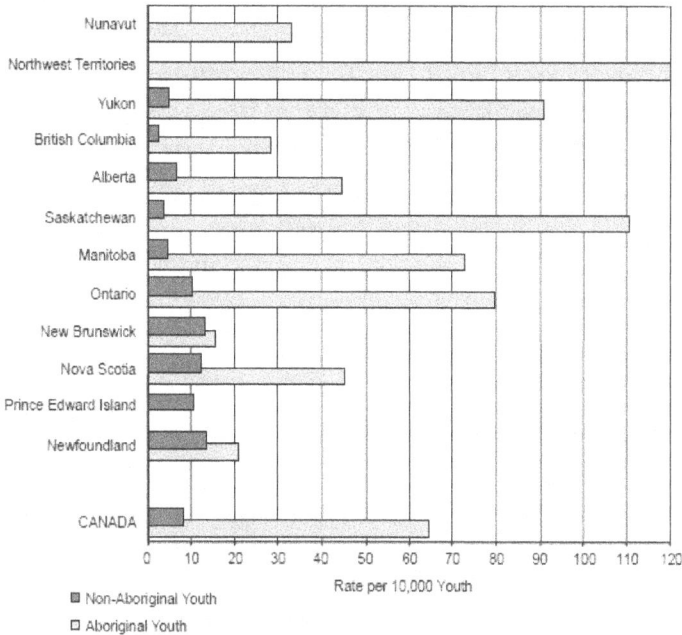

Figure 12. Source: Justice Canada. 2004. *A One-Day Snapshot of Aboriginal Youth in Custody Across Canada: Phase II* http://www.justice.gc.ca/eng/rp-pr/cj-jp/yj-jj/yj2-jj2/yj2.pdf

The disparities in the use of incarceration that we observed across jurisdictions are undeniably compounded by the distinctly harsh treatment of First Nation's youth. In provincial jurisdictions like Saskatchewan and Manitoba, there are four times as many Aboriginal adults incarcerated compared to non-Aboriginal adults; for children and youth, the ratio increases dramatically. In fact, for Canada overall, the ratio is about 7 to 1. The extreme racial skew illustrated here is endemic to most regions in Canada and tells us much about the history of the country and the aggressive displacement of Aboriginal people and cultural genocide of First Nations and about the current inability of Canadian society to break free from the habit of treating people differently in the justice system on the basis of race and culture.

The undeniable reality for the Canadian justice system and its treatment of the young is that it is a system that is not working; it is based on historical habit that prefers incarceration, and it has not changed very much since its inception. It conflates issues of individual and collective health with criminality, and it makes judgments about young people, in part, dependent upon where a young person lives, the colour of his/her skin, and how well s/he is doing in school.

The use of incarceration as a solution for young offending leads us down a very dangerous path. The greatest predictor of recidivism for young people is whether they have been incarcerated in the past—a predictor that is 4 times as strong as gang membership. Spending time in prison also reduces the likelihood of a return to school or success in the labour market. Incarceration also dramatically increases the likelihood of self-harm, depression, and suicide. In the calculus of social justice and healing, prison is a tragic mistake, if our intentions are to do the best by young people (Holman and Ziedenberg 2006).

Theoretical Arguments/Explanatory Issues

In the end, we need to be able to understand how the violations of the human rights of children and youth, sometimes critiqued but most often ignored, come to be acceptable global practice. While there is considerable global anxiety about the treatment of young people, especially in war zones and child labour contexts, the reality is that young people do not receive the protections that adults receive, nor do they have the opportunity to express their wishes in effective political contexts. These realities speak somewhat to the place of children and youth in global politics, a place in which their labour provides corporate and government administrations with the potential to maximize profit while ignoring workers' rights. In a global context in which countries are compelled by the IMF and the World Bank to increase their national productivity by reducing public spending, the search for cheap labour thrives. Cheap, unsecured labour is part of the answer to increased productivity and maximized profits. And this is where young people enter the equation: they often need to work, they live outside the protections of constitutional protections, and they are vulnerable to egregious exploitation. They are the consummate slaves. And, as we have come to see, this reality extends to first world countries where profit maximization overrides moral consciousness. This all occurs in a global context in which young people have little voice: they cannot vote, and they have no formal venue for influencing local, national, and international politics, other than becoming activists, often times to their own peril.

The denial of the rights and capabilities of the young occurs within a deep-seated belief system that diminishes the capabilities and the value of young people. Such a powerful ideological framework lives within the discourses of Science, Education, and Criminology/Law, conjoined under the "paradigm of risk." The language of "at-risk," generation-at-risk," and "risk-assessment" all provide the linguistic and academic contexts in which adult stakeholders can talk, with authority, about the "social and scientific" origins of school shootings, child-murderers, and online abusive children. Certainly, the media has fostered images of young people and dangerousness through selected depictions of high-profile cases of children as perpetrators, cases which are often presented as normative or at least understandable within a paradigm of risk (Schissel 2006)

Embedded in the view that children need to be assessed for their potential to do deviance is what I call the "conundrum of competence." In public consciousness, children are too young to protect themselves because of their physical, emotional, and cognitive immaturity. They are at the same time, because of their immaturity, a potential threat as incompletely socialized beings. Their incapacities demand that they be protected (hence a child welfare response), but those same incapacities demand that society be protected from them (hence the harsh justice response).

Finally, it is a reality that the baby-boom generation is the most powerful generation: demographically it is largest; economically it has the most wealth invested in the global economy; and politically, it is the political power-elite worldwide. It is not difficult to comprehend, based on these realities, that older-generations have a vested interest in protecting their wealth, much of which is tied up in pension and stock-market investments. And, certainly, those investments are perceived to be threatened by many things: social justice programs that demand relatively high rates of taxation; or equity and fairness programs that demand a minimum standard of living and a wage system that distributes the wealth fairly. It is arguable, that older generations, given their economic and political power, will not jeopardize their place of privilege by advancing the cause of young people. Importantly, the discussions around space and place give evidence to this. While public space shrinks and private space grows, as a consequence of the growing wealth of a minority of people, young people become increasingly dispossessed of their physical and social space in the world. They are relegated to designated places like schools that are highly controlled environments created around the adult-driven principles of physical efficiency, restraint, discipline, and productivity. Children and youth's tenancy is not of their making; their space and place is increasingly in jeopardy.

A CHILD/YOUTH RIGHTS APPROACH: A PARADIGM SHIFT IN LEGAL STUDIES

So what, then, would a new paradigm of rights look like that provides a way out of the dilemma that seems to be "the universal abrogation of the rights of the young"? The "new childhood studies" movement (Liebel 2012) provides an initial answer: children need to be perceived as a social group that lives under certain conditions. In other words, children are not "beings in development," but individuals with human agency. They are members of an identifiable social group living within the constraints of larger society and because of this, they have the right to have rights. In this context, they have the right to self-determination, the liberty to formulate their place in society as a collectivity. In short, they have the right to participate in their own destinies.

Such an approach stands against the assumption of biological incompleteness and concentrates, instead, on the abilities and competencies of children to advocate for themselves and to establish agendas for the future. It shrugs off the language of modern science that equates maturity with competency, and ultimately, with superiority.

> By conceiving childhood as social category, and by recognizing children as social subjects, new childhood studies have opened a new view on children and childhood(s). They represent a paradigm shift that could advance the equality of children and adults on the level of

social co-determination without negating the particular
and special needs of children. (Liebel 2012, 20)

CONCLUSION: THE IMPLICATIONS FOR PUBLIC CRIMINOLOGY

The role of the public criminologist in the context of
child-rights might seems a little elusive at first blush, but
the arguments presented in this paper, I believe, set an
agenda for action that is clear, straightforward, and consistent with principles of legality, fairness, and democracy.
Criminologists need to broaden their mandate and speak to
issues of social justice before they speak to issues of crime
and justice. They need to see the criminal justice system
as often at odds with social justice, either by design or by
omission. They need to see the denial of the right to self-
determination for young people as a foundational roadb-
lock to public policy. They need to see the discourse of
dangerousness and public security, especially in relation to
young violators, as the language of generational politics
that is unproductive at best and dangerous at worst. They
need to see that there are vested interests that lobby, often
in subversive ways, to keep young people out of the political economy. Finally, they need to understand that the
right to place and space is a fundamental human right, that
the world is shrinking rapidly for young people, and that
forcing young people out of places and spaces is a type of
physical and cultural relocation that is reminiscent of the
relocation of peoples throughout history. Such relocations
have always resulted in great social tragedy.

References

Aber, J., S. Jones, & C. Raver. 2007. "Poverty and child development: New perspectives on a defining issue." In *Child development and social policy: Knowledge for action,* edited by J. Aber, S. Bishop-Josef, S. Jones, K. McLearn, & D. Phillips, xvii (311): 149-166. Washington, DC: American Psychological Association.

Arneil, B. 2002. "Becoming vs being: A critical analysis of the child in liberal theory." In *The moral and political status of children,* edited by D. Archard & C.M. Macleod, pp. 70-96. New York: Oxford University Press.

Bastos, A., C. Machado, & J. Passos. 2010. "The profile of income-poor children." *International Journal of Social Economics,* 37(12): 933 – 950.

Borer, T.A., J. Darby, & S. McEvoy-Levy. 2006. *Peacebuilding after peace accords: The challenges of violence, truth, and youth.* South Bend, Indiana: University of Notre Dame Press.

Boyle, E.H., T. Smith, and K. Guenther. 2007. "The rise of the child as an individual in global society." In *Youth, globalization, and the law,* edited by S. A. Venkatesh and R. Kassimir. Palo Alto, CA: Stanford University Press.

Campaign 2000. 2000. *Report card on child and family poverty in Canada.* Toronto: Campaign 2000.

Campaign 2000. 2008. *Family security in insecure times: The case for a poverty reduction strategy for Canada.* Toronto: Campaign 2000.

Campaign 2000. 2011. *Report card on child and family poverty in Canada - 2011 Revisiting Family Security in Secure Times.* Report Card of Child and Family Poverty in Canada. http://ywcacanada.ca/data/research_docs/00000223.pdf

Canadian Institute for Health Research. 2008. *Reducing Gaps in Health: A Focus on Socio-Economic Status in Urban*

Canada, 2008. Ottawa: Canadian Institute for Health Information/Institut Canadien d'Information sur la Sante, https://secure.cihi.ca/estore/productSeries.htm? pc=PCC448>.

Canadian Population Health Initiative. 2009. Improving the Health of Young Canadians. Ottawa: the Canadian Institute for Health Information. https://secure.cihi.ca/free_products/cphi_enewsletter_20090 7_e.pdf.

CIA World Factbook. 2014. https://www.cia.gov/library/publications/the-world-factbook/fields/2091.html

Cockburn, J., & J. Kobubo-Mariara. 2010. *Child welfare in developing countries.* Ottawa: IDRC.

Drydyk, J. 2006. Globalization and Human Rights. In Christine Koggel (Ed.), *Moral issues in global perspective: Moral and political theory, 2nd.* Toronto: Broadview Press. Frey, Frey, Darcy. (2004). *The last shot: City streets, basketball dreams.* (New York: Mariner Books.

Haché, A., Dekelver, J., Montandon, L., Playfoot, J., Aagaard, M., & Elmer, S.S. 2010. "Research and policy brief on ICT for the inclusion of youth at risk: Using ICT to re-engage and foster socioeconomic inclusion of youth at risk of social exclusion, marginalized young people and intermediaries working with them." European Commission.

Holman, B, & J. Ziedenberg. 2006. *The dangers of detention: The Impact of incarcerating youth in detention and other secure facilities: A Justice Policy Institute Report.* Washington, DC: The Justice Policy Institute.

Justice Canada. 2004. *A on-day snapshot of Aboriginal youth in custody across Canada: Phase II.* Ottawa: Department of Justice Canada. http://www.justice.gc.ca/eng/rp-pr/cj-jp/yj-jj/yj2-jj2/yj2.pdf

Kaime, T. 2009. *The African charter on the rights and welfare of the child.* Pretoria: Pretoria University Law Press.

Liebel, Manfred. 2012. "Framing the issue: Rethinking children's rights." In *Children's rights from below* edited by M. Liebel, pp. 9-28. New York: Palgrave Macmillan.

Luxton, M. 2005. "Feminist perspectives on social inclusion and children's well-being." In *Social inclusion: Canadian perspectives* edited by T. Richmond & A. Saloojee, pp. 82-104. Halifax: Fernwood Publishing.

Lynch, K. 2010. *The global drivers of change.* Montreal, Canada: Policy Options.

Milloy, John. 2000. *A National Crime: the Canadian Government and the Residential School System, 1879 to 1986.* Winnipeg: University of Manitoba Press.

Paperny, A.M. 2011. "Canadian youth crime plans bewilder international observers." Toronto: *The Globe and Mail.* Tuesday, July 19.

Pollis, A. & P. Schwab. 2006. "Human rights: A Western construct with limited applicability." In *Moral issues in global perspective: Moral and political theory,* edited by Christine Koggel. Toronto: Broadview Press.

Raykov, M, & A. Taylor. 2013. "Health and safety for Canadian youth in trades." *Just Labour: A Canadian Journal of Work and Society,* 20(Summer): 33-50.

Schissel, Bernard. 2011. *About Canada: Children and youth.* Halifax: Fernwood Publishing.

Schissel, Bernard. 2006. S*till blaming children: Youth conduct and the politics of child hating.* Halifax: Fernwood Publishing.

Schlosser, Eric. 2002. *Fast food nation: The dark side of the all-American meal.* New York: Perennial.

Skott-Myhre, H.A., & D. Tarulli. 2008. "Becoming-child: Ontology, immanence, and the production of child and youth rights." In *Child rights: Theory and practice* edited by T. Oneill and D. Zinga. Toronto: University of Toronto Press.

Statistics Canada. 2015. Table 251-0008 - Youth correctional services, average counts of young persons in provincial and

territorial correctional services, annual, CANSIM
(database), Using E-STAT (distributor).
http://estat.statcan.gc.ca/cgi-win/cnsmcgi.exe?
Lang=E&EST-Fi=EStat/English/CII_1- eng.htm

Statistics Canada. 2011. *Income in Canada, 2010.*Table 802,
Cat. No. 75-2-2-X. Ottawa: Statistics Canada.

Statistics Canada. 2013 *Infant mortality rates by province and
territory*. http://www.statcan.gc.ca/tables-tableaux/sum-
som/l01/cst01/health21a-eng.htm

Statistics Canada. 2007. *The Canadian labour force survey.*
http://www.statcan.gc.ca/daily-
quotidien/080111/dq080111a-eng.htm

Thomas, E.M. (2009) "Canadian Nine Year Olds at School."
Ottawa: Statistics Canada

Thompson, Isha. 2012. "Cut the Western diet and get moving."
AMMSA Aboriginal Multi-Media Society Association, 30(2).

UNICEF. 2013. *Child Well-being in Rich Countries: A
Comparative Overview. Innocenti Report Card 11*. Unicef
Office of Research, Florence. http://www.unicef-
irc.org/publications/pdf/rc11_eng.pdf

Venkatesh, S., & Kassimir, R. (Eds.), *Youth, globalization and
the law* (pp. 255-283). Stanford, CA: Stanford University
Press.

Watson, M. 2008. "Social networking: An opportunity for
health and social care?" *Journal of Integrated Care, 16*(1):
41-43.

York, Geoffrey. 1992. *The dispossessed: Life and death in
Native Canada.* Toronto: Little, Brown.

DRIFT: A CRIMINOLOGY OF THE CONTEMPORARY CRISIS

JEFF FERRELL[1]

D ifferent historical periods trace different trajectories by way of prospects and perception. For those who rode the ascending wave of mid-twentieth century modernism, one moment after another often seemed connected along a straight line to a better future—a future fulfilled by the insights of science, the convenience of technology, and the satisfactions of material prosperity. Within and against this modernist ascension, fundamentalists have often sought to reverse its trajectory, to return the social order to the past principles of founding fathers and founding documents. In periods of rapid social change, political revolutionaries often see, or long to see, a trajectory that resembles that of a rocket launch—a new social order, blasting free from the old, taking flight, roaring upward toward a firmament of previously unimagined possibility. When on the other hand the social order fails of its own accord,

---

[1] For the author's biography, see the endnote on page 168

rotting from inside its own contradictions, some find themselves caught in an opposite trajectory, descending quickly and deeply into economic ruin and existential despair; others ride a sad social spiral, a process of circling back time and again on the same recurring problems, yet each time a bit farther from their solution; and some sense

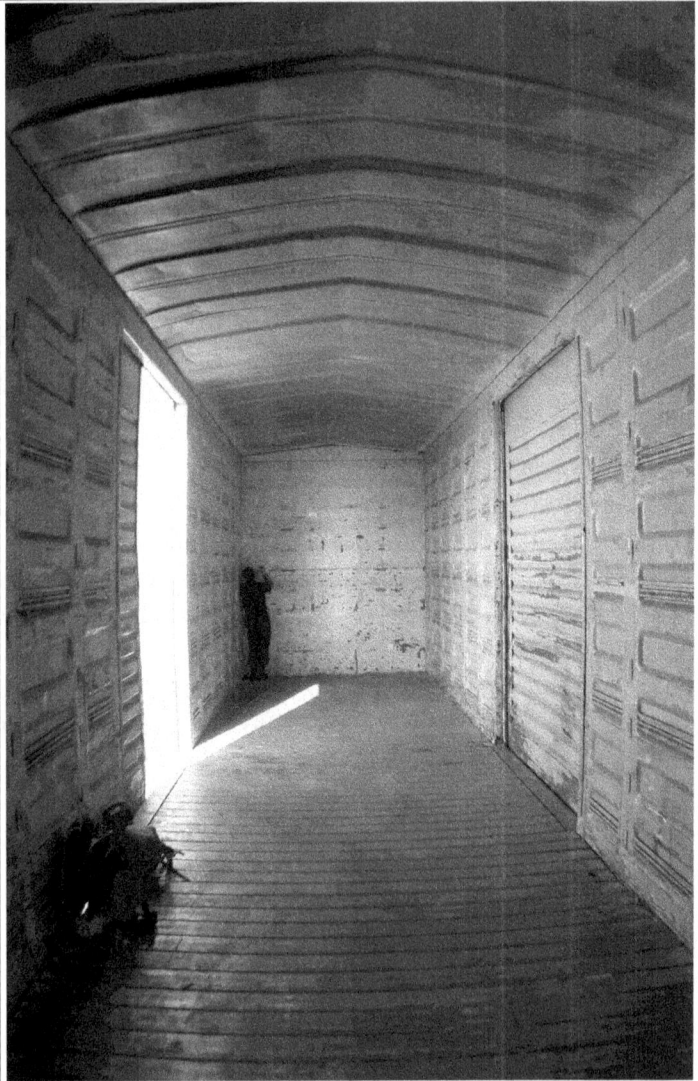

"Boxcar" by Jeff Ferrell.

a dispersal out from the middle, a centrifugal failure of social bonds and cultural cohesion.

Yet other times, historical periods seem to embody a trajectory that is, oddly enough, not much of a trajectory at all—or perhaps a trajectory defined by its lack of definition. This is the trajectory of drift. Drift follows neither the straight-line forward motion of progress nor the stern reversals of fundamentalism or economic failure. It neither ascends nor descends, and it remains too uncertain a motion to maintain even the circling arc of a spiral. Sometimes drift comes close to the unraveling trajectory of the failed social order—but even here it is uncertain in its uncertainty, since as we shall see, drifters may consider their unsettled circumstances a new set of social possibilities. Likewise, drift is often the trajectory of the disengaged and dispossessed—but disengaged from what, dispossessed of what, and on whose terms? Certainly drift suggests some sort of personal and social disruption, and some degree of spatial and temporal dislocation—yet even this implies some degree of prior certainty, some coordinates of time and space, against which such disruption can be measured.

In North America, for example, the period of the 1930s Great Depression was founded on systemic economic and ecological failure, and came to embody horrific economic hardship—but it also came to be experienced by many as a time of profound and unprecedented drift. The failure of crops and farm economies meant dislocation from one's land, and in many cases a wandering search for something better. Joblessness spawned not only the loss of career identity, but the necessity of drifting away from the social networks that had once supported it. One survivor of the Great Depression recalled that, 'a man had to be on the road. Had to leave his wife, had to leave his mother, leave his family just to try to get money to live on.... The shame I was feelin'. I walked out because I didn't have a job' (in

Terkel, 1970: 58). In *Waiting for Nothing*, his haunting account of hoboing through the Great Depression, Tom
Kromer (1933: 52) confirms this. "When a guy loses his
job in his hometown, he has to go on the fritz," says
Kromer. "He has to grab himself a drag out of town. A guy
can't be dinging back doors for hand-outs and flopping
behind signboards when his girl lives in the next block."
Once out of town and on the road, the dislocation only re-
doubled. Continuing the tradition of hoboing and hopping
freight trains which had begun with the westward expan-
sion of the railways after the U.S. Civil War, millions
hoboed their way across the continent looking for work.
Yet even the small stabilities of a hobo camp were subject
to the brutal disruptions of the "bulls," or railroad police.
Hoboes "huddle around their fires in the night," Kromer
(1933: 114) reported. 'Tomorrow they will huddle around
their fires, and the next night, and the next. It will not be
here. The bulls will not let a stiff stay in one place long.'
Others wandered in rickety automobiles or trucks, most
famously in the lyrics of Woody Guthrie songs like *Hard
Travellin'* and *I Ain't Got No Home*, and in the pages of
John Steinbeck's *Grapes of Wrath*. As Dorethea Lange
and Paul Taylor (1939: 108) documented in their pioneer-
ing photo-ethnography of these wanderers, their experience of perpetual drift mirrored that of the hobos. 'People
has got to stop somewhere. Even a bird has got to rest,' reported one of those interviewed in the book. 'What both-
ers us travellin' people the most is we cain't got no place
to stay still.' Like the Great Depression itself, this sweep-
ing dislocation transcended the boundaries of North America as well. Some of the unemployed youths who hoboed
across Canada, for example, found that their rough wandering eventually led them to—and prepared them for—
the physical pain and radical politics of participation in
Spain's anti-fascist Civil War (Kish, 1975). Cut loose from
any certain trajectory, they and millions others had be-

come what Kromer (1933: 115) said of himself: a 'restless ghost.'

THE CONTEMPORARY CRISIS

Today, the restless ghosts are with us again, and in growing numbers. Lives adrift, folks waiting for nothing or on the way to nowhere: these circumstances now circle the world once more. A mounting global crisis that interweaves economic inequality and ecological decay with conflicts over immigration, development, and consumption has set these circumstances in motion. Ongoing civil and transnational warfare continues to spawn swelling refugee populations. Repressive governmental regimes engage in the forced expulsion of dissidents and minority groups—and when these regimes are confronted, even successfully, further dislocation often results. Within China, across Europe and North America, and around the globe, economic migrants wander in search of work, or are simply moved en masse from one work locale to another as economic demands change. In the U.K., Europe, and North American, the corporate criminality of the mortgage/banking crisis, the ongoing destruction of low-cost housing as part of urban redevelopment schemes, and the proliferation of part-time and low-wage service work all conspire to preclude certainties of home, shelter, or destination. Moving from house to house or country to country, sleeping in cars or temporary encampments, haunting streets and train stations, those cut loose from certainty find little in the way of spatial or social stability.

In this world, impoverished Central Americans risk sexual assault and extortion to hitch rides through Mexico atop freight trains bound for North America. In North America, more and more young adults live on the streets, sometimes couch surfing or crashing with friends, other times hitchhiking from one city to the next, uncountable and unaccounted for. The newly homeless and unemployed drift from city to city, sleep in flood drains beneath the streets of Las Vegas, or become semi-permanent residents of cheap motels. Migrant farmworkers continue to face family disruption, limited educational opportunities, and deportation; graduate students, part-time instructors, and non-tenure-track instructors now make up three quarters of college faculty; and an economist reports that, in general, 'we're in a period where uncertainty seems to be going one forever. So this period of temporary employment seems to be going on forever' (Rich, 2010: A1; Lewin, 2011: A15; Brown, 2011: 17, 21; Raymer, 2011).

In southern Europe a native-born generation finds that today, even advanced degrees leave them lost between dead-end jobs and unemployment—and so they sleep in their cars, and make plans to travel abroad in search of work. So dire is the situation in Portugal that, amidst a prison overcrowding and abuse crisis brought on by budget cuts, prisoners nonetheless refuse to apply for prison leave—since 'at least their meals are paid inside.' Says one ex-convict, who has departed for part-time work in Switzerland, 'if you come out of jail in Portugal now, you've got almost zero chance of not going straight back in. There's just nothing for you to do except sit around and stay poor and depressed' (in Minder, 2012: A12). In Spain, where unemployment stands above fifty per cent for young people, pervasive home foreclosures and evictions lead to a surge in homelessness, the squatting of buildings, and the scavenging of trash bins that is 'so pervasive... that one Spanish city has resorted to installing locks on supermarket trash bins' (Daley, 2012a, b). In the more affluent north of Europe, a German 'shadow labor market' of poorly paid temporary workers is now seen as essential to the country's 'global competiveness'. A 'floating generation' of young people likewise haunts the internships, part-time jobs, and unemployment offices of France. There, millions of young people search in vain for employment, or simply give up; and among those that do find work, eighty per cent are offered only temporary contracts. 'In our parents' generation, you had a job for life,' says one young woman, unemployed at age 25 with a master's degree in management, 'Now we constantly have to change jobs, change companies, change regions' (in Erlanger, 2012: A6). Altogether, this 'lost generation' is reported to cost Europe 153 billion Euros a year, amidst fear that it 'could lead to upheaval like the Arab spring' (Malik, 2012: 3)

Across the globe, migrants from rural areas pour into sprawling encampments outside Rio de Janeiro, Mumbai, and Ulan Bator, or find themselves shuttled between one country and the next by political and economic upheaval. Young Arabs argue that 'it's impossible for us to get ahead here—there are no opportunities', and dream of moving abroad; North African refugees in search of work or safety crowd rickety boats to cross the Mediterranean, only to find themselves consigned to shantytowns or bounced back and forth across national borders (Erlanger, 2011: A8). Delhi, India, is 'ruthless in its use' of impoverished immigrants and wanderers, who nonetheless launch little schemes of survival and treasure their own *azadi*—freedom—until one of the city's regular demolition and redevelopment drives destroys even these possibilities (Faleiro, 2012: 22). In Japan almost half of the country's young workers are consigned to temporary, 'irregular' jobs amidst a collapsing career structure; in China, migrant workers from rural areas now make up a third of Beijing's population, and with no place to live, occupy abandoned air-defense tunnels underneath the city (Fackler, 2011; Ewing, 2011: B6; Wong, 2011). In post-Soviet, free-market Russia, 'the *bomzh*—a homeless person in dirty clothes, begging in the metro underpasses, at churches, lying on park benches or scavenging near train stations —has become omnipresent in Russian cities and towns' (Stephenson, 2006: 113).

These are indeed the trajectories of a world adrift. But what is the criminology of this contemporary crisis? That is, how are these drifting circumstances intertwined with issues of crime, law, and social control, and how are these issues in turn embedded in contemporary configurations of economic and political power?

CONTRADICTIONS AND CAUSES IN THE CRIMINOLOGY OF DRIFT

Answers to these questions aren't straightforward; they're contradictory, confounded, and oddly self-reinforcing. In fact, they rest on two foundational contradictions. The first is the degree to which drift is promoted both by contemporary economic failure and by successful economic development. The second is the related dynamic by which contemporary policing strategies both target drift in an attempt to stop it, and promote further drift as a result. Of these, the relation between economic failure and drift is perhaps the most obvious. A global banking crisis evicts millions from their over-mortgaged homes, and leaves millions more unemployed or shuttling between part-time jobs. Ecological crises engendered by global warming, and by global oil and agri-business, spawn conflicts over land and water, push small farmers off their plots, force itinerant farm workers into ever-wider arcs of travel, and lure millions of rural residents towards the false economic salvation of the city. Amidst collapsing national economies and civil wars, refugees—some of them already migrants from elsewhere—leave belongings behind to flee in crowded boats or on foot. With economic failure there arrive, all too often, the sorts of structural strain and anomic disruption so well understood by Durkheim (1984) and Merton (1938), and with them the spatial and normative experience of drift.

And yet many of the same drifting consequences today arrive with 'successful' economic development as well. Increasingly, world cities from Vancouver to Istanbul define success in terms of economies organized around consumerism, entertainment, tourism, and the large-scale service work necessary to support these endeavors. Theorists like Markusen and Schrock (2009: 345, 353) argue that this sort of new 'consumption-driven urban development...help[s] to attract skilled workers, managers, entrepreneurs, and retirees,' and they emphasize the 'significance of lifestyle preferences of skilled workers as an important determinant of economic development'. In this sense 'quality of urban life', as David Harvey (2008: 31) notes, has 'become a commodity, as has the city itself, in a world where consumerism, tourism, [and] cultural and knowledge-based industries have become major aspects of the urban political economy.' But in the same way that these consumerist economies and available 'lifestyle preferences' benefit those affluent enough to consume them, they harm the far larger population of low-end retail workers left to provide them. For them, the social contract that once linked worker to employer over time, and hard work to career advancement, has been annulled. Their work lives are now defined by pervasive and low-wage service work, the vulnerability of missing medical and retirement benefits, the profound uncertainty of temporary employment and flexible scheduling, and the experience of sequential contract or freelance jobs in place of career. For every old industrial factory successfully converted into high-end lofts or attractive retail spaces there are a hundred workers left to drift between unstable employment, low-wage work, and economic failure.

In addition, corporate developers, city planners, and zoning commissions regularly carve out the city spaces needed for new 'consumption-driven urban development' —'consumption spaces', as Zukin (1997) calls them— from existing low income neighborhoods and older mixed-use industrial areas. This revanchist reclaiming of urban space—what Harvey (2008: 28, 34) describes as 'the capture of valuable land from low-income populations that may have lived there for years'—further tips the balance of urban life towards privileged populations. And with this land captured, with its low-cost housing obliterated and local shops bought out, there is also the great likelihood that those dispossessed by this development will now be cut loose and cast adrift in ways that they were not before. The new boutique hotel or row of artisanal shops, built in place of an old motel or row of modest homes, signals a shift in the city's class character and the terms of its employment. It also signals that many residents of the economically 'successful' late modern city will now suffer increased instability of occupation and residence—and that this instability will now be legally encoded in imminent domain procedures, zoning laws, and no trespassing enforcement.

Here we begin to see the second of the contradictions that underlies drift: the way in which contemporary law and law enforcement both target those set adrift and at the same time promote further drift. As a number of scholars have shown (Ferrell, 1996, 2001, 2006; Amster, 2008; MacLeod, 2002; Mitchell, 2003), the policing of new urban consumption spaces—and more broadly, the policing of late modern urban economies—often operates as aesthetic policing. That is, the goal is to guard the carefully constructed appearance and appeal of the city and its new consumption spaces, and so to protect the city's 'quality of life' from those whose public presence would intrude on its ensemble of high-end attractions and profitability. Here policing comes to focus on perceptions as much as populations, and on minimizing risk and intrusion as much as solving crimes. During an urban revitalization campaign, for example, an economic official in the U.S. argues that panhandling is a problem precisely because 'it's part of an image issue for the city'—and an American legal scholar agrees, positing that 'the most serious of the attendant problems of homelessness is its devastating effect on a city's image' (in Ferrell, 2001: 45; in Mitchell, 2003: 201). Or as Aspden (2008: 13) concludes, commenting on how a 'corporate city of conspicuous consumption' has recently emerged from what was a decaying British industrial city, 'There seems to be no place in the new Leeds for those who disturb the rhythms of the consumer-oriented society.' Homeless populations, undocumented immigrants, seasonal workers, uprooted residents—much of contemporary urban policing focuses on these groups, and is designed to make invisible those unlucky enough to be displaced and adrift.

At times this approach is implemented with straightforward legal simplicity: existing streets, sidewalks, or parks are deeded to private developers, and so made unavailable to the displaced and the unprofitable (Amster, 2008). More generally it is enforced though a variety of popular crime control approaches. In Britain, the United States, and elsewhere, authorities employ dispersal borders, banishment orders, exclusion zones, and curfews to push undesirables away from consumerist havens. In the United States, built-environment policing programs like CPTED (Crime Prevention Through Environmental Design) seek to reduce crime by building social control into the spatial environment; such programs are employed, for example,

to discourage 'loitering' by the homeless and other vulnerable populations in public areas or transit stations. By re-
moving waiting facilities, installing uncomfortable benches, and closing public toilets, authorities are indeed often
able to force such populations from public parks or town
squares, thereby 'cleansing' these spaces for preferred
populations of tourists and short-stay retail consumers.
But in doing so, of course, such programs undermine even
the fragile spatial communities that emerge among the
vulnerable populations that occupy such spaces, and so
put these populations back on the move once again. Like
the old U.S. 'move on' laws used to roust laborers and labor organizers a century ago, like the bulls busting up
hobo camps in the 1930s, CPTED programs today force
vulnerable populations to move on, and move on again, in
search of even minimal comfort or convenience (Ferrell,
2001).

   Similarly, the contemporary criminal justice embrace of
the 'broken windows' model of crime prevention, with its
focus on the policing of low-order street violations like
begging and writing graffiti, operates to push vulnerable
populations out of areas targeted for gentrification or
tourism. This approach, in conjunction with parallel
'place-based' crime prevention approaches, also produces
programs like the Los Angeles Safer Cities Initiative
(SCI). This 'place-based policing intervention' deploys
police officers to move through Skid Row areas, 'breaking
up homeless encampments, issuing citations, and making
arrests for violations of the law' (Berk and McDonald,
2010: 813, 817) for the purpose of dispersal. Such initiatives are designed specifically to address the alleged problem of 'spatial concentration' among the homeless—that
is, spatial stability—with such initiatives to be comple-
mented by the 'dispersal of homeless facilities' and support services throughout urban areas as well (Culhane,

2010: 853). Vitale (2010: 868, 870) argues that, due to aggressive fines and arrests, such initiatives only further entrap those targeted in homelessness. Importantly, they also force the homeless into ever more dislocated ways of living; as before, they are 'moved on' whenever and wherever they settle. Recalling the dynamics of consumption-driven urban development, Vitale in turn wonders if 'the primary goal of the SCI [is] really to reduce crime and homelessness or instead to remove a large concentration of poor people forcibly from Skid Row in hope of encouraging the subsequent gentrification of the area.... A major effort to gentrify Skid Row has been underway for years...'

Together these developments begin to suggest a multi-faceted criminology of contemporary drift. Mortgage fraud and insider trading—particularly costly forms of corporate criminality—force millions from their homes and their livelihoods, in the process dislocating them from neighborhood ties and career security. Others forfeit home and neighborhood to the revanchist spatial and legal politics of 'consumption-driven urban development', and find that hopes of life-long career have been replaced by the reality of part-time retail work. Cut loose and cast adrift, they are subsequently pushed off privatized sidewalks, excluded from public spaces, criminalized for loitering or trespass, and cited and dispersed for the crime of spatial concentration. In this way the infatuation with consumption-driven urban development spawns the very sorts of populations who are imagined to threaten it—and in this way the forms of legal control and policing designed to protect such development from transient populations at the same time serve to make such populations more transient.

A variety of global dynamics add other facets and contradictions to the criminology of drift. In China, a strict household-registration system consigns the hundreds of millions of citizens now moving illicitly from village to city to 'an uncomfortable world that is neither urban nor rural, isolating them from their own children, [and] preventing them from becoming full members of the country's economy' (Saunders, 2010: 16). In Russia, a similar system of 'administratively organized territorial affiliations' guarantees that for homeless populations 'a lack of place also means a lack of any social recognition, employment rights or recourse to public welfare' (Stephenson, 2006: 145). As refugees and undocumented immigrants cross international borders, they are likewise often left with no legitimate place to settle; even the millions of global refugees whose journeys take them to refugee aid camps nonetheless remain adrift in many ways. As Bauman (2002: 344; 2000: 102) argues, such 'non-places' or 'nowherevilles' originate as 'a totally artificial creation located in a social void', and so incorporate an 'extra-territoriality' absent meaning or belonging for those forced to occupy them. Describing these massive collectivities as 'city-camps' (*camps-villes*), Agier (2002: 322) likewise notes that they are designed to induce 'the social and political non-existence of the recipients' of their aid.

A similar sort of legal non-existence confronts many others across the globe who migrate from rural to urban areas. Such migrant populations often first settle in the relatively unplanned, unregulated zones that surround established cities, thereby forming what Saunders (2010) calls informal 'arrival cities'. These arrival cities function as tenuous footholds for those seeking a life in the city, with migrants both arriving and at times returning home; with their fluid links to both rural areas and the city itself, they operate as ongoing, two-way conduits for subsequent generations of migrants as well. At the same time, such areas often suffer from the neglect of established urban authorities; allowed a tenuous existence, these areas nonetheless remain outside the orbit of water and sanitation services, legal protection, and urban citizenship. In this sense arrival cities are both extra-territorial and *extra-legal*—and over time this legal and spatial marginality may itself be transformed, moving either in the direction of incorporation into the formal urban grid, or outright criminalization, demolition, and enforced exclusion from it. The arrival city, Saunders (2010: 11) concludes, is 'both populated with people in transition…and is itself a place in transition'. For the millions who settle in such cities, life remains nonetheless unsettled and uncertain.

DRIFT AS ACTIVISM AND ALTERNATIVE

Sociologists often explore the dynamic between structure and agency—that is, the way in which large, structural forces impinge on and determine human behavior, but also the ways in which individuals and groups retain their agency in responding to and making sense of such forces. For criminologists, the task is similar: to investigate powerful forces of law, policing, and social control, but also the ways in which individuals and groups respond to victimization, criminalization, and more general attempts at controlling their behavior. So far, the criminology of contemporary drift outlined here has analyzed a variety of social structural forces—global economic failure and programs of economic development, strategies of law and policing, and patterns of migration and resettlement. A fuller criminology of drift, thEough, must also account for the attitudes, experiences, and agency of those cast adrift by economic forces or targeted by legal campaigns. Turning our attention to a few of these people and groups, we not only begin to build a broader criminology of drift, but uncover a third essential contradiction that animates the contemporary politics of drift: Often, those activist groups and alternative subcultures who are victimized by eco-

nomic and legal forces don't wholly reject the drifting circumstances that result. Instead, they embrace dislocation,
drift, and uncertainty on their own terms, finding in them
new guides for political resistance, shared survival, or social change—but often finding themselves once again the
targets of legal control.

The group Food Not Bombs, for example, salvages
wasted food in urban areas and serves it to the homeless,
recent immigrants, and others cut loose from the security
of home or career; put differently, Food Not Bombs seeks
to attend directly to those victimized by the contemporary
crisis, and understands itself as intervening in a system
that 'values wasteful consumption over common sense'
(CrimethInc., 2004: 248). Hundreds of Food Not Bombs
chapters reclaim and serve food throughout North America, Europe, Africa, and around the globe—and yet they do
so not through centralized organizations, but in ways that
are intentionally fluid, imprecise, and unstable. As 'an anarchist dis-organization' (Clark, 2004: 28), Food Not
Bombs disavows hierarchical structures and political authority, promoting only the general principles of consen-
sus, non-violence, and vegetarianism while emphasizing
that 'the core of [its] philosophy is that each local group is
autonomous' (Butler and McHenry, 2000: 73). In this way
Food Not Bombs itself drifts along with others cast adrift,
open to changing circumstances and emerging problems.
But by doing so—by openly feeding the hungry in public
urban areas, with a minimum of organization, and with
neither the permission nor the assistance of legal and political authorities—Food Not Bombs itself becomes part of
the problem for those invested in the sorts of consumerist
economic development and attendant legal controls already noted. Legal harassment is common, as with the arrest of hundreds of Food Not Bombs food servers in San
Francisco, or the more recent arrest of Orlando, Florida,

Food Not Bombs 'food terrorists,' as the local mayor labeled them (Butler and McHenry, 2004; Ferrell, 2001, 2006; Maxwell, 2011).

Meanwhile, the ongoing economic crisis in southern Europe has generated a loosely organized 'precarity' movement among young people who are now consigned to a shifting mix of unemployment, migration in search of work, and unpredictable part-time or 'flex scheduling' conditions in what work they do find. As those involved in the movement argue, their generation has been denied the conventional social anchors of set career and spatial stability—and so has been left to drift within a life of social and economic 'precarity' (Ross 2008; De Angelis and Harvie 2009; Seligson 2011). In developing their critique of precarity, though, those associated with the movement have also begun to explore its cultural and political potential. Christina Morini (in Galetto et al 2007: 106), for example, argues that while precarity can suggest the trauma of uncertainty, 'it is at the same time also connected with the idea of re-questioning, of becoming, of the future, of possibility, concepts which together contribute to creating the idea of the nomadic subject without fixed roots.... The precarious subject has no fixed points and does not want any. He/she is always forced to seek a new sense of direction, to construct new narratives and not to take anything for granted.' Embracing this sense of nomadic drift, the feminist collective Precarias a la Deriva has undertaken to 'drift through the circuits and spaces of feminized labor' as a way of highlighting the overrepresentation of women in precarious service work. Drifting through the spaces of female domestic workers, telemarketers, and food service workers, the members of Precarias a la Deriva have been able to 'find points for commonality and alliance', and to 'find ways to turn mobility and uncertainty into strategic points of intervention' through collective gatherings, workshops, and other techniques (Shukaitis 2009: 152-6). The recent development and growth of groups like the Canadian Freelance Union, and the Freelancers Union in the United States, suggest that this model of loose affiliation among those cut loose—'a federation of the unaffiliated', as the Freelancers Union calls itself—may be emerging more broadly.

Food Not Bombs, Precarias a la Deriva, and similar groups constitute collective attempts to assist those who have been cast adrift by contemporary economic and political forces. In their attempts, though, they do not simply reject drift; instead, they convert it into new styles of activism and resistance, and in so doing begin to craft an alternative culture of drift. These new styles are as fluid and dislocated as are the lives of those who create them; this new culture spans spaces and situations as readily as do those whose lives it reflects. Because of this, such groups can perhaps be understood less as formal organizations than as drifting 'dis-organizations'. As already seen, this term has been used to describe Food Not Bombs; it is also used by contemporary groups like Critical Mass bicycle activists and Reclaim the Streets members, who work to reclaim urban spaces from cars and capitalism. In a press release entitled 'On Disorganization', for example, Reclaim the Streets emphasized that it is 'a non-hierarchical, leaderless, openly organized public group. No individual "plans" or "masterminds" its actions and events. RTS activities are the result of voluntary, unpaid, co-operative efforts from numerous self-directed people attempting to work equally together' (Reclaim the Streets 2000). Chris Carlsson (2002), one of Critical Mass's founding activists, affirms this sort of open-ended, self-directed activism, and describes it in terms of yet another contradiction: 'assertive desertion.' Drift, uncertainty, lack of direction: these are pains imposed by the contemporary crisis, certainly, but as these groups suggest, they can also operate as assertive dis-orientations for knowing the world, for moving through it, and for crafting collective alternatives to it.

Among such groups there is one in particular that most fully embraces this notion of assertive desertion, and with it an alternative cultural politics of drift. These are the gutter punks. Beginning in the 1970s, punk emerged as an aggressively alternative subculture that rejected cultural and political authority while embracing anarchic 'dis-organization' and do-it-yourself music and style. From the beginning, though, there was also a tension within punk, a tendency toward punk's being coopted into corporate culture or reduced to a mere stylistic affectation, and so over the years the rowdy ethos of punk has been debated, lost, reborn, and parceled out among various versions of punk culture. The gutter punks chose one way of resolving this tension—to live as punks with a militant dedication to independence and autonomy, to become punks who were punker than punk. For gutter punks, their assertive desertion from mainstream society and their radically do-it-yourself alternative lives were taken as givens, and over the past couple of decades these hallmarks of gutter punk culture have tended to play out in various ways. In place of money, and the dullingly obedient retail work required to earn it, gutter punks generally scavenge trash bins for the food and materials they may need. As the anonymous, unemployed, dumpster-diving author of the book *Evasion* put it: '"Money?" they ask, the implication being that without money our system was flawed, incomplete. When in fact our lifestyle had stripped money of its value, reduced it to an inefficient and indirect means of acquiring...' (Anonymous, 2003: 80). When a bit of money does sometime become a necessity, though, gutter punks 'fly a sign'—that is, hold up a hand-made sign on a street corner asking for whatever donations may be available—or perhaps busk on the streets for spare change. And when gutter punks want to be on the move—which they generally do—they disavow car ownership or costly bus rides in favor of hopping freight trains. Living hand-to-mouth and on the streets, crashing in abandoned houses or other happenstance spaces, hopping freights from one city to another—gutter punks are drifters of the first order.

Because of this they are also, from the view of the contemporary legal system, a collection of serial miscreants and career criminals. Over the past three decades the 'broken windows' policing model, with its focus on the hardnosed policing of low-order criminality, has spawned an aggressive criminalization of public begging, curb-side performances, and other autonomous forms of street-level economic activity on which gutter punks rely (Ferrell, 2001). Likewise, with the growth of consumerist urban economies, 'dumpster diving' and trash scavenging have come under increasing surveillance and legal control, with some cities now criminalizing even the unauthorized lifting of a trash bin's lid (Ferrell, 2006). Hopping freight trains is of course also soundly illegal, with those apprehended regularly charged with trespass, destruction of property, or other offenses. Public consumption of alcohol —another gutter punk pastime—constitutes yet another violation of high-end urban economies and their public aesthetics, and so also regularly draws an aggressive policing response to those whose neighborhood bar is the street. Short on cash and on respect for legal authority, gutter punks in turn tend to let the resulting tickets go unpaid, and so fines accumulate, warrants are issued—and the crime of being a drifter builds on itself.

As for me, I first hung out with gutter punks and became acquainted with their status as legal outsiders vis-à-vis consumerist urban economies some fifteen years ago, while researching and writing a book on battles over urban space (Ferrell, 2001). Recently I got reacquainted.

Out on my bicycle, doing some trash scavenging of my own (Ferrell, 2006), I came upon a young kid named Zeke with a cardboard sign, soliciting money from drivers stopped at a red light. I guessed from his black clothes and railroad tattoos that he was a gutter punk, and he confirmed it. He 'grew up riding trains and going from [punk] show to show to show by way of freight trains,' Zeke told me—and as for 'housy punks', kids with homes and money and stability, well, 'more power to them, I'm not doggin' anybody out. But that's the difference between us. I'm a gutter punk.' He also told me he was just out of jail on probation, having been convicted on an assault charge he picked up while passing through town on a freight train a few months back, and was now just hanging out down by the rail yards, homeless, waiting for his next probation hearing. 'You wake up breaking the law drinking in public, you go to sleep breaking the law sleeping in public, how are you going to do that probation time?' he asked me. I didn't have an answer, but I did figure I'd help him out. One thing led to another, and a few days later, having taken care of the probation hearing, we agreed on the spur of the moment…to hop the next freight heading west.

Outside a convenience store we hitched a ride with a couple of drunks, who dropped us off at a 'catch out' spot that Zeke knew—a hidden spot for illicitly boarding outbound freight trains as they leave the rail yard, its walls adorned with the signatures of other gutter punks and hobos who had 'signed in' on their way through. After a while Zeke noticed that a big freight was about to depart, and so we scrambled toward the train, and the moment of 'catching out', or hopping the train, was here. 'Most hobo autobiographies …refer to this moment of 'catching out' as the location of their subcultural power', John Lennon

(2007: 214, emphasis in original) writes. 'By using their physical and mental skills in life-threatening situations, they *proactively* become invisible on the moving train.' Become invisible we did, dropping down into a little sunken space at the back of a container car and staying there until we were well out of the yards. Significantly, Zeke had picked out a 'double-stack'—a mile-long train carrying big global shipping containers double-stacked on each car—and because of this, the train was also a 'hot shot', it's global supply chain content giving it priority to pass other trains that would pull over on sidings along the route to let it through.

After a few hours of rocketing through the countryside, the train ground to a halt in the Abilene, Texas, rail yards. We hunkered down and waited, hid in the dark from some railroad officials checking the train, disembarked to go on a beer run, climbed back aboard as the train was pulling out, and rode on to Sweetwater, beers in hand and thunderstorm lightning flashing around us. There another beer run caused us to miss the train as it pulled out, so we had cold beans and beer for dinner, then wandered around looking for a place to sleep out of the rain, finally settling under the little metal overhang of a building near the yards. In a few hours the journey would continue, as we'd hop another train and ride on west the next day to Big Spring, Odessa, Pecos, and beyond. But it was here, stuck and drunk in the rain in the middle of the night on the edge of the Sweetwater rail yards, that I began to understand some things. To begin with, I now understood the name of the train-hopping crew of which Zeke had long been a part: Slow Drunk Krew. Beyond this, I began to understand how the radical, moving uncertainty of train hopping mixes with the independent intentionality of those caught up in it. I began to see how decision-making occurs within a larger swirl of immediate contingencies, vulnerability to the volatility of emerging situations, and the inevitability of eventual disorientation. Most importantly, I began to realize that being lost doesn't necessarily mean you're looking for a map—and that missteps, failures, and slow drunk detours may constitute for some fleeting signs of autonomous success.

Interestingly, gutter punks and train hoppers have their own term for this phenomenon: 'the drift'. 'For me, the drift occurs when I migrate from the linear world, neat with its processes and models, to the road, where everything happens at once,' says veteran train hopper Todd Waters. 'You've got a general direction, but it doesn't have much glue on it. The plan has equal weight to every new direction that comes along' (in O'Connell, 1998). Likewise, in the course of the train-hopping travels that she documents in her film *Train on the Brain*, Alison Murray (2000) happened to meet Wendy, a veteran gutter punk train hopper, when they discovered that they were riding a car apart on a freight train rolling across western Canada. 'Wendy's told me about "the drift,"' Murray reports in the film, 'a carefree state of mind that overtakes you on the train. I'm losing all sense of time and place.' Riding with train hoppers, a reporter for *Esquire* magazine lost it, too, writing that the 'magic of the freights', their 'sudden rush of movement,' left her with 'an incredible feeling of lightness…on the freights, time flows around you—there is no goal other than movement' (Ferguson, 1994: 74). And when a *San Francisco Weekly* reporter set out to ride freights with some veteran train hoppers, she found herself lost in the same state of mind. 'I have no idea what time it is', she says as they rest in a track-side hobo camp between rides. 'Welcome,' replies Ballast, one the group. 'Time doesn't matter after a while' (in Tudor, 2001).

In this sense gutter punks seem the very embodiment of drift: drift as historical artifact and contemporary crisis, drift as structured social problem and active human agency, drift as assertive desertion and cultural dis-orientation. All of their essential endeavors are shaped by the dynamics of drift, by a mercurial mix of self-determination and abandon amidst situations beyond their control. Theirs is a sort of survival surfing; the ocean of global consumer society generates the wave, but they figure out how to surf it —and upon wiping out, as they always do, they figure out how to catch the next one. To dig in a trash bins or 'fly a sign' is to scavenge the remains of consumer-driven economies, to violate the legal strategies meant to protect those economies, and to create an alternative culture to them—all at once. To hop a loaded freight train is to assertively and illegally abandon the matrix of precarious work, automotive transit, and enforced timetables by which others move through life while at the same, quite literally, riding the flow of goods that will eventually circulate through those lives; to hop a fast-moving 'hot shot', as Zeke knew to do, is to understand as well the priority now given global supply chains and global capitalism over local economies. 'Hobo punks hop trains, squat abandoned buildings, collect welfare, and dumpster food,' that *Esquire* reporter wrote in summary. 'Anything, in short, to exploit and condemn the consumer culture they so despise' (Ferguson, 1994: 70). Drifting this way, they circulate among the other restless ghosts of the contemporary crisis, among displaced workers and undocumented immigrants, and they call forth past ghosts as well. That next day, after we made it out of the Sweetwater yards and on to Pecos, I couldn't resist asking Zeke what he knew about an earlier generation of hobos, about those cast adrift by the Great Depression of the 1930s, and about the culture they created. In response he started to sing. I recognized the song—it was Woody Guthrie's *Hard Travellin'*.

Photo by Jeff Ferrell

REFERENCES

Agier, M. (2002). 'Between war and city: towards an urban anthropology of refugee camps' *Ethnography* 3(3): 317-341.

Amster, R. (2008). *Lost in Space*. New York: LFB.

Anonymous. (2003). *Evasion*. Atlanta: CrimethInc.

Aspden, K. (2008). *The Hounding of David Oluwale*. London: Vintage.

Bauman, Z. (2002). 'In the Lowly Nowherevilles of Liquid Modernity' *Ethnography* 3(3): 343-349.

Bauman, Z. (2000). *Liquid Modernity*. Cambridge, UK: Polity.

Berk, R. & McDonald, J. (2010). 'Policing the Homeless' *Criminology and Public Policy* 9(4): 813-840.

Brown, P. L. (2011). 'Itinerant Life Weighs on Farmworkers' Children' *The New York Times* (13 March): 17, 21.

Butler, C.T. and McHenry, K. (2000). *Food Not Bombs*. Tucson, AZ: See Sharp Press.

Carlsson, C. (2002). 'Cycling Under the Radar—Assertive Desertion', in C. Carlsson, ed., *Critical Mass*. Oakland, CA: AK Press, 75-82.

Clark, D. (2004). 'The Raw and the Rotten: Punk Cuisine' *Ethnology* 43(1): 19-31.

CrimethInc. (2004). *Recipes for Disaster*. Olympia, WA: CrimethInc.

Culhane, D. (2010). 'Tackling Homelessness in Los Angeles' Skid Row' *Criminology and Public Policy* 9(4): 851-57.

Daley, S. (2012a). 'Spain Recoils as Its Hungry Forage Trash Bins for a Next Meal' *The New York Times* (25 September): A1, A6.

Daley, S. (2012b). 'Wave of Evictions Leads to Homeless Crisis in Spain' *The New York Times* (12 November): A4.

De Angelis, M., & Harvie, D. (2009). '"Cognitive Capitalism" and the Rat-Race', *Historical Materialism* 17(3): 3-30.

Durkheim, E. (1984[1893]). *The Division of Labour in Society*. Basingstoke, UK: Macmillan.

Erlanger, S. (2012). 'Young, Educated, and Jobless in France' *The New York Times* (3 December): A6, A11.

Erlanger, S. (2011). 'On Journey to New Lives, Young Tunisians Need Only a Final Destination' *The New York Times* (20 April): A8.

Ewing, J. (2011). 'Temp Workers In Germany Dismay Unions' *The New York Times* (20 April): B1, B6.

Fackler, M. (2011). 'Japan Blocks Young, Stifling the Economy' *The New York Times* (28 January): A1, A9.

Faleiro, S. (2012). 'Invisible Economy' *The New York Times Book Review* (25 November): 22.

Ferrell, J. (2006). *Empire of Scrounge*. New York: New York University Press.

Ferrell, J. (2001). *Tearing Down the Streets*. New York: Palgrave/St. Martin's.

Ferrell, J. (1996). *Crimes of Style*. Boston: Northeastern University Press.

Ferguson, S. (1994). 'Meet the Crusties' *Esquire* (January): 69-75.

Galetto, M., Lasala, C., Magaraggia, S., Martucci, C., Onori, E., & Pozzi, F. (2007). 'A Snapshot of Precariousness' *Feminist Review* 87: 104-112.

Harvey, D. (2008). 'The Right to the City' *New Left Review* 53: 23-40.

Kish, A. (dir.). (1975). *Los Canadienses*. Toronto: National Film Board of Canada.

Kromer, T. (1933[1986]). *Waiting for Nothing*. Athens: University of Georgia Press.

Lange, D. & Taylor, P. (1939 [1969]). *An Amercian Exodus*. New Haven: Yale University Press.

Lennon, J. (2007). 'Too Dirty To Be a Hobo?' in A. Greenberg, ed., *Youth Subcultures: Exploring Underground America*. New York: Pearson/Longman: 212-223.

Lewin, T. (2011). 'Survey Finds Small Increase in Professors' Pay' *The New York Times* (11 April): A15.

MacLeod, G. (2002). 'From Urban Entrepreneurialism to a "Revanchist City"?' *Antipode* 34(3): 602-624.

Malik, S. (2012). 'Lost generation costing Europe 153bn a year, research finds' *The Guardian Weekly* (26 October): 3.

Markusen, A. & Schrock, G. (2009). 'Consumption-Driven Urban Development' *Urban Geography* 30(4): 344-367.

Maxwell, S. (2011). 'Breaking Bread and Breaking the Law' *Orlando Sentinel* (7 June), at http://articles.orlandosentinel.com/2011-06-07/news/, visited 2 January 2012.

Merton, R. K. (1938). 'Social Structure and Anomie' *American Sociological Review* 3: 672-82.

Minder, R. (2012). 'Crowding and Austerity Strain Portugal's Prisons' *The New York Times* (27 November): A12.

Mitchell, D. (2003). *The Right to the City*. New York: Guilford.

Murray, A. (dir.). (2000). *Train on the Brain: A Documentary by Alison Murray*. London: MJW Productions.

O'Connell, P. (1998). 'A Different Breed of Freight-Hoppers' *The New York Times* (20 August).

Raymer, B. (2011). 'The Upside of Foreclosure' *The New York Times Magazine* (10 April): 23.

Reclaim the Streets. (2000). 'On Disorganization' @ http://rts.gn.apc.org/disorg.htm, accessed 15 July 2011.

Rich, M. (2010). 'Weighing Costs, Companies Favor Temporary Help' *The New York Times* (20 December): A1, A4.

Ross, A. (2008). 'The New Geography of Work: Power to the Precarious?' *Theory, Culture and Society* 25(7-8): 31-49.

Saunders, D. (2010). *Arrival City*. New York: Pantheon.

Seligson, H. (2011). 'Job Jugglers, on the Tightrope' *The New York Times* (26 June): 1, 6.

Shukaitis, S. (2009). *Imaginal Machines*. Brooklyn, NY: Autonomedia.

Stephenson, S. (2006). *Crossing the Line: Vagrancy, Homelessness and Social Displacement in Russia*. Aldershot, UK: Ashgate.

Terkel, S. (1970). *Hard Times: An Oral History of the Great Depression*. New York: Avon.

Tudor, S. (2001). 'Railroaded' *San Francisco Weekly* (October 31), at http://www.sfweekly.com/2001-10-31/news/railroaded/, visited 25 January 2013.

Vitale, A. (2010). 'The Safe Cities Initiative and the Removal of the Homeless' *Criminology and Public Policy* 9(4): 867-73.

Wong, E. (2011). 'The Labyrinth' *The New York Times Magazine* (24 April): 16.

Zukin, S. (1997). 'Cultural Strategies of Economic Development and the Hegemony of Vision' in Merrifield, A. & Swyngedouw, E., eds., *The Urbanization of Injustice*. New York: New York University Press, pages 223-243.

About the Author

Jeff Ferrell is Professor of Sociology at Texas Christian University, USA, and Visiting Professor of Criminology at the University of Kent, UK. He is author of the books *Crimes of Style, Tearing Down the Streets, Empire of Scrounge*, and, with Keith Hayward and Jock Young, *Cultural Criminology: An Invitation*, winner of the 2009 Distinguished Book Award from the American Society of Criminology's Division of International Criminology. He is co-editor of the books *Cultural Criminology, Ethnography at the Edge, Making Trouble, Cultural Criminology Unleashed*, and *Cultural Criminology: Theories of Crime*. Jeff Ferrell is founding and current editor of the NYU Press book series *Alternative Criminology*, and one of the founding editors of *Crime, Media, Culture: An International Journal*, winner of the ALPSP 2006 Charlesworth Award for Best New Journal. In 1998 he received the Critical Criminologist of the Year Award from the Critical Criminology Division of the American Society of Criminology.

PUBLIC CRIMINOLOGY IN AN AGE OF AUSTERITY: REFLECTIONS FROM THE MARGINS OF DRUG POLICY RESEARCH

ANDREW D. HATHAWAY, PHD[1]

The idea of academics as democratic underlabourers derives from John Locke's famous *Essay Concerning Human Understanding*. Locke equates the role of the philosopher with that of a groundskeeper or custodian whose task is 'to clear the ground a little and remove some of the rubbish' lying in the way of truths revealed by scientific knowledge. There is a certain irony that this was the assumed role of a thinker as preeminent as Locke, whose contributions to political philosophy alone rival those of scientific luminaries like Newton as among the most important ideas of the Enlightenment. Locke's position has been criticized as sorely understating philosophy's essential contribution to humanity (Winch, 2008).

Philosophy is much more than a method tasked with purely negative objectives like the Lockean imperative to remove impediments to the advance of science. Surely its role is more positive insofar as the philosopher is in a position to facilitate or work toward a better understanding of the world in her own terms. Arguably, moreover, Locke's apparent lack of hubris, and corresponding defer-

[1] Department of Sociology and Anthropology, University of Guelph

ence to strict empiricism, is less of an admission of the limits of philosophy than a demonstration of its power. The scientific masters he was there to serve would surely never have ascended from the depths of mysticism without the power of revolutionary philosophical ideas.

FOR PUBLIC CRIMINOLOGY?
A CRITICAL PERSPECTIVE

The role for 'public criminology' is similarly fraught with contradictions, challenges, and trenchant criticisms that are not the primary focus of this paper. Nonetheless, a brief review of arguments presented in the emerging literature on public criminology is warranted to situate the author's orientation as one who has not previously contributed, identified, nor thought about the issues raised in the same terms before.

The role of criminologists as democratic underlabourers has been articulated variously as one that advocates for scientifically informed 'justifiable action.' The primary role is to challenge or question the conventional wisdom in criminal justice, to debunk myths and scare tactics, to evaluate and reframe hegemonic, prejudicial cultural images of the criminal (Loader and Sparks, 2010; Uggen and Inderbitzen, 2010). Put otherwise, the task is largely to attempt to "cool things down"—to appeal to rationality and scientific method, and to create new institutions that might insulate crime policy from the heat of politics and populist demands.

One might justifiably contend that in some cases it would seem more appropriate to 'heat things up' a little—domestic violence, for example, abuse of children, the environment, and other crimes committed by the powerful which are often downplayed or neglected by the criminal justice system. Notwithstanding this objection, it does not preclude commitment to a calm and calculating bureau-cratic ethos that fosters use of expertise and evi-dence-based knowledge, which presumably is optimal for meaningfully informing criminal justice policy and prac-tice.

Loader and Sparks (2010), like Latour (2004), are at-tentive to the importance of maintaining a skeptical orien-tation to those espousing promises of 'evidence-based' policy, or the desire to replace politics with "calculative devices." The idea of criminology as a civic enterprise has been rightly challenged by those wary of extending the complicity of academia in serving the technocratic aims of a neoliberal state.

All claims about crime are political in nature, suggest-ing what is needed is neither better science or manage-ment, but a better understanding of the forces that shape these discussions in the public sphere. Being 'political' does not mean acting more like politicians, or even more like activists. Wacquant (2011) is unequivocal that it is im-perative for the social scientist to maintain independence from the state and political pressure groups, for otherwise engagement is bound to become service, if not servitude, to outside vested interests.

The democratic underlabourer must be committed first and foremost to generating knowledge, rather than scoring political points. The task is to interpret 'facts' and other hard-won knowledge and bring it to bear on political is-sues that are matters of public concern. This role ought not be reduced to simply giving evidence. Academics must maintain the freedom to be critical and be at liberty to refuse to take the world for granted. We can and should be skeptical about institutional arrangements based on 'com-mon sense,' or what everybody knows.

The trade-off is that criminologists must put aside illusions of possessing knowledge that trumps other types of claims in public policy debates (Loader and Sparks, 2010). There is a need for more humility in what can be accomplished, coupled with more certitude in asserting our own principles—including, most importantly, to follow our own instincts, rather than conforming to any particular style of engagement or label (Wacquant, 2011).

Such labels are inevitably restrictive, and they fail to capture the fluidity of academic work. Since every social science discipline is 'public' by necessity, such assertions are redundant, one might similarly argue. Far from a call to action and political engagement, such developments, for Wacquant (2011), are more like intra-disciplinary turf wars, which confuse the territory marking and politics of the profession with the real world politics and problems of society.

The formation and development of 'public criminology' is inseparable from the "field of power" (Bourdieu and Wacquant, 1993) in which academics operate—i.e., within a neoliberal context of degraded work conditions, marked by the devaluation of teaching and research that do not correspond with managerial priorities (Côté and Allahar, 2011). Neglect of institutions is problematic, Wacquant (2011) continues, given the proliferation of alternative knowledge producers.

The influence of 'think tanks' has transformed the policy landscape, acting as selective magnifiers that function to buffer politicians from alternative perspectives. Staffed by semi-scholars (e.g., high ranked police as 'research fellows'), these coalitions capitalize on administrative authority, political connections, visibility, and access to sympathetic journalists.

Against such organizations, specializing in production of digestible soundbites and executive summaries of the kind sought after by state managers, how can so-called 'public criminologists' compete? (Waquant, 2011).

New emerging online quasi-scientific journals—with often dubious credentials, editorial boards, and funding sources backed by right-wing political organizations—now seek to level out the playing field by neutralizing critical research and advocacy in the field of power that counts. Cuts to social science research serve a similar agenda, as these reinforce the status quo by limiting resources and the visibility and reach of opposition.

To illustrate, despite the mounting evidence of harms due to drug laws and policing, versus the effectiveness of harm reduction programs, the latter initiatives receive a tiny fraction of the total funding marked for drug use by the Canadian government. Research also receives a thin portion of the budget, with harm reduction programs and research combined accounting for one-tenth of the tax dollars devoted to funding for drug law enforcement (see De-Beck et al., 2007; Hathaway and Tousaw, 2008).

Accordingly, the contexts of production, validation, and reception to academic work require more frank articulation and reflection by criminologists, if we hope to develop a more politically engaged, conducive, and coherent public role. It is important to remain humble, as Wacquant (2011) advises, and follow our own instincts, rather than attempting to conform to a particular style of engagement, or label such as 'public criminologist.'

Intentions of this sort are not unique to criminology. Nor are they distinctive to the social sciences. Rather they recur throughout the history of science. And typically (predictably) they have not generated much interest or discussion outside of academia, nor among scholars outside our own respective disciplinary boundaries.

To be clear on my position, I am all for academics assuming an active role in public policy discussions. But it is important that we do not take for granted what that role entails and be as honest as we can be about related challenges and prospects. One must guard against developing too lofty aspirations. At the same time nonetheless, when opportunity comes calling we are professionally and publicly obliged to 'make it count.'

CONFESSIONS OF A CANADIAN DRUG POLICY OBSERVER

The foregoing observations are consistent with my own experience as a sociologist whose work has, on occasion, been cited or presented in drug policy discussions outside standard academic literature and fora. Similar concerns were raised by Hathaway and Tousaw (2008) in their commentary on the controversy over supervised injection in the city of Vancouver. In particular, they argue for a clearer articulation of the values that inform drug policy discussions. Advocates for law reform in academic circles, accordingly, need not play down the humanistic values and respect for rights informing their position in support of harm reduction programs and initiatives like InSite.

Avoiding moral arguments as a tactical concession, harm reduction has made inroads on pragmatic grounds alone as a necessary step toward drug policy reform in many jurisdictions where confronting prohibition is seen as too politically contentious. Harm reduction is a tactical form of criticism that accepts official definitions of 'the problem' but not the remedies employed by status quo supporters. It may therefore be described as a stepping stone towards the more humane enforcement of our drug laws on the way to more significant or meaningful drug policy reform (Hathaway, 2001).

Maintaining an aura of value neutrality has undoubtedly been useful, or politically expedient, allowing for some common ground that benefits drug users by sidestepping ideological disputes (Reinarman, 2004). Yet, 25 years since setting forth an official mandate to develop more pragmatic drug policies in Canada, support for harm reduction is no less marginal in practice. Indeed, along with funding cuts to harm reduction programs, public health initiatives like InSite in Vancouver have been disavowed explicitly by the Harper government as condoning drug abuse and fostering addiction.

It appears that no amount of data or sidestepping value-laden arguments will resolve the fundamental ideological division between those who seek to challenge oppressive anti-drug laws and those who seek to maintain the war on substance users. With clear evidence that the war on drugs is ineffective, costly, inhumane, and harmful to the user and society, the choice to stay the course as a societal response is ultimately a moral choice with drastic consequences.

A CONSTRUCTIONIST FRAMEWORK

"Public criminology," criminology in general (and every social science discipline, more broadly, for that matter) is concerned with better understanding social problems and, less often, though not rarely, advocating for solutions. My training in the social constructionist tradition informs my understanding or approach to social problems as being products of collective definition or *claims making*—as opposed to facts about conditions to be determined through assessment of objective evidence *per se*.

From this standpoint, theoretically, even scientific evidence brought to bear on arguments concerning social problems should be seen as part of the claims makers' efforts to persuade (Gusfield, 1981). The constructionist perspective is primarily concerned with what people say about the putative conditions, rather than the so-called facts or truth about conditions, which are the subject of contested or competing sets of claims. Whereas the prevalence of substance use may or may not change, these kinds of facts are less important, for example, than the fact that people understand drug use as a social problem.

Often independently of changes in the actual conditions or objective situation, certain drugs or 'types' of users are targeted as problems by authorities, or segments of the general population in society. From the temperance movement to the reefer madness era(s)—to drug panics about LSD, PCP, and crack, heroin and ecstasy (and model airplane glue)—a wide variety of substances, at one time or another, have generated disproportionate attention and concern.

The target of drug panics, and the ways we understand drugs, have undergone significant transitions throughout history. These are often a reflection of the way we understand drug problems as belonging to a certain type. Different types of problems call for different solutions. Thus it is noteworthy that 'the problem' has been variously defined and understood as a sin or moral failing, as a criminal behaviour, and as a sickness or disease requiring medical attention. Constructionist analyses focus on examining rhetorical styles and strategies to further understanding of the specific nature of the claims making process through which social problems are constructed (see Best, 1987; Ibarra and Kitsuse, 1993).

Gusfield's early work in this tradition emphasizes the influential role of science and scientific experts in legitimating official definitions of drug problems. Writing forty years ago, he observed an evident transition in the US toward what he described as a more rational style of drug policy discourse:

> The rules of the game now demand that ideas be set forth in the language and tactics of rational debate and analysis.... It is a game of persuasion. The expert assumes importance in this game because he or she assumed an informed and impartial position. As knowledge is disseminated, it sets limits to the public acceptability of ideas (1975, p. 13).

Research by experts in the drug field can serve to challenge the factual basis for maintaining status quo arrangements and are subversive in the sense that they "...break down the public appearance of a united and consensual society on the question of drug use" (p. 12). Four decades afterwards, however, although the more outrageous claims of the past seem less appropriate than ever in the context of informed drug policy debate, the wealth of scientific evidence continues to have little actual impact on criminal justice policy (see also Blumstein, 1993; Erickson, 1998; Hathaway and Erickson, 2003).

Notwithstanding his assertions to the contrary, moreover, Gusfield (1975, p. 13) acknowledged that in matters of drug policy it appears that "...knowledge makes less difference than conventional theory will admit." More specifically, he pointed out that "...scientific knowledge is only one of a number of factors that bear upon the symbolic and instrumental character of official public action." Recognizing that most claims about social problems incorporate both moral and rational themes (Best, 1987), academic researchers participating in these forums are encouraged to consider using a fuller range and interplay of rhetorical devices (Hathaway, 2002).

Since claims making inevitably involves making certain choices about the kinds of arguments considered most persuasive in light of the specific audience and circumstances, different types of claims have currency in different contexts. Arguably, however, as democratic under-labourers, criminologists ought to be more open about the value commitments that inevitably guide our research and advocacy (see also Gouldner, 1968). Sacrificing deeper moral warrants in exchange for an illusion of neutrality that is rarely respected outside academic circles, and increasingly distrusted by social scientists within them, appears politically shortsighted in this democratizing context. The moral and the empirical are inexorably entangled, for the interpretation of empirical reality ordinarily entails employing certain moral standards (Putnam, 1993).

The following case study seeks to shed light on the value of critical engagement with ideological commitments that underpin the war on (certain) drugs—and, by extension, other forms of crime control, state violence and oppression that raise questions about what is meant by *justice*. With respect to Public Criminology, to be candid, the closest I have came to influencing public policy came early on in a career that is primarily devoted to academic teaching and research—when time allows the latter (which is rarely). In May 2001 I was invited to a hearing to testify in Ottawa as an "expert witness" before the Senate Special Committee on Illegal Drugs. Excerpts from this testimony and other work submitted are cited in the September 2002 report of the Committee entitled, *Cannabis: Our Position for a Canadian Public Policy*.

THE TESTIMONY

The bulk of testimony was derived from data gathered through structured interviews conducted with adult marijuana users recruited through an ad in a Toronto free newspaper seeking experienced cannabis users. Study data were presented to the Committee indicating that, even at high use levels, the experience of problems is a relatively low occurrence. In addition to this research, other findings were submitted in the form of academic papers which presented qualitative data from the author's MA thesis—and more ideologically contentious points developed in my recently completed and, at that time, unpublished doctoral work. Excerpts from the studies examining use patterns occupy approximately a single page in total—which amounts to mere footnote—of the 627-page final report on cannabis produced by the Senate Committee.

My other work, presenting more polemical assertions, is not directly cited in the 2002 report. However, (unexpectedly) the Chair of the Committee requested it be outlined in my presentation, so it would be included in the official testimony (in addition to my presentation of the data derived from structured interviews with marijuana users). Thus the testimony is comprised of observations based on an array of social scientific methods. The specific forms of analysis included the use of tables and statistics, inductive qualitative research, and more explicitly interpretive polemical inquiry.

This paper focuses on aspects of the submitted testimony that were deemed by the Committee of sufficient interest to be included in their final report. The invited presentation was prepared for in advance of the Senate hearing in May 2001. New data were presented from a recently completed study that examined use patterns and experiences of marijuana users in the city of Toronto.

Survey Data on Dependence

Survey data were presented on a range of drug effects, including self-perceptions of both benefits and problems, utilizing standard measures of dependence and abuse (for further details on the study, see Hathaway, 2003). The findings are interpreted as evidence supporting a non-pathological perspective on marijuana use as rational insofar as, for respondents (n=104), the perceived benefits of using outweigh any adverse consequences they experienced. The most common reasons for using marijuana were for relaxation and enhancement of activities followed by coping with stress and anxiety.

The data showed that there was no significant relationship between levels of consumption reported by respondents and any indicator of dependence or abuse. Users generally acknowledge the potential adverse outcomes and adapt their use levels when problems are experienced. Some participants were worried about developing dependence or respiratory problems in the future. To address these health concerns, the data are interpreted as indicating needs for harm reduction education, and replacing criminal sanctions with a public health approach.

Excerpts from this testimony appear in Chapter 7 of the Senate Report (2002) which examines cannabis effects and consequences. In a section on the topic of cannabis dependence, under the sub-heading *Studies on long-term users*, the following findings appear. Nearly one-third of respondents reported having ever experienced three or more symptoms of cannabis dependence. This is the standard threshold for a diagnosis of dependence, based on the DSM-IV criteria for substance use disorders. When asked about more recent use, however, only half of the group diagnosed 'dependent' had experienced three or more symptoms during the *past year*.

Accordingly, as cited from the transcripts of the hearing:

> In light of this finding, the most frequently encountered problems with cannabis have more to do with self-perceptions of excessive use levels than with the drug's perceived impact on health, social obligations and relationships, or other activities. Lending support to the highly subjective nature of his (sic) evaluative process, no significant correlation were found between amounts nor frequency of use and the number of reported DSM-IC (sic) items. For those whom cannabis dependency problems progress to the point of seeking out or considering formal help, however, the substantive significance of perceived excessive use levels cannot be overlooked (p. 158).

The selection of this excerpt, from all the testimony given, suggests that the Committee found the evidence persuasive. The statistical analysis presented indicates that diagnosing cannabis dependence is not easy. Standard diagnostic tools are better at detecting more objective indicators of dependence and abuse that correspond with serious drug problems. Cannabis-related problems tend to be subjective; they are not necessarily related to use levels, nor to the kinds of symptoms found with other kinds of drug use, such as problems with health or meeting social obligations.

The selected findings and interpretation given have important implications for informing harm reduction and treatment services for users with cannabis-related problems. These observations based on findings from a quantitative study were considered interesting enough for the Committee to cite them verbatim in their eventual Report.

In addition to my oral testimony at the hearing, I was invited to submit published articles and works in progress that could be of interest to the work of the Committee. The documents submitted for their consideration included research papers from a qualitative study which conducted interviews with experienced users who were committed to continuing their marijuana use.

IN-DEPTH INTERVIEWS WITH USERS

Marijuana use is argued to have undergone transition from a practice documented within deviant subcultures to one now widely tolerated throughout most western cultures (Hathaway, 1997a,b). With diffusion of the practice in the general population, particularly among the middle classes, it has become more personal or individually determined. Accordingly, more research is needed to develop a better understanding of how marijuana use develops in the context of conventional everyday behaviour.

Based on unstructured interviews with 30 adult users, this research examines motivations and use patterns. My emphasis was on exploring its use for work and leisure, among other patterns that challenge the assumption that using marijuana is a substance use disorder, or motivated by involvement in a deviant subculture. Excerpts from this study appear in Chapter 6 of the Senate Report, which is on users and uses of cannabis.

In a section labeled use patterns and circumstances, under the sub-heading *Trajectories of use*, the Senate noted the following findings. It is reported that new research shows experienced, long-term users regulate their use independently of other users, integrating marijuana use into their daily lives. As cited in the Report from the article submitted (Hathaway, 1997b):

> ...moving from a pattern of use that is dependent on one's level of participation with other users to one that is independently regulated marks a crucial transition in

the marijuana user's relationship to the drug. (...) their continuing use of the drug does not necessarily suggest an inability to commit to adult roles. Instead, adapting one's marijuana use to suit an otherwise conventional way of life appears to make the practice significant on a more personal level than that previously fostered through affiliation with marijuana-using groups (Senate, 2002: p. 116).

Thus it was important, in the eyes of the Committee, to recognize perceptions and experiences of users which do not correspond with the perspective that use patterns are determined by involvement in a deviant subculture. Other testimony from the written work submitted, which was not included in the 2002 Report, was nonetheless brought forward at the hearing by the Chair. Accordingly, the witness gave an impromptu summation of the arguments developed in the submitted work in progress (see Hathaway, 2001), followed by a final round of questions from the Committee.

MORAL WARRANTS FOR REFORM

Notwithstanding recognition of his role as 'expert witness' and commitment to developing new evidence-based knowledge, today's disputes about drug policy, according to the witness, are fundamentally moral arguments which cannot be judged according to professional standards of rationality or harm. Whereas liberal reformers commonly concede the immorality of prohibited conduct and then go on to discuss the excessive costs of preventing it, efficiency-based arguments have had little success in reducing the scope of criminalized conduct in practice.

Where decriminalization has occurred—as in the case of contraception, abortion, and consensual sexual relations between adults, for example—it has resulted from a shift in moral judgements as opposed to regard for cost-effi-

ciency assessments. Where moral judgements remain unchallenged, as with illicit substance use, movement toward
decriminalization has been negligible. By contrast a
rights-based orientation, with commitment to upholding
legal equality and fairness, calls on constitutional protections that put the onus on state regulators and enforcers to
justify infringing on personal freedoms.

A fundamental precept of the liberal tradition is that
only threats to public safety justify state intrusion or coer-
cion. Intervention must be limited to behaviour that is
threatening to civil order or public security, and repressive
action by authorities is limited so as to minimize disruption of citizens' rights. The scope of criminal law is restricted such that acts may be made criminal only if they
inflict concrete harm on assignable persons. This means
that it is never proper to criminalize an act solely on the
grounds of preventing harm to the actor or because the act
is seen as offensive by others.

To say that a person has a right to use drugs is not to assert such a right should be exercised. To assert the existence of such a right is rather to make a legal-political
claim that the conduct must be protected from coercive
prohibition by the state. Respect for the right to use drugs
preserves individual experience from a cultural hegemony
rooted in an absolutist conception of public morality. Accordingly, reformers should be more explicit about promoting arguments that challenge prohibition by seeking to
uphold constitutional protections—such as the "right to
life and liberty and security of the person" which is guar-
anteed in Section 7 of the *Charter*.

Invoking social norms of tolerance and respect for personal freedom, advancing the drugs debate in Canada and
other western nations is, arguably, contingent on developing more liberal normative interpretations of protected
rights and freedoms. 'Rational' assessments of the prob-

lem, utilizing 'value-neutral' arguments and scientific data, are accordingly in need of a rhetorical foundation that denounces prohibition as a morally objectionable intervention in the private lives of individuals. Although such a strategy is boldly out of step with the noted trend toward more use of scientific arguments, a human rights perspective is as viable in western culture as the continuing commitment to criminalizing substance users and appeals to value neutral warrants for reform.

To illustrate the argument, a 1997 landmark court case that challenged the legitimacy of existing marijuana laws (*R. v. Clay*) was examined by the witness in the written work submitted. Considering both factual and constitutional assessments of arguments presented to the Court, more weight was ultimately given to upholding normative standards than to the weight of scientific evidence submitted. To find guidance on questions concerning the enforcement of morality, it is essential that we must look beyond conclusions based on 'science' to larger normative debates in law and politics about power and autonomy, equality and freedom, and other social values that give meaning to the evidence about what kind of arguments ultimately matter.

Drawing on insights from constructionist theory about the role of claims making in shaping social problems, the above case study of the Clay trial indicates that arguments for law reform based on rationality are limiting because they lack a foundation of accepted principles from which to maneuver in legal-political arenas. Whereas evidence-based arguments have certain advantages in the context of ostensibly rational debate, the underlying issue of personal autonomy is ultimately central to drug policy debates.

As a matter of strategy, it is thereby essential to articulate an understanding of the 'problem' in which freedom to pursue one's own ends, including use of drugs, without undue interference takes on primary significance. From this standpoint, it is argued that challenging anti-drug laws requires commitment to developing a morally invested rights-based perspective on drug policy in Canada.

INTERPRETATION AND DISCUSSION

To summarize in general terms, the testimony given is that marijuana users are responsible and rational, and that it is important to respect their motivations, perceptions and experiences of use. Criminal justice policy development would benefit from further recognition that drug users have rights, and that drug users have voices worth hearing. The persistent 'us' versus 'them' point of view overlooks the obvious, but nonetheless worth raising, objection that drug 'users' are parents, siblings, sons and daughters. Put otherwise, drug users are first and foremost people too. Academics accordingly have an obligation to challenge and compel the powers-that-be to listen.

The data that were shared at the hearing by the author, in a 'value-neutral' way (as protocol suggests is an expectation of any 'expert witness'), are combined with arguments informed by more polemical moral-legal judgements and assertions. The research that the witness was invited to present might be considered more 'objective' than the qualitative study (which was not discussed directly at the hearing but nonetheless included in the subsequent Report). Evidently in-depth interviews with 30 cannabis users (who were friends and friends-of-friends of the researcher as a student) were no less convincing or persuasive than the data from the later, larger survey using quantitative methods.

Both types of data naturally have strengths and limitations. The latter are considered more reliable and valid, and representative of users in the general population. The qualitative data are more detailed and descriptive; they are considered more subjective, open to interpretation, and subject to the biases of the interviewer. Despite the limitations of the study, still the interviews gave a voice to marijuana users who would not otherwise be 'heard' by interested politicians. This suggests the qualitative research was at least as equally compelling, in the view of the Committee, as the survey data and statistical analysis presented by the author in his primary report.

One might also argue that the qualitative data were neither more nor less persuasive, but rather served to complement the findings from the survey. In turn, the survey data, in combination with the interviews, gave a fuller picture of marijuana users than either method alone could provide. Furthermore, the more polemical statements by the witness (which he viewed as secondary and submitted as appendices) seemed to correspond with the aims of the Committee, and they requested that he put them 'on the record' at the hearing.

Sentiments like these are ordinarily avoided by academics taking part in drug policy discussions. They are not informed by hard or even soft facts, as such evidence is often understood in social scientific terms. These are rather claims informed by values and commitments to the rights and freedoms and constitutional protections ostensibly observed in Canada and other jurisdictions influenced by democratic principles. From this perspective, prohibition is an affront to human dignity and a violation of fundamental human rights.

No amount of scientific reasoning or argument can influence these principles of fundamental justice. They are essentially contested ideological commitments, of the kind in opposition that justify the drug war. It needs to be asserted that these values are not just viable, but *more* legitimate than those that seem to favour prohibition. They have the moral weight of deeper values and convictions that are necessary to challenge overreaching drug laws.

Value-neutral arguments and scientific data are in need of a rhetorical foundation based on values that ultimately give meaning to the work of criminologists. In this light, it is noteworthy that the Senate Committee argued for developing a set of guiding principles to inform drug policy discussions in the future. As concluded in the final report of Committee (2002, p. 50):

> ...public policy on illegal drugs, specifically cannabis, ought to be based on an ethic of reciprocal autonomy and a resolve to foster human action. It ought to defer to criminal law only where the behaviour involved poses a significant direct danger to others. It ought to promote the development of knowledge conducive to guiding and fostering reflection and action.

Therefore the ideological arguments submitted were consistent with their overall objective to consider democratic principles and values in addition to scientific evidence or facts. From my own perspective as an academic advocate for meaningful drug policy reform, this is an indication of endorsement for the view that academics on the outside or the margins of these fora ought to be encouraged by the prospect of employing a broadening array of rhetorical resources in stating policy positions as independent 'experts.' Avoiding moral warrants for reform is less authentic, and thereby less strategic in some ways, than being open to engaging in discussions about values.

In today's austere neoliberal context, it is increasingly important that social scientists endeavour to develop and articulate foundations for inquiry informed by left-liberal ideological commitments. As democratic under-labourers, public criminologists ought to be as humble as John Locke was in asserting their role as independent academics.

While it may amount to sorting 'rubbish,' that role gives us the freedom to be open about having certain values, and an array of powerful tools at our disposal.

REFERENCES

Best, J. 1987. Rhetoric in claims-making: Constructing the missing children problem. *Social Problems* 34: 101–121.

Blumstein, A. 1993. Making rationality relevant. *Criminology* 31(1): 1-16.

Bourdieu, P. and Wacquant, L. 1993. From ruling class to field of power. *Theory, Culture & Society* 10: 19-44.

Côté, J.E. and Allahar, A.L. 2011. *Lowering Higher Education: The Rise of Corporate Universities and the Fall of Liberal Education*. Toronto: University of Toronto Press.

DeBeck, K., Wood, E., Montaner, J., and Kerr, T. 2007. Canada's 2003 renewed drug strategy—An evidence-based review. *HIV/AIDS Policy & Law Review* 11(2–3): 4–12.

Erickson, P.G. 1998. Neglected and rejected: A case study of the impact of social research on Canadian drug policy. *Canadian Journal of Sociology* 23: 263-280.

Gouldner, A.W. 1968. The sociologist as partisan: Sociology and the welfare state. *American Sociologist* May: 103–116.

Gusfield, J.R. 1975. The (f)utility of knowledge?: The relation of social science to public policy toward drugs. *Annals of the American Academy of Political and Social Science* 417, 1-15.

Gusfield, J.R. 1981. *The Culture of Public Problems: Drinking-driving and the Symbolic Order*. University of Chicago Press.

Hathaway, A.D. 1997a. Marijuana and tolerance: Revisiting Becker's sources of control. *Deviant Behavior* 18(2): 103-124.

Hathaway, A.D. 1997b. Marijuana and lifestyle: Exploring tolerable deviance. *Deviant Behavior* 18(3): 213-232.

Hathaway, A. D. 2001. Charter rights of Canadian drug users: A constitutional assessment of the Clay trial and ruling. *Canadian Journal of Law and Society* 16(1): 29-43.

Hathaway, A.D. 2003. Cannabis effects and dependency concerns in long-term frequent users: A missing piece of the public health puzzle. *Addiction Research & Theory* 11(6): 441-458.

Hathaway, A.D. and Erickson, P.G. 2003. Drug reform principles and policy debates: Harm reduction prospects for cannabis in Canada. Journal of Drug Issues 33(3): 467-496.

Hathaway, A.D. and Tousaw, K.I. 2008. Harm reduction headway and continuing resistance: Insights from safe injection in the city of Vancouver. International Journal of Drug Policy 19: 11-16.

Ibarra, P.R., & Kitsuse, J.I. 1993. Vernacular constituents of moral discourse: An interactionist proposal for the study of social problems. In G. Miller and J.A. Holstein, Eds. Constructionist Controversies: Issues in Social Problems Theory. N.J.: Aldine.

Latour, B. 2004. Politics of Nature: How to Bring the Sciences into Democracy. Cambridge, UK: Cambridge University Press.

Loader, I. and Sparks, R. 2010. What is to be done with public criminology? Criminology & Public Policy 9(4): 771-781.

Locke, J. 1975. (1690). An Essay Concerning Human Understanding. Oxford, U.K.: Oxford University Press.

Putnam, H. 1993. Objectivity and the science-ethics distinction. Pp. 143-157 in M.C. Nussbaum and A. Sen, Eds. The Quality of Life. Oxford: Clarendon Press.

Reinarman, C. 2004. Public health and human rights: The virtues of ambiguity. International Journal of Drug Policy 15: 239–241.

Senate Special Committee on Illegal Drugs. 2002. Cannabis: Our Position for a Canadian Public Policy. Ottawa: Available on the Parliamentary Internet: www.parl.gc.ca/illegal-drugs.asp.

Uggen, C. and Inderbitzen, M. 2010. Public criminologies. Criminology & Public Policy 9(4): 725-749.

Wacquant, L. 2011. From 'public criminology' to the reflexive sociology of criminological production and consumption. British Journal of Criminology 51: 438-48.

Winch, P. 2008. The Idea of a Social Science and its Relation to Philosophy. NY: Routledge.

SOCIAL REGULATION OF DRUGS: THE NEW "NORMAL"?

PATRICIA G. ERICKSON, PH.D[1]

INTRODUCTION: THE ROLE OF PUBLIC CRIMINOLOGY IN THE DRUG POLICY ARENA

The purpose of this commentary is to draw attention to the growing disconnects among drug use behavior, the perspectives of users, the research on drug use framed within the normalization perspective, the archaic drug laws governing illicit drug use, and the failure of current policy responses. Academic research can and should inform more enlightened policies. As an example of public criminology, this body of research challenges official definitions of the drug problem. The role of public criminology is to make this research evidence part of the public discourse on drug policy reform. An earlier analysis of the lack of the impact of social research in Canadian drug policy, characterized as "neglected and rejected," illustrates the difficulties of challenging the moral sway of a century of drug prohibition and the entrenchment of criminal justice bureaucracies dedicated to maintaining it (Erickson, 1998).

[1] Department of Sociology and Centre for Criminology and Socio-Legal Studies, University of Toronto

Nevertheless it is vital that criminologists continue to exert their efforts to produce alternative knowledge that challenges the status quo (Wacquant, 2011). In this tradition, I shall endeavour to trace the tensions between the law as it exists and the changing social evaluation of this drug using behaviour, considering developments from 1970 onwards. I shall draw at times on my own experience as researcher, policy analyst and presenter at government hearings dedicated to considering changes to drug law. As an applied researcher in this tradition, I have attempted to provide evidence on a perplexing social problem, to a wide range of citizens and stakeholders, and set out some guideposts to effective and humane resolution (Erickson, 1992; 2011).

Nowhere is the gap between the ongoing punitive response to drug use and the widespread social acceptability of this use more apparent than for cannabis (marijuana and hashish). While nearly half of the adult Canadian population has experience with this drug, more than 60,000 possession offences are recorded annually (Health Canada, 2010; CDPC, 2013). Thus it is the best candidate to illuminate the normalization perspective, both in Canada and in much of the rest of the world (Erickson and Hathaway, 2010; Beckley Foundation, 2009). The hallmark of normalization is *recreational* drug use, defined as the occasional use of certain substances in certain settings and in a controlled way" (Parker, 2005:206). This relatively new depiction of drug use as pleasurable, persistent and part of everyday life has been described as "the most important development in the sociology of drug use in several decades" (Sandberg, 2013:64). The criminal law, of course, recognizes no such distinctions, and considers possession of any amount of cannabis, for any purpose, to be illegal and the offender deserving of punishment (Erickson, van der Maas and Hathaway, 2013).

HISTORICAL BACKDROP OF DRUG POLICY: SEVERAL DECADES OF INDECISION

Few areas of public policy have been so fraught with misconceptions, stigma and contesting of evidence as the ongoing debate over how society should respond to illicit substance use. For over a century, Canada has experienced alternating waves of "panic and indifference" as each new or rediscovered drug provokes a moral panic that this is the one that will live up to the "demon drug" mythology of individual ruin and enslavement (Giffen, Endicott and Lambert, 1991). Such imagery combined with racist sentiments fanned the flames of the first "narcotics" (i.e, opium, morphine, heroin, cocaine and cannabis) prohibition laws in 1908, 1911 and 1923, and their ever escalating penalties during the 1920's to the 1960's (Solomon and Green, 1988). The criminal justice system became the first line of defence against this perceived threat, and special powers for police, prosecutors and severe sentencing options for judges ensured that "dope fiends" would be caught and their contaminating influence removed from society (Solomon, 1988). Then, starting in the mid-1960's, use of banned substances moved from the fringes of society to the mainstream, as more and more youth began to experiment with cannabis, LSD and other mood altering drugs. The era of a global "drug culture" had begun, and 50 years later, has become entrenched in most western nations. The legacy of prohibition and its applied arm of criminal justice, however, continue to dominate Canada's policy response.

In Canada, illicit drugs are prohibited by federal criminal law, found in a statute, *The Controlled Drugs and Substances Act* [CDSA]. This law prohibits the possession of any amount of cannabis, subject to a maximum penalty of a $1000 fine and a 6 month jail sentence. Penalties can be doubled for a subsequent offence. There has been no change in the possession offence since 1969, when the *Narcotic Control Act* was amended to allow a "fine only" option (instead of only jail or probation). A change to the *Criminal Code* in 1972 created a non drug-specific provision for absolute and conditional discharges. While most of those sentenced do not receive the maximum penalty, with small fines or discharges the norm, some are jailed and all do become labelled with a criminal record (Erickson, 1980; 2005). It is estimated that upwards of one million Canadians now have criminal records for cannabis possession. This then is the current situation; now I shall turn to a historical recap of how this gap could grow and persist, and how the normalization perspective can be helpful in understanding these developments.

Several overviews of the efforts to reform Canada's drug laws over four decades are available (Fischer, 1988; Giffen and Lambert, 1988; Hyshka, 2009a) and only the key events will be summarized here. In the 1970's, the Royal Commission on the Non-Medical Use of Drugs, known as the Le Dain Commission after its Chair, was formed to examine the rising wave of illicit drug use, and accompanying criminalization, among ordinary, non-delinquent young people (Erickson, 1980). It held hearings, conducted research, and produced four landmark reports. The one entitled *Cannabis* (Le Dain, 1972) contained a majority report recommending the repeal of the offence of simple possession, one minority report arguing for its retention with a maximum penalty of a $100 fine (no jail), and another minority report calling for the abolition of prohibition and the setting up of a regulated distribution system. None of these options was favoured by the Liberal government of the day, choosing instead to retain the existing maximum fine and jail penalties in the *Narcotic Control Act*, and to provide the sentencing alternative of discharge. Since the latter still required the accused to come to court, allowed him or her to be fingerprinted and photographed, and created a criminal record of guilt (though not conviction), an application for a pardon would still be required to "seal" the record. The Chairman of the Law Reform Commission of Canada, presenting at the subsequent Senate hearings when an automatic pardon for cannabis possession was being discussed, noted plaintively, "why did the machinery bring the person through the whole criminal justice system in to a position where he was convicted (or discharged) in the first place, when there are many other methods of coping with and dealing with the situation?" (Senate, 1975, quoted in Erickson, 1980:144). A bill to place cannabis in its own special section of the *Food and Drugs Act*, still a criminal statute but with lesser penalties at that time for amphetamines, barbiturates, LSD and other hallucinogens, never progressed to final reading and died on the order paper of Parliament in 1975 (Erickson, 1980).

The early 1980's was a fairly quiescent period, recording declines in both use and arrests for cannabis. Then in 1986 US President Ronald Reagan announced the relaunching of the War on Drugs, followed two days later by a statement from Prime Minister Brian Mulroney that "drug abuse has become an epidemic that threatens our economic and social fabric." As a high ranking Health official told me, "when he [the PM] made that statement, then we had to make it a problem" (quoted in Erickson, 1992:248). The result was Canada's Drug Strategy, formed with strategic input from a wide range of community groups, agencies serving drug users, and addiction professionals, to include not only illicit drugs but the whole range of addictive substances including alcohol and pharmaceuticals; it declared an emphasis on demand reduction through prevention efforts and more provisions for treatment (for a review, see Erickson, 1992). Thus while distancing itself from the more supply focused enforcement thrust of the US War on [Illicit] Drugs, the infusion of resources into policing, combined with new powers for antidrug efforts, meant that drug arrests again increased as local, provincial and national police forces demonstrated high levels of "productivity." Cannabis remained the major component of drug-related offenses, 64% in 1990 (Erickson, 1992:250). The ambivalence inherent in the Strategy, launched in 1987 with the official objectives of "reducing the harm to individuals, families and communities from the abuse of drugs," was captured in the Minister of Health's comment in 1990: "We believe that the first course of action in combatting drug abuse is to help the drug user or potential drug user. While the major priority is demand reduction, curbing supply is equally important, especially as a complement to demand reduction efforts" (quoted in Erickson 1992: 248, 255).

In the 1990's, the increased emphasis on criminal justice solutions favoured by the Conservative government led to the introduction of a new drug bill (C-85, *The Psychoactive Substances Control Act*) that provided basically the same classifications and penalties for drugs as the existing law, *the Narcotic Control Act*. It even proposed to double the maximum penalties for the first offence of cannabis (to 12 months and $2000 fine). The legislative sub-committee was given 2 weeks to conduct hearings and move the bill forward; then an election was called in 1993 and C-85 died on the order paper of Parliament. While in opposition, the Liberal members had severely criticized the proposed bill; now in power, the newly elected Liberal government introduced the nearly identical bill (C-7, *the Controlled Drugs and Substances Act*) in 1994 (Fischer, 1988). In more hearings on this, the first new drug legislation to be presented in Canada since the 1960's, Liberal members stated that "this is not a policy bill, so it should not be confused with drug policy," and "the government is not in favour of the decriminalization of marijuana" (cited in Fischer, 1988:55-57). Despite considerable criticism from many witnesses reflecting a wide range of stakeholders, the CDSA was passed in Parliament on October 30, 1995 (amidst the distraction of Quebec Referendum Day on possible secession from Canada) with the triumphant claim that "this new law will put Canada in the forefront of leading the War on Drugs from a perspective of harm reduction." After final review and approvals by the Senate, it became the law of the land in 1997. With the slight modification of returning the maximum penalties for cannabis possession back to where they were before, and putting it in its own section of the CDSA, apart from opiates and cocaine for the first time since 1923, the punitive prohibition of cannabis remained intact.

A novel aspect of the process of moving the CDSA forward had been the promise to conduct a policy review *after* it became law. This was carried out by two committees of Parliament, one from the House of Commons and one from the Senate, and after travelling and hearing witnesses, they both reported in 2002 (Hyshka, 2009a; Senate, 2002). while the elected members on the House committee proposed decriminalization of cannabis possession, the appointed senators went further and argued for legalization in the form of a regulated approach that would permit those 16 and older to purchase the drug. For the next four years, from 2003-2006, further hearings on a series of bills examined a Liberal Government proposal to make possession of no more than 15 grams of marijuana or 1 gram of hashish a non-criminal, ticketable offence under a *Contraventions Act* amendment to the CDSA. It was defended by the Justice Minister of the day as increasing deterrence, because it was expected that the police would charge more people than before, while increasing revenue from the fines imposed (Hyshka, 2009a). In the end, political inertia prevailed, and the proposed reform disappeared when a Conservative government was elected in 2006 (Hyshka, 2009b). The National Drug Strategy was quickly transformed into an Anti-Drug Strategy, and harm reduction was removed from its mandate, leaving three pillars of enforcement, prevention and treatment (Hyshka, Erickson and Hathaway, 2011).

Another important development in the first decade of the new millennium pertained to the right of medical access to cannabis. After a series of cases and challenges that went to the Supreme Court of Canada, it ruled in 2000 that the ability of sick individuals to obtain cannabis for their conditions was a constitutionally protected right that must not be thwarted by arrest or stigmatization (Hathaway, 2001). Thus, in addition to compassion clubs which already dispensed cannabis in a grey area of legality, the *Medical Marijuana Access Program* was created. This allowed patients (with prescription from a physician) to purchase their own marijuana from Health Canada's sole source provider, cultivate their own supply, or designate a third party to grow for them (limit of 2 patients per grower). This health protection bestowed by the *Canadian Charter of Rights and Freedoms*, however, was not extended to cannabis for personal use. Another series of legal challenges led to a Supreme Court ruling in 2003 that deemed recreational use "trivial" and "supported the present prohibition against the use of marijuana...under the criminal law power" (quoted in Erickson, Hathaway and Urquhart, 2004:26, note 59). The judges also added that "it is open to Parliament to decriminalize or otherwise modify any aspect of the marijuana laws that it no longer considers to be good public policy." The door was open constitutionally, but no corresponding motivation for re-

form was evident among law makers, and in fact the following decade of 2010 onwards witnessed both tougher
laws and plans for commercial production. This was in the
face of considerable survey data that indicated widespread
use and considerable support for lesser penalties.

PUBLIC USE AND PERCEPTION: THE GROWING GAP BETWEEN THE LAW AND SOCIETY

Recent surveys, opinion polls and interview studies provide a current picture of cannabis use in Canada where
some of the highest prevalence rates in the world have
been reported (Adlaf et al, 2005). More than half of Canadians aged between 15 and 44 have tried cannabis at least
once in their lifetime, with 13% having done so in the past
month (Health Canada, 2010). A history of use is highest
among the 18-24 year old age group, about 70%, and
overall it is estimated that 2.17 million Canadians used
cannabis in the past 3 months (Health Canada, 2010).
About half of university undergraduates across the country
have experience with cannabis, and the data from our recent study of a large class at University of Toronto, with
about 40% reporting some use, reflected these previous
national survey results (Kolar, 2012). Nor is use confined
to younger cohorts; recent Ontario data show that the average age of users is now about 30 years (Duff, Asbridge,
Brochu, Cousineau, Hathaway, Marsh and Erickson,
2012).

The public has repeatedly been canvassed regarding
their views on appropriate sanctions for cannabis use.
These have overwhelmingly supported medical access,
with more split views on penalties, but growing support
for liberalization (Erickson, Hyshka and Hathway, 2010).
Despite some confusion around legal terminology, however, endorsement of decriminalization (no possession offence or reduced penalties for user) or some form of legal-

ization (providing regulated means of obtaining the substance) has become the majority viewpoint of about 2/3 of
the population overall in contemporary polls. A survey in
Toronto in 2004 provided more details of those who
favoured relaxation of the laws, indicating that a majority
of all age groups, including those over 50 years, would
prefer to see cannabis regulated "more like alcohol"
(Hathaway, Erickson and Lucas, 2007).

The statistical picture provided by survey data, while
giving a snapshot of population views, does not provide
the more detailed insights as to how users actually view
their drug use and any role the law might play in their decisions. An interview study with socially integrated, long
term adult users provided these perspectives (Duff et al,
2012): "a lot of my friends don't even consider it (marijuana) a drug anymore;" "pot seems to be the vice that fits
into your moral code now;"" it's a small part of who you
are rather than like your identity." For users such as those,
for whom cannabis is an established part of their lifestyle,
not only is a view of use as "wrong" absent, but also many
were somewhat oblivious to the risk of arrest (Brochu,
Duff, Asbridge and Erickson, 2011): "[arrest is] highly unlikely. I never carry more than a couple of grams; I don't
sell it, I don't traffick; I don't do anything *too* illegal;" "I
would say zero percent. I don't feel like I would ever get
arrested for use;" "I'm happy with the status quo whereby
it's totally tolerated although it's not technically legal."
Yet the chances of getting caught and charged are not re-
mote in Canada, as it also has the distinction of one of the
highest cannabis arrest rates in the world, increasing by
16% from 2001 to 2011 (CDPC, 2013). Nevertheless,
those who do enter the maw of the criminal justice system
are only a small, atypical minority of all current users of
the drug, reflecting only about 1% or less of all who used
cannabis in a given year, a figure not different than the es-
timate of the Le Dain Commission over 40 years ago,
(Brochu et al., 2011; Le Dain 1972).

In the decade of the 2010's, the Conservative government, with the strength of a majority for the first time, introduced the *Safe Streets and Communities Act* in an *Omnibus Bill* in 2011. Embedded in a number of provisions affecting the criminal justice system, were several amendments to the CDSA. While the possession offence remained unchanged, mandatory minimum penalties were introduced for all the other distribution offences related to trafficking, possession for the purpose of trafficking, importation/exportation and cultivation. For example, growing 6 or more cannabis plants could lead to 6 months minimum jail time. A number of aggravating features were listed, such as using someone else's property or operating near a school, that could justify longer terms of imprisonment. These penalties took effect on November 6, 2012, and how they are being implemented is not known at this time.

Health Canada announced in June 2013 that the system for medical access to cannabis would be revised under the *Marijuana for Medical Purposes Regulations*. By April 01, 2014, the only legal source to obtain medicinal cannabis will be licensed producers approved by Health Canada and meeting its requirements for safety and surveillance. In late 2014, about 14 companies out of nearly 200 applications have been approved in what is estimated to become, by 2024, a $1.3 billion commercial market serving an estimated 450,000 Canadians (compared to less than 40,000 under the current scheme)(Canadian Press, 2013). Valid prescriptions from a physician or a nurse practitioner, will still be required for approved users to receive their cannabis by mail. How this initiative will affect medical users who want to continue to grow their own, or obtain it from compassion clubs, is unknown, but it is possible they could be subject to arrest for possession, cultivation and/or trafficking. In response, a class action lawsuit that has challenged the constitutionality of the removal of the prior provisions has succeeded in halting the full application of the new regulations until a hearing by a higher court (Coalition Against Repeal, 2013). With this background of policy development and public perception in mind, I will now turn to the experience of cannabis users as viewed within the normalization perspective. I will argue that despite the ongoing prohibition, social regulation is much more a reality than legal bans, stigma, and fear of punishment.

APPLICATION OF NORMALIZATION: CANNABIS AND LIVED EXPERIENCE

The normalization perspective, first applied to drug use by Howard Parker and colleagues in a longitudinal study of young people in the UK (Parker, Aldridge and Measham, 1998) and further developed in several articles and a second book (Aldridge, Measham and Williams (2011), presented drug consumption as part of contemporary lifestyles of otherwise conventional and ordinary young people. Centered on recreational rather than dependent or excessive drug use, the user was viewed as making "reasoned choices" considering potential interference with other valued aspects of life, including family, work, reputation and health. Overall, the process of normalization in society reduces the stigma attached to deviant or illegal activities, as these behaviours become progressively viewed as a normal part of everyday life and an acceptable leisure activity (Parker, 2005). The originators identified six indicators of drug normalization: (1) increasing access and availability of illicit drugs in the community; (2) increasing prevalence of this drug use; (3) increasingly tolerant attitudes towards drug use among both users and non-users; (4) expectations among current abstainers regarding future initiation of illicit drug use; (5) the "cultural accommodation" of drug cultures in youth oriented film, TV and music; and (6) more liberal policy shifts (Parker, 2005:206-7). The normalization thesis has provoked much discussion (Measham and Shiner, 2009) and further modifications, including its potential application not just to youth but across the life course (Erickson and Hathaway, 2010), the relation of perceived health risks to more tolerant attitudes (Duff and Erickson, under review), and the actual practice of enforcement in the absence of significant policy changes (Brochu et al., 2011).

While cannabis is also viewed as the exemplar of normalization in a global setting where it is the most widely used illicit drug by far, cultural variation in preferred and permitted intoxicants must also be recognized on the normalization spectrum (Beckley, 2009; Duff, 2005; Erickson and Hathaway, 2010). In Canada, the survey data reviewed earlier and other research on the experience of users has indicated that the process is well underway for cannabis (Duff et al, 2012; Osborne and Fogel, 2008). There are several reasons why this evidence is important to insert into the current Canadian debate over drug policy: it focuses on *recreational* cannabis use, the norm for most users; the patterns of widespread use described above show a shift in moral boundaries despite the persistence of criminal prohibition; opinion polls also illustrate the changes in social evaluation from a subcultural to mainstream practice; the reliance on the criminal law as the major policy approach is not compatible with public health, user practices of moderation, or a respect for the rights of people who use drugs. Hence its elucidation is congruent with the critical stance of public criminology.

While the epidemiological and survey evidence sets the groundwork for a portrayal of normalization, the lived experience of users provides the insights into the acceptability and cultural tolerance that are also required components. Now I shall present some additional findings from our qualitative interview studies of 165 long term (average about 15 years), socially integrated adult cannabis users recruited in four provinces (for a description of sample and method, see Duff et al, 2012). Here are some typical quotes of how these individuals describe their ongoing cannabis use as integrated into their lifestyle: "people who casually smoke a joint here and there, even if a little bit every night, but it's not interfering with their life or with their productivity, I don't really see the harm," and "for my generation, we've been using since we were young, and most of us will continue to use and can still be successful as long as we are average users and don't go in for heavy using." These are clear reflections of the importance of a sense of control and self-monitoring that are central to normalized patterns of use.

Even inter-generational use was not uncommon in this group: "I grew up in a family that smokes pot...I've smoked with my dad and my mom. It's just like part of family." While the large majority expected to still be using in 10 years, others saw a gradual turning away: "Pot plays the role of recreational activity...in 10 years I'll have different responsibilities and I don't see it being as much part of my life." For many, appropriate use of cannabis was often compared to alcohol: "We have social norms with alcohol, like it's inappropriate to have beer with breakfast, but it's ok to have wine with dinner. Well what we're doing there is, we're mitigating the negative effects. I try and to do the same with pot, to work out the right amount to have, when to have it, what about its effects on me, my work my friends; it's all about making sure things don't get out of hand." This quote echoes the "reasoned choices" that Parker describes as central to the normalized use of drugs.

Our respondents were asked about situations when and where it was, as importantly, *not* acceptable, to use cannabis. The list included funerals, baby showers, at church, around animals and around children. Many also emphasized avoiding use when efficient functioning to do work, school or other tasks was required: "anything work related;" "if I have anything else to do including dishes or laundry;" "before a test or while studying." Interestingly, when we asked the participants (68 out of 165) who were also cigarette smokers about what they considered inappropriate use of tobacco, this comment was typical: "I don't smoke around children, inside, or around pregnant people....or around people who don't want me to or who don't have a choice." When users of both substances were asked to compare others' responses to knowing about their habits, much more stigma was expressed about cigarette use: "I'd rather have them find out about marijuana because tobacco is 'dirty.' I think it's a dirty habit, I think most people think it's a dirty habit. I don't have the same conception or opinion of smoking pot. Because it's like in the same category as drinking I guess." The emphasis placed by smokers of both cannabis and tobacco on setting boundaries and being considerate of others, despite the vast differences in legality, demonstrates a convergence of norms on acceptable social behaviour.

In summary, the available evidence from various sources (including the surveys and our own research and that of others) strongly supports a conclusion that normalizing trends for cannabis use are well underway in Canada. Access is reported as easy with friendship networks as the main source. Use is widespread across society, not limited to a subculture or deviant group. Most users have many friends who are also users, but report acceptability among non-using peers as well. Little stigma is experienced in most settings but some reservations are expressed regarding employers and family members. Tolerance does not extend to heavy use or to "hard' drugs like cocaine or opiates. The vast majority do not fear arrest but also are cautious about public settings and exposure to police, though many are not aware of the existing law and penalties that could apply to possessing even small amounts. While the law had not changed, the exercise of police discretion not to charge in all instances may also reflect a significant policy shift towards leniency "on the street," at least for certain, less marginalized segments of society.

Growing Disconnect and the Rise of Activism: Prospects for Reform

This disconnect between policy and behaviour leads us to the contrast between formal and informal types of social control, the former inherent in the criminal law and the latter found in social regulation. Both set out standards or demarcations of forbidden versus acceptable behavior among members of society, but with vastly different mechanisms and consequences. Criminal prohibition, Canada's current dominant policy that has persisted for over a century, relies on the threat of certain and severe punishment to deter use. Selective enforcement, with quotas and proactive targeting, results in arrests of a small minority of the more vulnerable drug users by virtue of age and visibility. Illicit markets supply cannabis and other illicit drugs of unknown potency and purity, and generate violence as their major means of handling market competition. Despite royal commissions, special committees, numerous hearings and proposed decriminalization bills, no changes to the criminal justice model have occurred, and it was re-entrenched in the beginning of the 2010 decade with even harsher penalties and more resources for enforcement and interdiction.

In contrast, social regulation supports recreational use, within limits, relying on social disapproval to contain problematic use. The social context is central to determining acceptable use, with variation according to time, place and who else is present in the social situation. As opposed to classical deterrence which aims to prevent all use, restrictive deterrence operates to channel users not to quit, but rather to avoid potential risky situations in public where detection may occur. Thus displacement is the main impact of the criminal ban. Users obtain drugs through friendship and social networks, where few need to have connections to larger scale suppliers. This social supply means of distribution has been found to especially characterize cannabis markets.

Central to the normalization perspective, our interview studies show that cannabis consumption is shaped by a sensitivity to the individual use environment which helps to determine when, where and with whom use is appropriate, and also importantly, inappropriate. We observed similarities to the social norms governing alcohol and increasingly, both public and private use of tobacco. When a substance is legally regulated, as these are, in a public health oriented model, various bylaws and non-federal statutes set out acceptable conditions for obtaining and using them, e.g. age and place restrictions and licensing of sale outlets. Thus the law is applied to set standards rather than to punish, and infractions tend to result in non-criminal penalties such as fines or loss of licenses. In the next section, I shall consider the possible future drug use and policy directions that we might witness in Canada in the short run of the remaining years of this decade. This is primarily a speculative exercise, but one informed by past developments and those that are occurring in the broader global context.

From the earlier discussion of several decades of indecision, regardless of which party was in power, followed by the current Harper government's toughening of the CDSA provisions with mandatory minimum sentences, it would seem unlikely that change will occur at the federal level during its term of office (a federal election must be held by October 2015). Nevertheless, many shifts have been happening globally in both national and local policies that may eventually influence Canada. About 25 other countries have instituted significant decriminalization policies, not just for cannabis but for other drugs (The Economist, 2013). Uruguay has set a state wide system of cannabis regulation in motion, and voters in the states of Colorado and Washington recently passed voter initiatives legalizing the use and commercial sale of marijuana (Keefe, 2013). The international treaties governing drug policy, of which Canada is a signatory, explicitly ban such legal production, but compliance appears to be weakening; many Latin American countries have been criticizing them and proposals for opting out have appeared in prestigious journals (Room and Reuter, 2012), a far cry from when the treaties were presented as totally rigid requirements in the hearings on the CDSA (Fischer, 1997). Adding to the mix in Canada has been the new Liberal leader's (Justin Trudeau) comments in favour of "legalizing it, tax and regulate (cannabis)…the current model is not working" (July, 2013). However, a more feasible possibility may be the one presented by the Canadian Association of the Chiefs of Police to use the *Contraventions Act* to create a non-criminal, ticketing, possession offence (August, 2013). This of course is exactly the proposal put forward and much debated during the Liberal Government era of 2003-2006, and one which the CACP opposed at the time (Hyshka, 2009a;b).

A recurring thread in the drug policy debates since the Le Dain Commission has been the imposition of criminal records on otherwise non-criminal individuals, and the life-long consequences that can follow. A general amnesty has been discussed and rejected in prior federal policy reviews. A supposed safety valve for the hundreds of thousands of individuals with such records for cannabis possession is to seek a pardon which after a waiting period, an investigation, and a payment, is supposed to seal the record (Erickson, 1980). The Harper government recently re-named the pardon a "record suspension," increased the waiting period, and raised the fee (Erickson and Hyshka, 2010). The following email message, received by the author in the summer of 2013, illustrates both the persistent negative consequences of a criminal record and the limits of a pardon:

> I'm a Canadian living and working in New York City and presently trying to immigrate to the United States. Back in 1993 I was arrested for smoking a marijuana cigarette in Montreal. I was 21 and it was a first offense I ended up getting probation of 6 months, no fines. I have never been arrested or convicted again. In 2000 I requested a Pardon for this offense and most documents were destroyed—including the police report with a description of the single marijuana cigarette I had when apprehended. Since the US Immigration Service does not recognize the Canadian Pardon, the burden is now on me to prove the amount I was arrested with was less than 30 grams of cannabis. I still can't believe that this would follow me 20 years later but it has.

This story may have a happy ending, as this individual was able to find an old microfilm of his arrest, using the *Freedom of Information Act*, and add that to his application for immigration. But it is also clear that once a criminal record is acquired it is nearly impossible to eliminate the trail, or the effects.

An important ingredient in the prospects for reform of Canadian drug policy is the role of activists. Users themselves, such as the adults interviewed in our research, are emissaries of normalization and living proof of harm reduction. As they demonstrate self-regulation and long term use without problems or interference with their social roles and responsibilities, what end would be served by arresting them, taking them to court, and imposing criminal records? On a global level, the emergence of harm reduction has focused attention on recognizing the human rights of all drug users, across the spectrum, including the recreational users (Erickson and Hathaway, 2010). Despite being at the center of initial iterations of Canada's Drug Strategy, and shaping many provincial and city responses to their local drug issues, the Harper government removed harm reduction from its Anti-Drug Strategy in 2007. Nevertheless, groups such as Canadian Students for a Sensible Drug Policy have become active on many campuses, and the Canadian Drug Policy Coalition has provided a forum and a presence to critique current approaches and provide alternatives (CDPC, 2013).

While the future of Canadian drug policy remains a work-in-progress, public criminology can play an important role in this ongoing debate by bringing relevant research forward to inform a more just, humane and effective policy rooted in public health and the principles of harm reduction.

References

Adlaf, E.M., Begin, P., and Sawka, E. (2005) *Canadian Addiction survey (CAS): A national survey of Canadians' use of alcohol and other drugs:* Prevalence of use and related harms. Ottawa: Canadian Centre on Substance Abuse.

Aldridge, J., Measham, F., and Williams, L. (2011.) *Illegal Leisure Revisited: Changing Patterns of Alcohol and Drug Use in Adolescents and Young Adults.* London: Routledge.

Beckley Foundation (2009). *The Global Cannabis Commission Report: Cannabis Policy—Moving Beyond Stalemate.* Oxford: The Beckley Foundation.

Brochu, S., Duff, C., Asbridge, M., and Erickson, P.G. (2011). 'There's what's on paper and then there's what happens out on the sidewalk:' Cannabis users' knowledge and opinions of Canadian drug law. *Journal of Drug Issues* 41(1):95-115.

Canadian Drug Policy Coalition (CDPC) (2013). *Getting to Tomorrow: A Report on Canadian Drug Policy.* Vancouver: CDPC. Downloaded at: www.drugpolicy.ca/progress/getting-to-tomorrow

Canadian Press (2013). See The Globe and Mail and CBC stories at: http://the globeandmail.com/news and http://www.cbc.ca/news

Coalition Against Repeal (2013). http://www.johnconroycom/mmarcoalition/

Duff, C. (2005). Party drugs and party people: Examining the normalization of recreational drug use in Melbourne, Australia. *International Journal of Drug Policy* 16:161-170.

Duff, C., Asbridge, M., Brochu, S., Cousineau, M., Hathaway, A.D., Marsh, D., & Erickson, P.G. (2012). A Canadian perspective on cannabis normalization among adults. *Addiction Research & Theory*, 20, 271-284.

Duff, C. and Erickson, P.G.(2014). Cannabis, risk and normalization: Evidence from a study of socially integrated, adult cannabis users in four Canadian provinces. *Health, Risk and Society* (in press).

Erickson, P.G. (1980) *Cannabis Criminals: The Social Effects of Punishment on Drug Users*. Toronto: ARF Books.

Erickson, P.G. (1992). Recent trends in Canadian drug policy: The decline and resurgence of prohibitionism. *Daedalus* 121(3):239-268.

Erickson P.G. (1998). Neglected and rejected: A case study of the impact of social research on Canadian drug policy. *The Canadian Journal of Sociology* 23:263-280.

Erickson, P.G. (2005). Alternative sanctions for cannabis use and possession Pp. 39-43 in P. Begin and J Weekes (Eds.), *Substance Abuse in Canada: Current Challenges and Choices*. Ottawa: CCSA.

Erickson, P.G. (2011) Lower risk cannabis use guidelines—for whom? *Canadian Journal of Public Health* 102(5):328-329.

Erickson, P.G. and Hathaway, A.D. (2010). Normalization and harm reduction: research avenues and policy agendas. *International Journal of Drug Policy* 21:137-139.

Erickson, P.G. and Hyshka, E. (2010) Four decades of cannabis criminals in Canada, 1970-2010. *Amsterdam Law Forum* 2(4):1-14.

Erickson, P.G., Hyshka, E., and Hathaway, A.D. (2010). Legal regulation of marijuana: The better way. Pp. 109-118 in N. Frost, J. Freilich and T. Clear (Eds.), *Contemporary Issues in Criminal Justice Policy*. Belmont, CA: Wadsworth, Cengage Learning

Erickson, P.G. and Murray, G.F. (1989). The undeterred cocaine user: Intention to quit and its relationship to perceived legal and health threats. *Contemporary Drug Problems* 16(2):141-156.

Erickson, P.G., van der Maas, M. and Hathaway, A.D. (2013). Revisiting deterrence: Legal knowledge, use context and arrest perception for cannabis. *Czech Sociological Review* 49(3):1-22.

Fischer, B. (1997). The battle for a new Canadian drug law: A legal basis for harm reduction or a new rhetoric for prohibition? A Chronology. Pp. 47-68 in P.G. Erickson, D.M Riley, Y.W. Cheung and P.A. O'Hare (Eds.), *Harm Reduction: A New Direction for Drug Policies and Programs*. Toronto: University of Toronto Press.

Giffen, P.J., Endicott, S., and Lambert, S. (1988). *Panic and Indifference: The Politics of Canada's Drug Laws.* Ottawa: Canadian Centre on Substance Abuse (CCSA).

Giffen, P. J. and Lambert, S. (1991) What happened on the way to law reform? Pp.345-369 in J.C. Blackwell and P.G. Erickson (Eds.), in J.C. Blackwell and P.G. Erickson, *Illicit Drugs in Canada: A Risky Business*. Scarborough: Nelson Canada.

Hathaway, A.D. (2001). Charter rights of Canadian drug users: A constitutional assessment of the Clay trial and ruling. *Canadian Journal of Law and Society* 16(1):29-43.

Hathaway, A.D., Comeau, N.C., & Erickson, P.G. (2011). Cannabis normalization and stigma: Practices and processes of moral regulation. *Criminology & Criminal Justice*, 11, 451-469.

Hathaway, A.D., Erickson, P.G., and Lucas, P. (2007). Canadian public opinion on cannabis: How far out of step with it is the existing law? *Canadian Review of Social Policy* 59:44-55.

Health Canada (2010). *Canadian Alcohol and Drug Use Monitoring Survey* (CADUMS). Ottawa: Canadian Centre on Substance Abuse.

Hyshka, E. (2009a). The saga continues: Canadian legislative attempts to reform cannabis law 2003-2008. *Canadian Journal of Criminology and Criminal Justice* 51(1):73-91.

Hyshka, E. (2009b). Turning failure into success: What does the case of Western Australia tell usw about Canadian cannabis policymaking? *Policy Studies* 30(5):513-531.

Hyshka, E., Erickson, P.G., and Hathaway, A.D. (2011). The time for decriminalization has come again...and again. *Criminal Law Bulletin* 47:258-275.

Keefe, P.R. (2013). Buzzkill: How to grow a pot economy. *The New Yorker* Nov. 18:40-51

Kolar, K. (2012) Exploring drug acceptability among drug using and non-using undergraduate students. Paper presented at the Canadian Sociology Association annual meeting, Victoria, BC. June, 2013.

Le Dain Commission (The Commission of Inquiry into the Non-Medical Use of Drugs) (1972) *Cannabis*. Ottawa: Information Canada.

Measham, F. & Shiner, M. (2009). The legacy of 'normalisation': The role of classical and contemporary criminological theory in understanding young people's drug use. *International Journal of Drug Policy,* 20, 502-508.

Osborne, G. and Fogel, C. (2008). Understanding the motivations for recreational marijuana use among adult Canadians. *Substance Use and Misuse* 43:539-572.

Parker, H. (2005). Normalization as barometer: Recreational drug use and the consumption of leisure by young Britons. *Addiction Research & Theory*, 13, 205-215.

Parker, H., Aldridge, J., and Measham, F. (1998). *Illegal Leisure: The Normalization of Adolescent Drug Use*. London: Routledge.

Room, R. and Reuter, P. (2012). How well do international drug conventions protect public health? *The Lancet* 379 (Jan. 07):84-91.

Sandberg, S. (2013). Cannabis culture: A stable subculture in a changing world. *Criminology and Criminal Justice* 13(1):63-79.

Solomon, R. (1988). The noble pursuit of evil: Arrest, search and seizure in Canadian drug law. Pp. 263-290 in J.C. Blackwell and P.G. Erickson (Eds.), *Illicit Drugs in Canada: A Risky Business*. Scarborough: Nelson Canada

Solomon, R. and Green, M. (1988). The first century: The history of non-medical opiate use and control policies in

Canada, 1870-1970. Pp. 88-116 in J. C. Blackwell and P.G. Erickson (Eds.), *Illicit Drugs in Canada: A Risky Business.* Scarborough: Nelson Canada.

The Economist (2013). Towards a ceasefire: Winding down the war on drugs Pp. 57-59 in February 23-March 1, 2013.

Wacquant, L. (2011). From 'public criminology' to the reflexive sociology of criminological production and consumption. *British Journal of Criminology* 51:438-448.

[arts & culture]

WHAT IS A REBEL? A CONVERSATION WITH GUILLERMO TREJO

MARC JAMES LÉGER[1]

O ttawa-based artist Guillermo Trejo recently exhibit-
ed a series of prints during the 2014 Manif d'art in
Québec City (the Québec City biennial). Titled BAN-
DERAS (flags), these pieces draw from the iconography
of the Zapatista movement and related struggles, fusing its
symbols to that of the colour code of the Québec national
flag, thereby making links between the political history of
Québec and Latin America. Intrigued by this provocative
work, I interviewed Trejo by email in the summer of 2014.

Marc James Léger: I've been aware of your work for a
few years now and appreciate the simplicity of the techniques that you use, your avoidance of pop imagery and
your focus on what seems to me like the language and aesthetic of political protest. For these reasons I was very
much interested in your installation at the Manif d'art.
Could you describe the work and its references. I would
also be interested in knowing your thoughts on why

---

[1] For biographies, please see the end of the chapter, page 239

Québec nationalism could or should be compared to the struggles of the Zapatista.

Guillermo Trejo: Thanks for the comments. When I found out that I was going to participate in the biennial, my first idea was to create a project that reflected somehow my reality as Latin American, but also as a resident of Canada. The next thought was to create a project that was even more specific: Latin America and Québec. This established the parameters for *BANDERAS*—or flags.

BANDERAS consists of a series of eight flags. The flags where made using MDF (medium density fibreboard) relief cut plates. The idea was to make prints by using the simplest system of printing, as if you where in hiding and had limited resources, and from there were struggling along with different separatist or revolutionary movements from Latin America. I appropriated the designs of these flags and re-made them using only the colour blue so as to reference the Québec flag and by doing this tried to reflect the political history of this province and the relations I believe exist between Québec and Latin America.

PHOTO 1. Guillermo Trejo, BANDERAS, 2014.
Installation view. Eight relief prints on heritage
cotton, each print 60 x 90 cm. Photo by Ivan Binet.
Courtesy of Guillermo Trejo.

PHOTO 2 (&3-6 on following pages). Guillermo Trejo,
BANDERAS, 2014. Eight relief prints on heritage cotton,
each print 60 x 90 cm. Photos by Ivan Binet. Courtesy of
L'Oeil de Poisson, Centre de production et de diffusion
en art actuel et multidisciplinaire, Québec.

PHOTO 3.

PHOTO 4.

PHOTO 5.

PHOTO 6 (& ◄ 3,4 &5 ▲). Guillermo Trejo, BANDERAS, 2014. Eight relief prints on heritage cotton, each print 60 x 90 cm. Photos by Ivan Binet. Courtesy of L'Oeil de Poisson, Centre de production et de diffusion en art actuel et multidisciplinaire, Québec.

I am not sure how this idea came to me—maybe someone mentioned this to me, but I've been thinking about Québec as the forgotten Latin American state. They have a more or less a similar background and there has been constant resistance and political stand against a foreign force. For me, this was confirmed by the student protest in 2012. The reason for the protest, and the reaction of the society, was almost as if we were in Mexico or Chile.

There is then the question about whether Québec nationalism can be compared to the Zapatistas. In principle yes, I believe that all emancipatory movements have similarities. The main mandate of the Zapatistas is to have an autonomous government that respects their traditions and that is not racist towards the indigenous population. From what I understand and from what I have seen the Québec separatist movements emerged with the same ideal, to be independent and to have the right of self-government. I have read about the struggle of the Québécois and I was surprised to find that until the 1960s there were jobs in some places for only English people. There was the belief that the Québécois where somehow not equal. This is in some way similar to what happens with the mestizo and indigenous population in Latin American, where the European descendants have control over the main corporations and political institutions.

So yes, I think that historically there are similarities, especially if we add to the conversation the FLQ (*Front de Libération du Québec*), which is a far left organization like the EZLN (*Ejército Zapatista de Liberación Nacional*). I think though that it's important to mention that I use more than one flag because I'm trying to reflect the different faces of the idea of resistance. For example, the *Los Macheteros* (The Machete Wielders) are a group of citizen militants that have constantly fought for the independence of Puerto Rico. However, they are not "indigenous" to the land. They are Latin Americans that are against the social and political influence of North America over their nation, which is somehow similar to the language problems in Québec.

Do you think there are similarities between Latin America and Quebec? Could you see Québec as a forgotten Latin American state?

MJL: Well, thanks for asking. As a Franco-Ontarian I'm very aware of what Robert Choquette once referred to as *"le siècle de l'injustice"*—the period from before the rebellion of the *patriotes* in Lower Canada, in which the British project was to assimilate the colonial French—known at that time as simply *les Canadiens*—up to the *Révolution tranquille* and the *Crise d'Octobre*. I understand the history of imperialist conquest and capitalist exploitation in which French people in North America became second-class citizens, which is perhaps similar in some degree to what the Uruguayan historian Eduardo Galeano wrote about in *Open Veins of Latin America*.[2] In this light your *banderas* could possibly be seen as similar to the gesture of Hugo Chavez giving a copy of *Open Veins* to Barack Obama. But who are you giving this to? To those who don't know or to those who are already aware?

My immediate response, though, as both an internationalist and as a Lacanian, is to affirm that I have no interest in bourgeois nationalist projects and in petty bourgeois identity politics. In an essay I wrote recently, published in the journal *Third Text*, I refer to Slavoj Žižek's critique of cultural studies approaches to hegemonic contestation and

---

[2] Eduardo Galeano, *Open Veins of Latin America: Five Centuries of the Pillage of a Continent*, trans. Cedric Belgrage (New York: Monthly Review Press, [1971] 1997).

his reassertion of the communist project of universal emancipation.[3] Žižek argues that Frantz Fanon understood very well the notion of superego predicament when he asserted the possibilities for an emancipatory collective outside of the hierarchical particularisms in which he could be thought of an nothing more than a black man. "I will not make myself the man of any past," Fanon wrote in *Black Skin, White Masks*, "my black skin is not a repository for specific values."[4] Fanon's refusal to capitalize on the guilt of the colonizers rejects the negative universality of victim politics and asserts instead the space of universal emancipatory struggle. We all have identities, which our narcissistic selves can't do without, but the affirmation of this identity against someone else's difference from mine does not constitute a politics, except maybe the worst kind of liberal pluralist capitalism. If your politics cannot be universalized, if it cannot be imposed with force as the same for all, it's not a politics. It becomes increasingly urgent, then, and as capitalism becomes more coercive, for activists to be aware of how the culture wars function today in relation to the capitalist class war against revolutionary politics. Alain Badiou wrote about this in his 1997 book *Saint Paul: The Foundation of Universalism*, as did Tim Brennan in his 2006 book *Wars of Position: The Cultural Politics of Left and Right*.[5] In this regard it is clear that the Zapatista struggle is indeed a universal struggle,

---

[3] See Marc James Léger, "Art and Art History After Globalization," *Third Text* 26:5 (September 2012) 515-27.

[4] Frantz Fanon, *Black Skin, White Masks*, trans. Charles Lam Markmann (New York: Grove Press, [1952] 1967) 226-7.

[5] Alain Badiou, *Saint Paul: The Foundation of Universalism*, trans. Ray Brassier (Stanford: Stanford University Press, [1997] 2003). See also Tim Brennan, *Wars of Position: The Cultural Politics of Left and Right* (New York: Columbia University Press, 2006).

especially insofar as they have from the start linked their struggle with that of all Mexicans and anyone who struggles against neoliberalism. In this sense, the Zapatistas, as far as I know from reading the writings of Subcommandante Marcos (now Galeano), do in fact resist the logic of victim politics and instead remain very constructive and universal, rather than asserting specific interests at the expense of someone else's identity.

In terms of the Québec situation I also wrote about these questions in the introduction to my edited book *Culture and Contestation in the New Century*.[6] When I started this book I wanted to do something similar to what Hal Foster did with his 'little red book' on postmodernism, *The Anti-Aesthetic*. I wanted to write a book that would be useful to the new generation of politically-minded activists, artists like yourself, who are aware of what Badiou refers to as *"le réveil de l'histoire*," the return of emancipatory projects against the rule of the so-called free market and against the "democratic materialism" that reduces everything to languages and bodies, which has become little more than an adjunct to the worldlessness of the market.[7] I included in this book Mathieu Beauséjour's project *1½ Métro Côte-des-Neiges: Do They Owe Us a Living?*, a re-performance of Gaetan Montreuil's reading of the manifesto of the Front de Libération du Québec on Radio-Canada television on October 8, 1970. In this project the name of the FLQ is presented as an English logo alongside the Québec government insignia, as though this revolutionary group had succeeded in taking state power

---

[6] Marc James Léger, ed. *Culture and Contestation in the New Century* (London: Intellect, 2011). See also Hal Foster, *The Anti-Aesthetic: Essays on Postmodern Culture* (Seattle: Bay Press, 1983).

[7] Alain Badiou, *Le réveil de l'histoire* (Paris: Éditions lignes, 2011).

by abandoning most of its cherished ideals. Isn't this exactly the problem now that the Parti Québécois and the provincial Liberal Party share the same neoliberal policies of austerity? And to add insult to injury, the PQ embarked on a project of demagogic populism with its Charter of Values clause that it would not reconsider. In relation to this I had posted on my blog for a while Lenin's 1905 text "Socialism and Religion" in order to politicize this discussion—to politicize culture rather than to culturalize politics, as Žižek puts it. I also voted for the New Democratic Party in the last federal election but was extremely disappointed to see how the new leader, Thomas Mulcair, refused to pronounce himself on the Québec student strike, because it's a provincial issue, but he did weigh in on the Charter of Values question, because, ostensibly, this issue is more important to the constituents of his riding—so he has something to say about multiculturalism but nothing to say about social democracy. This gives you an idea of what social democratic politics has become in its rightward drift toward the neoliberal right.

About *1½ Métro Côte-des-Neiges*, which by the way is a project I think has an interesting relationship to *BANDERAS*, I argued that the work questions the relevance of the FLQ's radical ideas to *today's* Québec nationalism, now referred to by anti-capitalist leftists as "Québec Inc.," the Québec of Paul Desmarais and Pierre Karl Péladeau. In this context, leftist worker solidarity has been replaced, at best, by what Žižek refers to as the "postmodern racism" of tolerance, by conservative populism and the restoration of class power. Politicization is thus presented against the background of the privatization of public issues.

In relation to the student strike, which is undoubtedly the most important expression of anything here having to do with the struggles of the Zapatista, Badiou gave an interview that no doubt upset many people. He argued that the student strike has to be seen against the background of the brutal global phenomenon of transforming universities into corporations and is therefore an echo of May 68, and so the strike was beneficial to all of Québec society, even if it was divisive. He added that the "becoming world" of Québec has to do with the experience of contact among identities, nationalities, and with indigenous peoples. For this reason, he views with skepticism the shift towards independence. Everywhere in the world, he says, in Yugoslavia, Czechoslovakia, Somalia, the Congo, there is a pulverization of federalist agreements and a shift towards national identities. These negative phenomena of contemporary historicity are responsible for human tragedies.[8] One can see this playing out in Ukraine, where deputies in the Kiev junta are arming far right militias and in some cases calling for the extermination of ethic Russians. The U.S. and the E.U. are directly responsible for stoking this situation of civil war, just as they have done in Iraq, Afghanistan, Libya, and Egypt, and as you know, as they have done with impunity throughout Latin America. Americans rightly criticize Putin for his anti-gay laws, but they ignore that their ally, Saudi Arabia, kills people for the same reason. The obvious point is that they can't do without an enemy power that would justify their military-based economy. But this military power has absolutely no moral authority.

To come back to *BANDERAS*, I would have two questions for you about this work. One would have to do with what I see as something that operates like Emory Douglas' theories on revolutionary art. Revolutionary art, he argued, gives people "the correct picture of our struggle," "the

---

[8] See François Gauvin, "L'enjeu philosophique mondial du conflit étudiant," *Le Devoir* (June 11, 2012), available at http://www.vigile.net/L-enjeu-philosophique-mondial-du.

correct understanding of our struggle." In this vanguard
way he argued that art should raise awareness and educate
the masses through participation and observation.[9] So I
would ask you about the level of undecidability that you
talked to me about at the opening of the biennial—the fact
that you also want to avoid a clear propaganda message.
You mentioned something about Albert Camus. In this regard you also included in your installation a work from
your *Instigators* poster series, a print that shows a toppled
statue of a man and the words "everything ends with a beginning." Who would be a good statue candidate for you
in terms of your installation? Can this base actually be occupied or is it purely ideological?

GT: I'm a big follower of Emory Douglas, for his work
and activism, and also as an icon of political art. I also
think that for him, in his historic moment and reality, as an
African American, it was easy to find "the correct picture
of our struggle." Emory was maybe the first black American visual propagandist. His work has the intention to educate and to be accessible. In an interview he mentions that
he had to do all the posters with images because the
"brothers did not know how to read or write," and so he
had to develop a system of visual education where blacks
could be reflected and see the "correct picture."[10]

In my case it's harder to find the correct image. We are
in a time where idealism and ideologies are blended and

[9] See Emory Douglas, "Position Paper No 1: On Revolutionary Art,"
in Will Bradley and Charles Esche, eds. *Art and Social Change: A
Reader* (London: Tate Publishing/Afterall, 2007) 166-70.

[10] See the contribution by Kathleen Cleaver in Sam Durant, ed. *Black
Panther: The Revolutionary Art of Emory Douglas* (New York:
Rizzoli, 2007).

consumed as popular culture and sadly the fierceness of capitalism is that it consumes all idealisms and transforms them into soft ideologies. For the same reason, it's harder to find positions. Albert Camus starts his 1951 book *The Rebel*, with this question: "What is a rebel? A man who says no, but whose refusal does not imply a renunciation. He is also a man who says yes, from the moment he makes his first gesture of rebellion."[11] He then elaborates the rebel as a man who maintains his position against oppression at all costs.

I try to avoid propaganda with my work because I am not clear about positions. But I am clear that I want to maintain positions against oppression. My ambivalent position is not due to the fact that I am ambivalent in my beliefs but rather because I am ambivalent about the political and social structure of the world at this moment. You have to remember that I grew up in Mexico where the ideal of revolution was corrupted to the point that it was transformed into a dictatorial party called the INSTITUTION-AL REVOLUTION PARTY. In this context democracy is based on corruption and clientelism, the Green Party favours the death penalty and the left is completely fragmented. My beliefs are informed by this chaotic reality and so yes I am ambivalent. Still, although we no longer believe, many Mexicans are still calling for change.

---

[11] Albert Camus, *The Rebel: An Essay on Man in Revolt* (New York: Vintage, [1951] 1992).

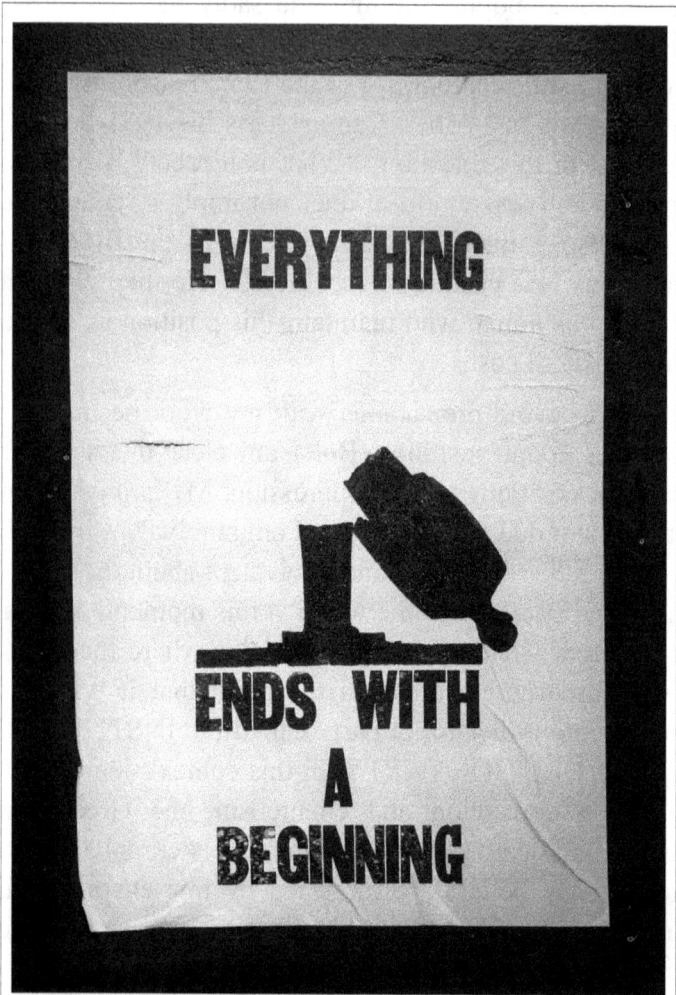

**IMAGE 7. Guillermo Trejo, everything ends…,
2013.** Letterpress and lino cut on paper weed
pasted to gallery wall, 90 x 60 cm. Courtesy of
the artist.

About the poster *everything ends…*, I think the base of
that statue could be occupied by almost any dictator and
so the image stands for any ideological position. However,
the poster was designed after a specific event that hap-

pened in Mexico. In 2010 or 2011 there was a celebration of Mexican independence. During the festivities, a massive sculpture was assembled in Mexico City. Afterwards the monument was disassembled, placed in storage and forgotten. The monument is supposed to represent a man of the revolution but I found this event to be a kind of parody, assembling and disassembling and with supposedly an ideological meaning but that cannot be permanent. It was as if the government was dismantling its own ideas. And by doing that they were opening a space for a new monument.

MJL: My second question has to do with the usefulness of the example of the Zapatista (and maybe also the Macheteros) for us here in Québec. There are various forms of anarcho- and combative syndicalism—like that used by the ASSÉ (*Association pour une solidarité syndicale étudiante*)—that balance the anarchist principles of horizontalism and participatory democracy with a willingness to take on state power through its representative institutions. There are forms of revolutionary movement that can work to bridge the anarchist-communist opposition. This points though to some of the limits of idealism. As Gene Ray argues, the Zapatista are tolerated only as long as they don't become a revolutionary threat to the Mexican government and as long as they do not reorient the whole of Mexican society along revolutionary lines.[12]

GT: I think it's true that the Zapatistas and other movements can exist in Mexico because they are somehow tolerated, but I also think that the reason why these groups

[12] See Gene Ray, "Antinomies of Autonomism: On Art, Instrumentality and Radical Struggle," *Third Text* 23:5 (September 2009) 537-46.

can exist is because the government has lost control of or is not interested in these mainly rural indigenous and ethnic communities. For example, at this moment there are several "community self-defense organizations." These groups are taking control of places in the centre of Mexico. These civil movements are possible because for years the different levels of government were not concerned about small towns, that is, until they started to organize against the drug lords and somehow create a self-government status. The only reason these groups were stopped was because they started using weapons and openly calling for armed resistance against politicians, against the corrupt police and the drug lords. If this had not happened the government would have allowed them to pursue self-government practices because it's cheaper for them and they basically could care less about these people.

I've recently heard a good description of the world that seems applicable to this conversation: There are two types of people on this planet—those with no security and those with some or lots of security. The ones who have no security have nothing to lose and so they can react. The others have the kind of security that stops them from reacting because they worry about losing their stability. Canadians are on the whole part of this second group and for better or for worse there is no real reason to react—or at least that's how I see it. But I also feel like this stability is damaging to democracy. The lack of social concern is reflected in poor electoral participation and civil society fails to be active in calling for change. I have to say that I'm disappointed that there were only two major demonstrations on Parliament Hill this year and these were for the legalization of marijuana and for the pro-life campaign.

MJL: There was also an action by the Council of Canadians and Frack Corp, who placed a 14-foot fracking rig spilling fracking wastewater on the federal government's front lawn in order to bring attention to the risks associated with this environmentally hazardous practice.

In terms of the relation between art and politics, is there a difference for you between a series like *Instigators*, which uses a simple poster style to present quotes from Friedrich Nietzsche, Albert Camus, Jean-Paul Sartre, Jack Kerouac and Buddha, and a series like *Black bloc*, or *We are angry*, which depicts front-page news events, mostly images of protest against poverty and violence? In the case of *Instigators* I'm reminded of Jenny Holzer's work, especially as she based many of her works on the political speeches of such people as Emma Goldman, Adolph Hitler, Vladimir Lenin, Mao Tse-tung and Leon Trotsky. Her work though was initially based in postmodern irony, attempting to rework ideas that had turned into media clichés and looking into how the mass media neutralizes the language of extreme situations. Like Holzer it seems that you maintain a kind of postmodernist's critique of authorial voice, of the violence of representation and power discourses. She also used simple, everyday vehicles such as printed matter and T-shirts. She has made more poetic and more emotionally compelling statements in larger and more monumental forms. How do you see your work evolving? Where would you like to see it go?

GT: I did not know about Frack Corp, that's great!

Yes, there are differences between the *Instigator* series and *We are angry*. Both came from the idea of appropriation and how to understand symbols. *We are angry* was a project that started by analyzing how western media depicts non-western countries. The idea was to take the free *Metro* newspaper and create a drawing based on the images in the international section. For me drawing is a system of observation and "visual research." This allows me to slow down the process of observation and to see more in the image. I consider this really important as an artist. The project evolved to a more complicated level, where it was not only about the representation but also about the relation of text and image, how images are constructed and not "reality." The series was influenced by the work of Roland Barthes and specifically the idea that a traumatic image cannot transmit information because the traumatic aspect cancels the communicative capacity of the image.

FIGURES 8 ▲ & 9 ► Guillermo Trejo, Untitled (2011) from the series We are angry, 2011. Carbon paper, ink and pencil on Bristol paper, 30 x 22 cm. SAW Gallery, Ottawa. Collection of the artist. Photo: Remi Theriault.

New jets could trigger 'Arctic arms race'

We are angry starts with a drawing of the newspaper image along with its caption. Beside this I place an abstract image that has as a caption the title of the column. The abstract image on the right is created at the same time and with the same material as the newspaper image on the left. The process for these "drawings," as I call them, is to draw with carbon paper and then to use ink for the tones. I then clean my paintbrush on another piece of paper the same size and type. In this way I am creating two images: one where the visual elements are organized in a way that can easily be understood, and a second for which the visual elements are not organized in such a way that we can understand it. The only obvious connection between the two is the text. This project was about how media can give meaning to images and how image lose their veracity when they are presented alongside a text.

This process was a strange way for me to understand images insofar as I was drawing dead people or people in terrible situations. This made me very uncomfortable. I became aware of the ethics of the image and how as an artist I have to question myself. That's why I stopped using these kinds of images and started working with concepts and words instead.

The *Instigators* series came from a personal question that was "why do people protest?" My thesis is that people who protest are in a collective adolescent stage, not in a negative sense, but as a period in life when things are changing rapidly and someone becomes aware of their existence. The adolescent has a need to kill the father and be emancipated. My posters were made with the idea that a protester thinks that the only way to make sense of their life is to protest. This is similar to the existentialist premise that we have to find a reason to exist because there is no external reason. I don't see this as necessarily political, but more a philosophical stance that connects somehow with the notion of ambivalence of position that I discussed. As you can see *Instigators* and *We are angry* came from different places, but I think that it's making *We are angry* that brought me to the second series.

I'm not sure about where my work will be going in the distant future. I can tell you that I have been moving more into abstraction. This only started recently but I'm still not sure yet where it's headed. My work is becoming more about how we understand symbols. Knowing how symbols create the visual world can be part of the evolution of how we understand political problems. I'm tempted to go into video but I want to avoid using new media simply because it's accessible. I don't like art that "looks" contemporary if only because of the technology and so I wouldn't want to go there.

MJL: Thanks for this interview.

GT: Thanks for the interview, Marc. I would later like to know what you think of abstraction.

~ * ~

Guillermo Trejo holds a bachelor's degree from the Escuela Nacional de Pintura, Sculptura y Grabado in Mexico City, where he specialized in printmaking and drawing. He recently completed a master's degree at the University of Ottawa. His work has been presented in the U.S., Canada and Mexico. He has recently presented solo exhibitions at The Ottawa Art Gallery and SAW Gallery. See http://trejoguillermo.com/home.html

Marc James Léger is an independent scholar living in Montreal. He is author of *Brave New Avant Garde* (2012) and *The Neoliberal Undead* (2013), both from Zero Books, and is editor of Bruce Barber's collected essays in *Performance, [Performance] and Performers* (2007) and *Littoral Art and Communicative Action* (2013) as well as editor of *The Idea of the Avant Garde—And What It Means Today* (2014).

[book reviews]

Re-reading Foucault: On Law, Power and Rights

Ben Golder, Editor
(New York: Routledge, 2013. 264 pages.)
http://www.routledge.com/books/details/9780415673532/

Reviewed by—Irina Ceric, (Criminology Faculty member, Kwantlen Polytechnic University), *Vancouver, October 2014*

*R*e-reading *Foucault* is an ambitious and mostly successful attempt to answer the question "Where is the law in Foucault and what has he done with it?" and the contributors' creative responses demonstrate the breadth of the interdisciplinary analyses emerging in the wake of the translation of Foucault's later lectures into English. The collection is dedicated to the "interpretive work of re-imagining law in, and through, Foucault's work" but the key themes—the

politics of rights, surveillance, biopolitics and Foucault's gestures towards the juridical in his lectures on history, knowledge and power—reflect a broader orientation of likely interest to readers in disciplines other than law. To some extent, however, this potential is belied by the book's initial focus on the so-called expulsion thesis, the notion that "Foucault had expelled law from any significant role in modernity." Initially straying into the minutiae of the existing literature, the authors taking up the expulsion thesis ultimately succeed in locating this debate within the context of Foucault's broader political and theoretical development.

In "Expelled Questions," Colin Gordon begins by admitting that "whether one likes it or not, [Foucault] does not have a master theory or thesis about law" but goes on to forcefully argue that naming this omission as a problem is a deliberate choice. Moreover, this choice, according to Gordon, is the result of Foucault's historical location within a particular politico-intellectual culture, one in which "a commitment to law" on the part of leftists can be traced to the demise of actually existing socialism, and the concomitant desire for a "permanent statement that the errors of socialist regimes have been understood, and will not be repeated" (20). In this context, Gordon contends, the apparent absence of law in the "bundle of innovations and challenges presented by Foucault's work" was less troubling if one could claim that he had failed to even attempt the topic "now judged to be compulsory for any thinker with a serious claim to advise Left political forces aspiring to the legitimate acquisition of sovereign power" (21). Whether or not one agrees with the description of this task as "compulsory," the foundation of Gordon's claim—the existence of a commitment to law and legality on the part of a left critical of actually existing socialism—continues to resonate, given contemporary debates on the left with respect to law, the state, and the limits of democratic legitimacy (arguably, most notably during the presidency of Hugo Chavez). Through his defence of Foucault, Gordon also succeeds in linking the expulsion thesis and the initial rediscovery/revival of Marxist legal theory in the 1970s to current iterations of a renewed Marxist approach to international law, and the resulting need to glean Foucault's relevant insights while moving beyond the confines of the expulsion thesis debate.

Perhaps it is not surprising then that Alan Hunt, a long-time theorist of socialist approaches to law, as well as one of the key figures in the expulsion thesis debate, provides two examples of exactly this sort of contribution. First, as does Gordon, Hunt canvasses Foucault's claims that the techniques that emerged with the "inquiry" continue to contribute to contemporary forms of legal knowledge production, generating—and explicating—juridical procedures still in use today. The focus of Hunt's piece, however, is the development of the concept of the "juridical assemblage" arising from Foucault's 1973 lectures in Rio de Janeiro. Juridical assemblages "designate the coexistence of different combinations of legal, judicial and normative elements," and make it "possible to bring together some of the disparate elements found in Foucault's engagement with the juridical field" (81). By deploying this concept, Hunt argues, we can stop "castigating" Foucault for the narrowness of his explicit engagements with law and instead "appreciate his focus on the interaction between different fields of power, knowledge and governance" with which forms of law interact.

More than an analytical tool, Hunt's juridical assemblage may be read as a form of praxis, and as an example of *Re-reading Foucault's* success in highlighting the contemporary utility of Foucault as both a theorist and a public (or in his own term, "specific") intellectual. Gordon's defense of Foucault relies on the "tactical and strategic context" underlying Foucault's now-apocryphal debates with Deleuze, Chomsky, and Lévy and Glucksmann, and especially Foucault's challenge to orthodox Marxism, while Jessica Whyte cites Lévy's questions to Foucault on the desirability of revolution as the genesis of a shift in his position on rights. In her accessible and timely chapter, Whyte charts the relationship between the emergence of a politics of rights in the 1970s and the constitution of a neoliberal governmental rationality that emerged at the same time. She concludes that in the absence of revolutionary intent, the "dissident" politics of human rights (as an example of Foucault's concept of "counter-conduct," specific forms of resistance emerging out of correlating governmentalities), provided a substitute utopia to revolutionary Marxism, one which largely accepted the "rules of the neoliberal game" (224). Whyte's exploration of the shift from Foucault as a strident critic of rights to a contributor—theoretically and practically—to the formulation of a new politics of rights exercised by the "governed" dovetails with Gordon's historicization of Foucault, tracing a similar trajectory of his changing relationship to the left, Marxism, and the prospects for resistance.

The contributions highlighted above constitute only a fraction of the breadth of *Re-reading Foucault*, but they are exemplary of the rigour and reach of the book's contribution to both critical legal theory and the seemingly bottomless body of research and reflection on Foucault's politics. Marcelo Hoffman recently underscored the potential of this project, arguing that in *Discipline and Punish*, Foucault was speaking back to participants in the prisoner support movement years after his withdrawal from that movement," suggesting that "a sort of dialectic" had arisen between Foucault's theories and practices, with his theories "both emerging from collective political practices and serving to further inform these practices."[1] At its best, *Re-reading Foucault* confirms Hoffman's hypothesis, sharpening our understanding of Foucault's entanglements with the juridical while shedding new light on the evolution of his work overall.

□ ◇ □□ ◇ □□ ◇ □

"Too Asian?" Racism, Privilege, and Post-Secondary Education
RJ Gilmour, Davina Bhandar, Jeet Heer, and
Michael C.K. MA. (Editors)
(Toronto: Between the Lines, 2012. 224 pages.)

Reviewed by—*Jakub Burkowicz* (Graduate student in Sociology & Anthropology at Simon Fraser University),
Surrey, March 2015

In 2010, *Maclean's* became the subject of popular controversy when it asked, in a piece entitled "Too Asian" by Stephanie Findlay and Nicholas Köhler (later retitled "The Enrollment Controversy"), whether university campuses across Canada were

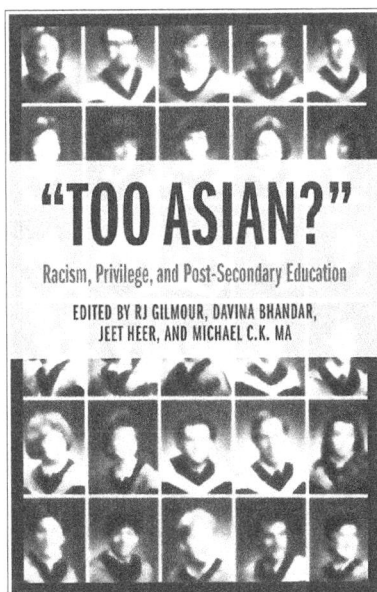

---

[1] Marcelo Hoffman, "Foucault and the "Lesson" of the Prisoner Support Movement" (2012) 34 *New Political Science* 21 at 24 and 36.

246 | Radical Criminology 5

not becoming demographically dominated by Asian students and, increasingly, Asian values. Findlay and Köhler
rang a proverbial alarm, alerting *Maclean's* readers to the
"single mindedness" of Asian students whose very presence turns top-tier institutions, such as the University of
Toronto, the University of British Columbia, and the University of Waterloo, into no-fun-zones of intense academic
devotion. While white students prefer to integrate social
activities into their university experience, Asian students
allegedly shun everything from athletics to alcohol. When
they do socialize, many of them, as the article points out,
have a tendency to create "segregated" organizations that
"balkanize" the campuses they attend (Findlay and Köhler, 2010).

The article's claim is not novel. And neither is its brand
of racism. Anti-Asian prejudice pre-dates Canadian Confederation. It has been, and is, still with us, as is evident
by the claims made by University of New Brunswick's sociology professor Ricardo Duchesne. Spotlighted recently
by the media, Duchesne went on record to claim that Vancouver has taken on too many Asian immigrants too
quickly and that as a result the "beautiful British city" has
acquired a "strongly Asian character" (*CBC News*, 2015).
I could just as well be quoting the claims of the Asiatic
Exclusion League on the eve of the 1907 anti-Asian riots
in the same city. The crowds that took part in the racial violence sang "Rule Britannia" before smashing windows
and looting businesses in Chinatown and Little Tokyo.
This is an old antipathy repackaged just like the article's
title. At its core lies an unease with Asian immigration itself and the presence of Asians in Canada, but this is represented variously as everything from the concern over the
Asian balkanization of education to the concern over the
transformation of urban space and employment. The idea
of an Asian outsider working insidiously from the inside

to uproot "our" way of life is a handy trope, readily deployed in the service of white settler Canada.

The edited collection *"Too Asian?" Racism, Privilege, and Post-Secondary Education* features 11 chapters that respond to the now well-rehearsed anti-Asian prejudice. Specifically, the text focuses on the racism endemic to Canadian society that makes such prejudice possible within the setting of post-secondary education. With contributions from academics and graduate students working in such fields as Canadian studies, education, history, and sociology, as well as from journalists, lawyers, and activists, this is a text informed by a radical and progressive sensibility. One of its notable strengths is that a number of the chapters are grounded in what may be called an activist epistemology. As Jeet Heer notes in his introduction, the book "takes its impetus from the outpouring of anger and activism that emerged in the wake of the *Maclean's* article" (2012, p. 9). A few chapters even evoke the well-known tradition of critical pedagogy. *"Too Asian?"* draws on and includes the recollections of those who protested—whether directly with their bodies on campuses across Canada, or by creating art exhibits, satirical music videos, or writing articles—against the original article. It considers the experience of those who went on to organize alternative classrooms, like the UBC hosted course "Way Too Asian", which employed Freire's dialogic method in order to turn the event into a "teachable moment" (Hsu and Paek, 2012, p. 100). The appeal of *"Too Asian?"* is that one is invited to read it as an extension of that activism, as an attempt to confront white privilege in education.

Following Heer's introduction, which provides a much needed context and which establishes a critique of the notorious article in question, the book is divided into three sections. Section I consists of three chapters that consider the role of meritocracy and affirmative action in university

248 | Radical Criminology 5   (ISSN 1929-7904)

education. It bears recalling that *Maclean's* did not dismiss meritocracy; rather, it suggested that something akin to what functionalist sociology calls a "dysfunction" characterizes it. From the magazine's point of view, Canadian meritocracy is worth defending, but it faces a "dilemma" owing to the overrepresentation of Asian students (Findlay and Köhler, 2010). In light of this claim, the chapters in this section take on the task of unmasking the ways that meritocracy actually *maintains* certain patterns of social stratification.

Meritocracy is addressed head-on by Henry Yu through an imaginary exercise he calls "the parable of the textbook" (Yu, 2012, p. 21-7). In his exercise, students are asked to consider what it might be like take a class in which only half the class, those whose last names start with letters A to K, were given the necessary textbook for several weeks. Understandably, such a system would give the students with the textbooks an upper edge—in the form of a stronger start—that would continue even once textbooks were distributed to the entire class. Yu's parable is a useful exercise in the use of the radical imagination. It invites us to consider how, once the old openly discriminatory "alphabetist" system is abolished, meritocratic colourblindness reinforces racial stratification by denying the racist contours of the past and present ("Unfair? I exclaim. What could you mean? … now that alphabetism is gone your failure must be your own responsibility. Why can't you just get over the past?" (Yu, 2012, p. 23)). Sarah Ghabrial provides an adroit critique of meritocracy as well in a chapter that compares the moral panic in education concerning the overrepresentation of women ("pink panics") to the panic concerning the overrepresentation of Asian students ("yellow perils"). Weighing the role of gender and race in Canadian education allows Ghabrial to perform an interlocking analysis of two forms of oppression. Her writing reveals a similar discursive element at work behind both panics, one that involves "the perceived slippage of white class-privileged men from a position of dominance" (Ghabrial, 2012, p. 50). Given the legacies of racism and sexism in this country, meritocracy cannot be regarded as a system that replaces the aristocracy, as Ghabrial brilliantly argues, "but simply [as] the reorganization of signifiers of mobility, falling largely on the same historically privileged groups" (2012, p. 38). This is to say that meritocracy allows for business-as-usual. It allows for the established racial hierarchies of the past to live on precisely by couching itself in a more legitimate colourblind discourse—a discourse that imagines that no longer seeing race is the equivalent of no longer being racist.

Besides skillfully interrogating meritocracy, the chapters in this section carry out the difficult task of remaining critical of the ability of affirmative action policies to redress racial inequities. This is not to say that affirmative action (or what in Canada is known as "employment equity") should be abandoned. As David Weinfeld, whose work compares the US and Canadian approaches to meritocracy, maintains, in US universities "the admission officers implicitly understand that the 1200 SAT score of a poor African-American student from a single-parent family in Harlem is worth more than the 1300 from a wealthy white kid living in a posh apartment overlooking Central Park" (2012, p. 35). While appreciating the capacity of affirmative action to stem systemic racism, the chapters in this section identify the ways that affirmative action—and more broadly antiracism—can be exploited by racist institutions and discourses. As Yu reminds us, today's racists are also capable of cloaking their language in a discourse of anti- or non-racism: "many political conservatives in the United States switched tactics. Rather than defending white supremacy, the argument now being made was that policies designed to counteract racism were themselves racist" because they admitted more whites and Asians than Latin American and African American students (Yu, 2012, p. 19). Such arguments, as Yu maintains, were made by those who wanted to dismantle affirmative action. Weinfeld too observes that by the mid-1980s some US universities attempted to deny affirmative action to Asian Americans on the grounds that such policies were failing to "add to 'diversity' of elite college campuses" (2012, p. 31), or, to the "balance" of the campus, as Ghabrial notes (2012, p. 51). Such observations echo the work of Pierre-André Taguieff (2001) who challenges antiracists today to be weary of assisting the enemy. As Taguieff maintains, we must pay attention to the ways in which the celebration of identity, community, and difference, as well as the arguments for affirmative action, can be picked up by racist discourses. This is not to reject affirmative action measures; it is only to heed Taguieff's reminder that 'difference' and 'diversity' do not form a foolproof antidote to racism.

Section II consists of two chapters that examine the role of settler colonialism in today's classroom. Both execute a far-reaching analysis of colonialism by performing work on material culture. Adele Perry tackles the subject by writing about graduation photographs on display in the hallways of the University of Manitoba. In what to me reads like a Foucauldian inspired approach to history, Perry dispenses with "linear and salutary stories of improvement and uplift" (2012, p. 55)—stories that perhaps would have us believe that the University and the city of Winnipeg are becoming less fortified, less defensive of their white privileges and more reasonable, tolerant, and even Indigenous overtime. "Winnipeg has always been an Indigenous city, and Indigenous people have been city-dwellers since cities exited in Canada", Perry maintains

(2012, p. 63). As such, "[i]nstead of seeing the late twentieth century as a new era, we might see the period between the Canadian takeover of Red River and the onset of a highly visible presence of urban Indigenous people in cities in the 1960s as the unusual years" (Perry, 2012, p. 63). To this end, she exposes, or rather creates, cracks in what looks like a neat Anglo past. The graduands in the photographs all appear white by today's racial standards. Perry, however, challenges "[t]his apparent homogeneity" for "mask[ing] a more complicated history" (2012, p. 55). In a time when "a quota system... limited the numbers of Jews, Poles, Ukrainians, and women" (Perry, 2012, p. 59), passing as white was a preoccupation of Indigenous people who strove for a university education, as well as of the peripheral Europeans who today can take their whiteness for granted. Mary Jane McCallum also does work on an object in order to read history. She demonstrates the complicity of Canadian history textbooks in settler colonialism. Such textbooks construct "Canada" by including Indigenous people only in terms of an excluded, pre-history of the country itself. As McCallum documents, Indigenous people are usually featured in the first chapter in history textbooks. Such first chapters serve the function of the literary "anteroom" (McCallum, 2012, p. 75) through which one must pass in order to reach Canada. Canada, as modern, living Canada thus only properly begins with European "discovery." This is an old strategy of exclusion through inclusion which normalizes colonialism while preserving it.

This section, in the space of two chapters, loses, however, something of the momentum and focus established in the previous section dealing with meritocracy. To be sure, Perry's and McCallum's chapters reflect sound scholarship on the understudied topic of settler colonialism. They offer much to students of racism. They are clear, penetrating, and provocative in the best academic sense. Yet their fit within this collection is haphazard. I say this because the relationship of both chapters to the *Maclean's* article is collateral at best. Only McCallum's chapter mentions it, but just once and then only as an afterthought in the last paragraph. There is no sense that either of these chapters have been written as a response to it. Settler colonialism certainly informs the white privilege of the *Maclean's* article, but those looking for something like a sustained analysis of anti-Asian racism in education, or even for its connections to settler colonialism, will have to look elsewhere.

Section III consists of six chapters that examine the ways that race features in the Canadian classroom. With the exception of Diana Younes' last chapter, which focuses on the role of whiteness in Canadian law schools, the first five chapters do restore the focus by bringing *Maclean's* back into the discussion, either by closely examining it or by treating it as a necessary referent for Canadian racism. Dan Cui and Jennifer Kelly, for example, respond in a point-by-point manner to the claims made in the "Too Asian?" article. Their work serves as a useful introduction to antiracist critique, but, I suspect, for most readers the myth/fact approach—debunking, for example, the idea that all Asian students study and work hard (Cui and Kelly, 2012, p. 89)—will not deliver any new insights. Rather than accepting the terms of the debate offered by *Maclean's*, the authors could have gone further by questioning the discursive formation that allowed the newsmagazine to make its claims. Similarly, Victoria Kannen provides an upfront denunciation of white privilege in the classroom that can serve as introduction to thinking critically about race and racism. However, the idea that whiteness shields white people from racial self-awareness (Kannen, 2012, p. 109) or that the question "where are you from?" is a technique of othering (Kannen, 2012, p. 111) does not deliver anything that has not already been established by scholars of race and racism.

The section does offer, however, a more far-reaching examination of racism in the classroom from a radical pedagogical perspective. Ray Hsu and Julia Paek consider the ways in which resistance to the *Maclean's* article took place in the classroom setting. They examine how "[t]he Way Too Asian (WTA) class was born out of a feeling of dissent" (2012, p.97). Peak speaks of WTA as an attempt to round out what was "missing from these forms of protest" (Hsu and Paek 2012, p. 96). In doing so, she echoes the insight of Jeff Shantz that movements have to at some point come off the streets and transform themselves into "infrastructures of resistance" (2013) if they are to offer more lasting alternatives. Following the tradition of Freire's dialogical method, WTA "was hardly a traditional classroom setting in that there was no syllabus, there were no course guidelines, and no expected outcomes" (Hsu and Paek, 2012, p. 97). Much like this edited collection, WTA was an open-ended event that solicited the participation of a diverse range of actors, serving as a kind of temporary ("it was a reactive course" (Hsu and Paek, 2012, p. 100)) infrastructure that facilitated the "effort to collectively 'take back' and update Eurocentric (i.e., *Maclean's*) definition of 'Asian'" (Hsu and Paek, 2012, p. 97). Like many antiracist attempts at education, WTA attracted whites along with visible minorities. Anita Jack-Davies' chapter complements Hsu and Paek's work by offering lessons to white allies as well as to non-white social justice teachers. As Jack-Davies points out, "the [*Maclean's*] article reveals that Canadians, like Americans, continue to engage in racial discourse that is simplistic, stereotypical, and fixed" (2012, p. 116). Any attempt to move in an antiracist direction must therefore move past simplistic racial discussions. Whites who attend in order to purge their white guilt, or in order to "[learn] about the 'politically correct' language for use in their interactions with racialized students and parents and behaviors they should avoid in order not to offend the racialized Other" (Jack-Davies, 2012, p. 116), are favoring aesthetic responses to racism. Their concern, as Jack-Davies shows, is misplaced, as merely appearing non-racist does not actually override the structure of racial privilege. And wanting to be taught by non-whites on how to appear non-racist is a subtle perpetuation of that very structure. Much can also be learned from Soma Chatterjee, Mandeep Mucina, and Louise Tam whose chapter considers anti-Asian and anti-East-Asian racism in the context of Canadian education. Sharing their own experiences in the first person, the authors draw on such personal examples as being automatically placed in ESL classes on the basis of their non-white skin colour, and of their own attempts to "model whiteness" (Chatterjee, Mucina, and Tam, 2012, p. 127). Having to constantly prove their self-worth, to "accept inequality by adopting self-help strategies or by contributing to white-centered social activities" (2012, p. 130), Chatterjee, Mucina, and Tam, demonstrate the outline of the dominant discourse of race that allows *Maclean's* to assume that universities are naturally white spaces. An undefined whiteness rules over Canadian post-secondary education and their chapter does much to name it.

"Too Asian?" features work that will be useful to scholars of race and racism and to antiracist activists. From advancing critiques of meritocracy; warning us against the capacity of racists to utilize affirmative action; considering the relationship between education and racism, as well as education and anti-racism; to frank, head on criticisms of the *Maclean's* article, this edited collection addresses a range of related issues. Despite the oc-

casional thematic divergence in the road, it is an invaluable source for those wishing to make sense of *Maclean's* claims from a radical, as opposed to liberal, position. Courses on multiculturalism, settler colonialism, anti-Asian racism, the media, and immigration will find a lot of well-written resources here. And given the continuity of anti-Asian racism (the fact that such racism is not just confined to *Maclean's* article but continues to re-emerge elsewhere) this edited collection is likely—albeit in a dreadful sense—to remain timely.

REFERENCES

CBC News. 2015. "UNB defends prof's academic freedom in wake of racism complaint." January 7. http://www.cbc.ca/news/canada/new-brunswick/unb-defends-prof-s-academic-freedom-in-wake-of-racism-complaint-1.2892206?cmp=rss

Findlay, Stephanie and Nicholas Köhler. 2010. "The Enrolment Controversy." *Maclean's*. November 10. http://www.macleans.ca/news/canada/too-asian/

Shantz, Jeff. 2013. "Taking it OFF the streets!" *Fifth Estate*, no. 388. Winter. http://www.fifthestate.org/archive/388-winter-2013/taking-it-off-the-streets/

Taguieff, P-A. 2001. *The Force Of Prejudice: On Racism And Its Doubles*. Translator and Editor: Hassan Melehy. Minneapolis: University of Minnesota Press.

□ ◊ □□ ◊ □□ ◊ □

Youth in revolt: Reclaiming a democratic future

Henry A. Giroux

(Boulder, CO: Paradigm Publishers, 2013. 216 pages.)

Reviewed by—*Jamie Thomas* (Criminology student, Kwantlen Polytechnic University), *Cloverdale, October 2014*

Henry Giroux's book *Youth in Revolt: Reclaiming a Democratic Future* does more than provide an analysis of the Occupy Movements that were predominate in the months following September 2011; Giroux's book carefully situates the Occupy Movements within both the historical structure of American society and the present political context. In his book, Giroux does not limit the scope of his argument by only discussing the repressive mechanisms used by the State to suppress youthful protesters or, as Giroux calls them, the "new generation of public intellectuals" (p. 132), but he also gives significant attention to the ideological mechanisms used by the State to maintain the status quo which subsequently perpetuates a vast acceptance of neoliberalism by society with little question. Giroux's book takes readers on a journey, as he illustrates the changing political atmosphere of the United States beginning with the terrorist attacks that took place on Septem-

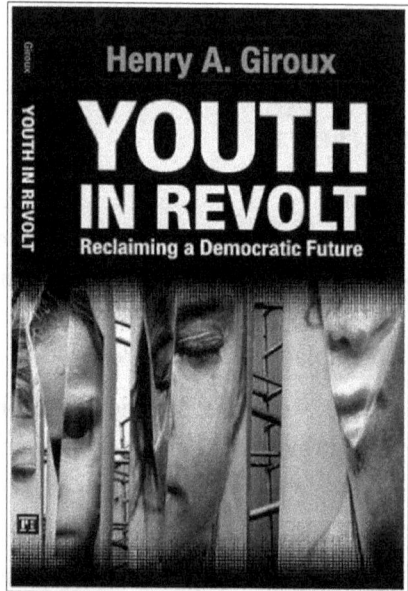

ber 11, 2001. Following his discussion of September 11, 2001, Giroux demonstrates the impact of two of the State's most formidable ideological mechanisms: the media and the education system, and he relates these mechanisms to the cruelty expressed within the greater political context. The journey outlined in Giroux's book ends with an assessment of the sheer lack of democracy in the United States of America, and he questions whether democracy in America will prevail. Although the journey explained in Giroux's book is one of struggle, it should not discourage readers but rather empower them, as it is only them who can reclaim our democratic future.

Given Giroux's experience as both a professor and advocate for radical democracy, it is no surprise his book is written from an alternative globalization perspective, a perspective that denounces the systemic inequalities created by neoliberalism. Giroux clearly aims to provide a critical voice in the depiction of Occupy Movements and the State's response to those movements, as these events are often reduced to simplistic, yet horrifying, media images. The story told in *Youth in Revolt* serves the purpose of addressing the complex interrelationship of historical and contemporary factors that have resulted in America's youth experiencing extreme frustration, as they no longer see a viable future for themselves within the warfare state of America. Giroux's book adds an important layer in the analysis of social movements and the criminalization of dissent, as he carefully assembles a broad framework for understanding the economic and political influences that have endorsed the rise of neoliberalism and the subsequent reduction of civil liberties. Giroux emphasizes it is the lack of critical analysis in education that has allowed neoliberalism to carry on unchallenged and thus an ideological response to the State's repressive attacks on youth is the only way to reinstate true democracy.

Giroux's passion for education and youth come together in chapter four appropriately titled, "Disposable Knowl-

edge, Disposable Bodies." The title clearly indicates the
way in which neoliberalism has written off the next generation as "disposable" (p. 71). Chapter four seems to be especially relevant to readers of Giroux's book, as it is likely
the majority of readers are students, like myself, or individuals who have spent a significant amount of time in educational institutions. Giroux reflects on the "literacy
purge" that occurred in Nazi Germany over eighty years
ago. Giroux compares the Nazi's "literacy purge" (p. 72)
with Arizona's elimination of ethnic studies classes and
the removal of a number of books that focused on oppression as well as on America's colonial and racist roots. The
parallelism of these two events, for Giroux, indicates the
"silencing of dissent" (p. 88) is not isolated in history, as
often suggested by authoritarian governments and educational curriculum, but a permeating factor in contemporary
capitalist societies. It is the awareness of oppression that
poses the biggest threat to neoliberal conservatives, as the
oppressed become empowered through knowledge and engagement. Giroux explains these informed citizens can
then use their education to participate in critical conversa-
tions about the power structures that effect their lives and
thus present a threat to the status quo. Rather than empow-
ering minority groups, education in authoritarian societies,
such as the United States, function to "mobilize fear, self-
interest, and political conformity" amongst students. In its
goal of creating complacency among citizens, the American government makes it clear the "war on youth" (p. 88)
is a war on education and in this war the targets are the institutions and professionals determined to instill a critical
voice in the next generation.

Henry Giroux's book *Youth in Revolt: Reclaiming a
Democratic Future* offers a comprehensive analysis of the
Occupy Movements and perhaps more importantly an examination of the historical underpinnings that have permitted the erosion of democracy within the American
state. I would recommend Giroux's book to anyone,
young or old, who wishes to gain a critical understanding

of the criminalization of dissent that is becoming ever more prevalent in today's society. However I would suggest, this may not be the book for capitalist nationals or neoliberal supporters, unless of course they wish to open their eyes to the rampant inequality that spans across the United States of America. I must also mention that although Giroux's book focuses primarily on the United States, the themes discussed in *Youth in Revolt* apply to other authoritarian nations where similar forms of dissent have emerged just to be silenced by state sanctioned repressive force and, in a broader context, state control over ideological mechanisms such as the media and education. My critique of Giroux's book is a matter of perspective; I cannot help but question if democracy in its true sense, or what Giroux would explain as radical democracy, could ever re-emerge. Throughout Giroux's book it seems he is calling for a revolution, yet he continuously reverts back to the hope of restructuring "American democracy" (p. xxxiii). I cannot help but consider Giroux's emphasis on revolution and restructuring as a paradox. I believe the idea of anarchy, a society free from government control, may be the only way to truly regain equality and freedom from state oppression. Nonetheless, Giroux's book is critical food for thought and a tool of empowerment for the 99% who will no longer be silenced.

Radical Criminology,
an insurgent journal of theory and practice for struggle

Considering contributing to an upcoming issue?

Authors are encouraged to submit articles for publication, directly to our website: **http://journal.radicalcriminology.org**

We are actively seeking marginalized voices, not only in the field of critical criminological scholarship, but also artists, activists, and reviewers. Or, send us a letter!

All academic articles are subject to a blind peer review process. (This does not include "insurgencies," artwork, poetry and book reviews, which will be assessed by our editorial committee.)

Please visit our website for more detailed submission guidelines. (There are no submission nor publication fees.) Create a 'reader' and 'author' account there now...

We use the Public Knowledge Project's 'open journal' online submission system (http://pkp.sfu.ca/ojs), which allows authors to submit papers via the Web. This system speeds up the submission and review process, and allows you to view the status of your paper online.

Artwork, poetic submissions, and notes on insurgencies can also be posted to our website, e-mailed to <editors@radicalcriminology.org> or send us mail at:

Radical Criminology,
ATTN: Jeff Shantz, Dept. of Criminology,
Kwantlen Polytechnic University
12666 72nd Ave,
Surrey, B.C. V3W 2M8

(and on twitter...find us @critcrim)

www.ingramcontent.com/pod-product-compliance
Lightning Source LLC
Chambersburg PA
CBHW071352280326
41927CB00041B/2906